EUROPE
IN SEARCH OF HER
SOUL

Europe in Crisis:
Symptoms - Root causes- Way out

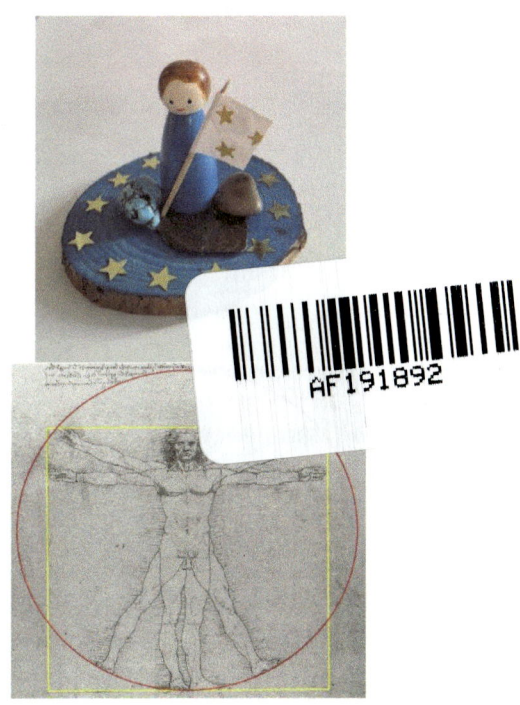

Georg von Goldbach

This book is a revised version of

selected chapters and the Epilogue of the book

Europe on the Way to her Apocalypse

History – Background – Perspectives

Bibliographic information from the German NationalLibrary:
The German National Library lists this publication in the German National Bibliography; detailed bibliographic data are availableonlineat https://dnb.de.
ISBN: 978-3-7693-0739-9

Manufactured in Leipzig, Germany(EU)
www.engelsdorfer-verlag.de
Euro (Germany)
Publisher: BoD · Books on Demand GmbH,
In de Tarpen 42, 22848 Norderstedt
Printed by: Libri Plureos GmbH,
Friedensallee 273, 22763 Hamburg

CONTENT

DEDICATION

I dedicate this book to the professors

Wolf-Dieter Narr, Freie Universität Berlin,

Eike Haberland, Frobenius Institute Frankfurt,

and Michel Izard, *Directeur de Recherche* at the
Centre National de Recherche

Scientifique and founding member of the
Laboratoire d'Anthropologie Sociale

of Claude Lévi-Strauss, at the *Collège de France*
in Paris.

Their trust in me has given me courage and
decisively promoted

my scientific education and academic career.

Our guiding principles and values

It may be helpful for the reader, if we give him some indications about the ideas, principles and values that have guided us in writing this book.

We believe that it is good, if people keep trying to improve their lives and also their living conditions. For us as modern humans, science and technology have become increasingly important tools to improve our living conditions. But there are at the same time other ways and means that man is deploying to improve living conditions and the quality of life. Most people will probably agree with us when we say that people strive to improve or enhance their living conditions and the quality of their lives through games, music, singing, poetry, dance, sports, various competitive games and many other activities. In anthropology, it is assumed that these are universal human activities, with which humans enrich their lives. While the natural sciences are mainly about technology and engineering, about the utilization and application of energy through instruments and tools, human life covers many more facets and aspects, taking into account a great diversity of values and interests.

The most important areas that we address here in this book, and which are not directly related to the application and use of energy through technology, concern the shaping of the coexistence of people, peoples and states. So we are dealing here with topics of politics, i.e. the shaping of public life, at the international level. This is what we mean by geopolitics.

The natural sciences are mainly about the application and use of energy and, issues that revolve around what we commonly call *matter*, or the physical world. In this sense, the most important functions of the natural sciences and of the technologies developed with their help are primarily linked to the improvement of our material living conditions.

In politics, it is *power and money* that are seen as the decisive factors, as the matter of politics, so to speak. At the end, however, the purpose and basic intentions that drive political action are not really different from those that are guiding science and technological efforts. In both areas, the purpose is the continuous improvement of living conditions and the quality of life.

In looking at things this way, we are also making a very personal commitment. We are expressing here our belief that we are able to make a sensitive contribution to the improvement of living conditions and the quality of life through improvements in the use of *power and money* as the essential factors and energies in the field of international politics, i.e. geopolitics. This belief infuses sense into our endeavor and is the *raison d'être* of this book.

This attitude is not self-evident. Because there are people out there, who think that, by principle, it is impossible to fundamentally improve geopolitics. Such attitudes are usually justified by the "nature" of man, by the belief that man's nature cannot be improved and does therefore also leave no room for any meaningful and lasting improvement in the shaping of the coexistence of people, peoples and nations. While it is acknowledged that humans are always striving to shape geopolitics, man's *eternal nature* seems to block off the way to real and lasting improvements. According to this thinking, many people ultimately assume that humans can develop a better way of life through technology and the application of the natural sciences alone. In the field of politics and geopolitics, they assume, however, that all these attempts to improve the modalities of coexistence will finally lead to nothing really useful. Since we have written this book, we admit that we do not share this point of view and therefore take a different stance.

We believe that it is important for people, for their living conditions and the quality of their lives, to try again and again to improve coexistence and the interaction and use of the factors of power and money in international relations among nations.

Due to our origins in Germany, we have taken a European perspective in this book. However, it should already have become clear that we are looking at the world as a whole, from the perspective of Germany and Europe. So we take a European perspective with the intention of understanding how we can improve our coexistence with other people, peoples and nations on earth.

We should also state here that we assume that the way, we shape our interactions between people, peoples and nations in Europe, is not necessarily the best, or should be seen as a role model for other people on earth. It remains to be seen what Europe can offer to improve the shaping of geopolitics, i.e. international coexistence. After all, other people, peoples and nations have to come in with their aspirations, beliefs and attitudes to check and co-decide on the making of geopolitics. So we are not going to take a Eurocentric position here. We do not claim that European, or Western geopolitics offer, basically and always, the best ideas or solutions.

It will be useful, if we finally give some further explanations about the values and principles that guided us in writing this book. We agree that it is not possible to define personal values and principles conclusively. We declare it desirable to work for a future political environment with more peace and less war and violent conflicts, attained through the shaping of geopolitics and international relations between peoples, peoples and nations. Furthermore, we see major deficits and opportunities for improvement concerning these questions of peace or war. Obviously, we do not consider war and violent conflicts to be good means of shaping the coexistence of people, peoples and states on earth. This is a clear statement that we want to make here.

Another value and fundamental principle that we consider important for the shaping of geopolitics is freedom. There is no question that there is not just one definition, one universally valid understanding of freedom. In the end, freedom and free development are very personal and depend very much on personal desires and aspirations. However, we believe that freedom, as a value and principle, should also be used and applied in the shaping of geopolitics. Taking into account the desires and aspirations of the great diversity of people will help define freedom. The definition of freedom cannot be provided by Government. The meaning of freedom is not theoretical, rather it is the perception of individual people that can teach us about the value and significance of freedom. As we see it, freedom is what people can realize in practice, in their *Human Action[1]*. In geopolitics, freedom therefore means to us that all people, peoples and nations can claim their right to contribute to the shaping of good and always better international relations, leading to improving living conditions and the quality of life on earth. Freedom means free participation in the *competition for the better ideas[2]*. We consider this *participation in the competition for the better ideas* to be a right that should apply not only to

---

[1] We refer here to "Human Action: A Treatise on Economics", 1949, by Ludwig von Mises.

[2] We refer here to lectures given in Buenos Aires in 1958, by Ludwig von Mises. They have been published in German under the title „Vom Wert der besseren Ideen", which we translate here with "The value of better ideas".

individuals, but also to individual peoples and nations. We will see later that the great challenge ahead is to find rules that enable us to really make these civil liberties possible in the interaction of peoples and nations. It is for this reason, that we intend in our book to provide useful practical indications for ways and means to find and apply such rules.

If the reader has followed us this far, then it should have become clear that our claim for personal peace and freedom, as we represent it in this book, is our fundamental *weapon* that we want to use in shaping the coexistence of people, peoples and nations. We contrast our weapon, *the competition for better ideas in search of peace and freedom*, with currently applied weapons, such as combat drones, intercontinental ballistic missiles, nuclear bombs and chemical weapons. This is our personal *declaration of war* and should be considered an appeal to strive towards ending the era of relentless rearmament and war.

We assume that there is no *a priori* plan for the course of human development. Likewise, no culture has an absolute claim to priority over any other culture. The dominant culture of the West, with science and technology at its center, has only asserted its dominance for the past 600 years. The African, Oceanic and Native American cultures have proven their value and importance for their people over hundreds of thousands of years. The cultural achievements of African, Oceanic and Native American cultures, expressed in languages, arts, and a great diversity of forms of social organization and kinship systems, are in no way less valuable or less complex than the achievements of Western or Eastern great cultures, such as China or India.

By principle, all cultures can therefore make a significant contribution to the further development of living conditions and the quality of life for people on earth. This understanding of the value of human cultures is one of the fundamental prerequisites for the future improvement of living conditions for humanity. All people, peoples and nations have the same right to participate in *the competition for the better ideas* to formulate new rules, according to which coexistence on our earth should be organized in the future.

.

Kiän - the Creative

The creative works lead to sublime success, furthered through perseverance.

I Ging, Book of Changes
in the translation of Richard Wilhelm

Foreword to the book

The personal motivation for this book comes from my realization that the creation of peace is, in our time, the most important concern of humanity. I was born in Germany and can therefore say that war is in my blood, as it is the case for most Europeans. A great number of wars have been waged on European ground among the European nations over the past centuries. In response to that, the European Union has been created and has progressively been shaped after the end of the Second World War as a "peace project". This hope is waning more and more, and Europe does not seem capable of escaping the claws of the evil of war.

In the decades after 1993, I had increasingly worked as a consultant for organizational development on behalf of the European Commission (EC). In the beginning, I was pleased and, to a certain degree, even enthusiastic to do this, as long as "international partnership" has been the EU's credible intention and guiding principle for our international advisory services and activities. After 2001, however, the situation started to change, and things went in a different direction. More and more, I had noticed how an intentional effort for dominance had come to the fore, thus changing progressively the foreign policy of the EU. Relations with partner countries became increasingly political and power oriented, less characterized by friendship and the honest dealings among partners. Of course, this change in attitude had also become obvious to many of our partners in the countries in which we worked. I am more of a free and liberal spirit by nature, and ideological narrow-mindedness has never been one of my personal traits. However, I have always endeavored to consciously guide my personal as well as my professional actions based on my ethical convictions and moral principles.

I can say that peaceful development among people and nations based on shared values and principles has always been a matter close to my heart. That is why I didn't feel challenged in particular when I was asked, consciously and with conviction, but without personal zeal or even fanaticism, to work for the healthy development of Europe and its relations with other countries in the world. My anxiety therefore increased more and more as certain authoritarian tendencies in the European Union (EU) and the European Commission became more frequently apparent to me. I then drafted an essay in 2017, essentially for myself, to sort out and clearly articulate my own thoughts, entitled "How Europe Lost Her Sovereignty". In it, I showed how, in the interplay between Germany and France, which had become a second spiritual home for me, the European Commission usurped the sovereignty of the European nation states and increasingly restricted their national responsibility. In addition, as a "participating observer", I recognized that a war was being prepared on European soil. Of course, that was not easy to see at the time. However, as I have been acting relatively close to the centers of political power, I could quite easily substantiate my perception. All the friends, acquaintances and business partners to whom I wanted to point out the issue of a looming war in Europe turned away or only looked into the air when I talked about it. Nobody wanted to know anything about it. I myself did not investigate this question deeper and, of course, could not know in what form this war would then begin and take place. I was personally surprised by the impressive way, with a flick of the wrist, Germany and the entire Europe were driven into this war, which was foreseeable by 2014 at the latest, and then turned into an open war in 2022.

Personally, this experience has shaken me very much, and my trust in people as a whole has been disappointed. I didn't want to believe how sensible and intelligent people could get involved in such stupidity. The experience of this general irrational behavior of the people in Europe still pains me very much. My grandfather was sent into the First World War in 1914 with the motto "Cannon thunder is our greeting". My father went to war in 1939 for the Hitler regime, from which he was not to return home from

Russian captivity until the end of 1947[3], severely damaged in physical health and also mentally. And now, at the end of my life, the war was to haunt me and perhaps plague my children as well.

I have always consciously enjoyed and never despised the great fortune of growing up in peace and being able to shape my life peacefully. Peace had always seemed to me to be a great and precious good that had to be carefully preserved. Unfortunately, we did not succeed in this.

---

[3] At a time when Russia is once again under strong ideological attack, it is necessary to confess that I have not developed any negative attitude or resentment from my father's experience in the mines of Russia. My father had been a prisoner of war (PoW), and his imprisonment was to be taken as the result of a war that had arisen and been waged in a criminal way.

The spiritual fathers of this book

The intellectual authorship of this book is held by two American thinkers and visionaries. The two have never met in person, but what they have in common is that they derive their thinking from cybernetics as a scientific means to understand and explain our world[4]. This is obvious in the case of Gregory Bateson[5], because he speaks of it frequently in his writings. In the case of R. Buckminster Fuller[6], the

[4] Cybernetics is the science of controlling and regulating machines in analogy to the functioning of living organisms by means of feedback processes that receive impulses from the sense organs. In social organizations, feedback works through information, communication and participant observation. The science of cybernetics was born from the cooperation of scientists in the "Vienna Circle". It was formulated by Norbert Wiener after 1945, after his emigration to the USA, when he came to the realization that intelligent behavior can be described as the result of feedback mechanisms.

[5] In the case of Gregory Bateson, we are essentially referring to the collection of essays published as "Ecology of the Mind" in 1985. The English edition of "Steps to an Ecology of Mind, Collected Essays" dates from 1972.

[6] At Buckminster Fuller, our main source is his book "Critical Path", which was published in 1981. Probably his best-known book is "Operating Manual for Spaceship Earth", from 1969. It can be downloaded online from the

reference to cybernetics is visible everywhere in his writings and also in his works, but he was more of a pragmatist and generalist nature. "Bucky" Fuller strove to live a life, in which he fought for the practical implementation of his ideas, mainly through the use and application of his design artifacts, while Gregory Bateson limited himself to theoretical and epistemological research, reflection and teaching.

What they both have in common is that they were very sharp observers of what was going on in the world and were always keen to understand how people acted. Both have always put people at the center of their efforts and have always looked at people in a larger, more comprehensive context and from a system view. In Buckminster Fuller's case, it was "man in the universe." For Gregory Bateson, a trained anthropologist and biologist, it was the systemic relation between man and nature. What both have in common is that they saw the fundamental fallacy in human thought and action in the fact that modern man saw himself disconnected from these necessary systemic

Buckminster Fuller Institute website. The German edition of "Instruction Manual for the Spaceship Earth and Other Writings" dates from 2011.

relations with nature and the universe. Both explained this as the result of the one-sided emphasis on the development of the natural sciences since the 17th century, which has led to a mechanistic world view. This paradigm of human isolation from nature and the universe, as both saw it, has slowly started to dissolve again since the early 20th century with quantum mechanics and new insights gained by biology in the self-regulating systems of life. These scientific discoveries generated progressively a new world view that related life and the role of humanity to the "uncertainty principle". A door into the unknown had opened. From now on, the meaning of life and human nature were perceived in a new light. It had become possible to reconnect with the nature of man and his relevance in the cosmos.[7] This sums up the experience shared by Gregory Bateson and Buckminster Fuller.

In order to better understand these two great minds, we would like to emphasize the decisive basic idea that is characteristic of each of them. Buckminster Fuller developed his fundamental ideas after 1930, formulated them in 1969 in his *Operating Manual for Spaceship Earth*, and

---

[7] Fritjof Capra gives a catchy account of this in his "Tao of Physics", of 1977.

summarized them with the formulation of *Synergetics* as *Explorations into the Geometry of Thinking*[8]. Intuitively, he seized the need for the application of "general principles and laws" to the understanding of the role and functioning of *Man in Universe*. He convincingly shows that it is not a lack of energy that inhibits the development of humanity. Rather, the fundamental deficiency lies in the fact that humanity has not found, not understood, the access to the infinite source of energy that is provided to us from the universe through the sun. This lack of access to understanding eternally regenerating energy has so far kept modern man caught in a self-made trap. According to Buckminster Fuller, this phenomenon can be traced back in particular to the work of the British economist Thomas Robert Malthus, who established at the beginning of the 19th century the principle, that humans would continue to reproduce with a necessary fatefulness, but at the same time they would have only limited natural resources at their disposal. Hence, the fight among humans for limited resources was inevitable. For Darwin, this became the struggle for existence and led

---

[8] This is the title of a book first published in 1975, in cooperation with E. J. Applewhite.

Darwinists to formulate the principle of "survival of the fittest". If we take these thoughts just a few steps further, we end up directly at the rationale for the demand for "unlimited growth" of the economy, and at the political level, for the hegemonic striving and the seemingly inevitable wars as a means of gaining power and access to supposedly limited resources. The critical analysis and examination of this rationale are at the center of this book.

Gregory Bateson is an anthropologist and a biologist by training. He has also worked successfully in the fields of psychology and psychiatry[9]. However, he has attained the most important significance as a researcher on epistemology, and in particular on the importance of cybernetics for the sciences and for the shaping of human living conditions on earth.

He says of himself that "the two most important historical events in my life were the Treaty of Versailles and the discovery of cybernetics"[10].

[9] The term "double-bind", i.e. the relationship trap, which is of common use in psychology and psychiatry, was coined by him.

[10] In this part, we essentially refer to Gregory Bateson, "Ecology of the Mind, Part VI, Crises in the Ecology of the Mind, from Versailles to Cybernetics", from his lecture in

This certainly sounds astonishing, because it is not immediately clear what the relationship between these two "events" looks like. We come closer to understanding what Gregory Bateson means when he says that, in his view, the "important question for history is: has the default[11] or attitude been changed?". He goes on to explain that "the most important points in history are... the historical moments... in which attitudes are changed", i.e. in which previous "values" change. He then shows that the Treaty of Versailles has not successfully changed the attitudes and values of the most important signatories of the treaty[12], i.e. Germany, France, Great Britain and the USA.[13] Therefore,

---

1966.

[11] The term "specification" here refers to cybernetics, as a system theory, and means "leadership variable" or "decisive reference value" to which the other parameters and elements of a system are oriented.

[12] We should note here that since the October Revolution of 1917, a government had taken power in Russia with which the United States did not want to come to an understanding.

[13] As we will show later, it was precisely this thought that guided Rudolf Steiner in his assessment of the events surrounding the First World War. He insisted that it was necessary to change the political "rules" in order not to prepare a new catastrophe. As we know, Max von Baden, the last Reich Chancellor of the German Empire, very soon

according to his understanding, the inevitable consequence of the Treaty of Versailles was the Second World War, with the same nations as principal protagonists. He calls the Treaty of Versailles one of the "greatest relapses in the history of our civilization" and says that "we will have to deal with the aftermath of this betrayal for a number of generations to come", before adding that "betrayal in an armistice or in peace negotiations is worse than a stratagem in battle." His conclusion: "It goes on and on. The tragedy of fluctuating, self-propagating mistrust, hatred and destruction through generations".

Gregory Bateson is aware that cybernetics, i.e. "the second historical event" of his time, will not in itself bring the solution to our geopolitical problems. But he sees that it can be a contribution to changing attitudes and behavior. At the same time, he knows that "any understanding can be used destructively". He summarizes his insight as follows: "In cybernetics itself there is integrity[14], which helps us not to be seduced by it into another madness,

---

ended Rudolf Steiner's advisory activities.

[14] Because cybernetics allows us to see the connections between events.

but we cannot trust that it will keep us from sin"[15] and then he adds in a more hopeful tone: "But this much is certain, that in cybernetics there is also the means to achieve a new and perhaps human worldview, a means to change our philosophy of power, and a means to see our own stupidities from a larger perspective". Obviously, he takes a system-view perspective.

---

[15] We would like to note here that Buckminster Fuller also sees integrity as a very important criterion for good and successful action. That's how he called one of his books, "Ideas and Integrities", from 1963. He also emphasizes this point in his "Critical Path".

Content and Structure of the Book

The purpose of the book is to look at the fundamental issues that are symptomatic of, and to identify and analyze the principal causes, that are at the root of the crisis in Europe. However, the book does not stop there, but shows ways to escape the crisis mode and the self-made traps by using her own will. Europe must now initiate the overdue paradigm shift to end the futile application of linear solutions in European politics. The book provides convincing examples to show that such a paradigm shift is possible. The prerequisite is political will and a determination built on new self-confidence. These political "virtues" will enable the EU and Europe to progressively move towards an end to the crisis mode. At the same time, a new self-confidence will enable Europe to reposition herself as an independent actor on the stage of geopolitics.

The book is structured in three distinct parts.

In Part One of the book, we will look at the Symptoms of the Crisis in Europe. The scientific approach in this part feeds on the historical analysis of the political economy, which is characteristic of Europe today. The critical result of the historical development of Europe's political economy over the past decades is her increasing involvement and even promotion of wars on the continent and beyond. We will bring to light the constituent role of the USA, which is at the origin of the root cause of this primordial symptom of Europe's crisis.

This is to say that the book does not intend to provide a sociological analysis of the crisis and its symptoms. In this book, we take an evidence-based approach and look at the most important symptom of the crisis in Europe.

We know from oncological medicine that patients with cancer usually develop various secondary symptoms, because the body is generally weakened and open to all kinds of secondary ailments. The physicists know, however, that they will have to focus their care on the root cause, which is cancer. The principal symptom of the crisis in Europe is, in our view, her involvement and the promotion of wars. A country, or a continent in war, will develop various other symptoms. This is what we call the crisis mode in Europe and the Western world in general.

Once we have a sufficiently good understanding of the symptoms, we will dedicate the second part of the book to the analytical description of the root causes of the crisis in Europe.

In Part Two of the book, we will focus our evidence-based approach on the descriptive analysis of the root causes of the Crisis in Europe. This approach will lead us to an epistemological understanding of the root causes of the crisis in Europe. This implies that we will describe and analyze the principal historical events and cultural factors that have shaped Europe and the social and economic life in her societies since the Renaissance. The origins of the historical memory and of modern Europe's self-image and consciousness are thus brought to light. This will eventually lead us to a thorough understanding of the principal root causes of the Crisis in Europe.

This examination will lead us deeply into the historical and cultural context of modern-time Europe. Our questions in this second part of the book will be complex. We will understand that the possible answers and potential solutions will be challenging for Europe on her way into the future of our globalizing world.

In Part Three of the book, we will intend to demonstrate that there are ways and means for Europe to get out of her self-inflicted crisis.

Building on the analytical results of the previous parts of the book, pragmatic solutions will be presented. It will become obvious that the main reasons for the continuing deep current crisis have their origins mainly in Europe herself. We will show that the root causes of the crisis are of a two-pronged nature. On the one side, they trace their origins to the historical and cultural development of Europe since the Renaissance. This is the ground on which the historical memory of modern Europe and the mental and psychological character of her people have grown. On the other side, the principal root causes can be found in its modern social, cultural and political history. Starting in 1919 and definitely realized after 1945, Europe has been incorporated into the American nation and its economic and political strategies, striving for global hegemony. This political process has attained its climax in our days, as Europe has lost her economic freedom and has been forced to change to an economy of war and to wage proxy wars on behalf of NATO and under US command.

Europe has lost the sovereignty to decide on her own destiny, mainly out of fear of taking responsibility against the forces that intend to keep her under their hegemonic influence and power. This fear of taking responsibility is further corroborated by the lack of moral honesty and intellectual courage to face the existing challenges. Europe's nations refuse to abandon their petty egoistic interests and to determine a common developmental strategy for the continent. These reasons lead to the complete lack of a vision for a sovereign and better future in Europe.

In our Epilogue to this book, we will eventually provide concrete indications of the first pragmatic steps towards a geopolitical paradigm shift that can lead Europe out of her imminent apocalypse and bring it back into the geopolitical arena as a sovereign actor and broker of peace and prosperity.

In addition, we will introduce initial reflections on the soul of Europe. For this purpose, we will briefly present our ideas and considerations concerning the meaning of this notion. On the basis of these reflections, we will explain, what we consider to be the principal conditions for Europe to find its way out of the crisis. Europe will have to build her future on her raising consciousness and new self-image.

PART 1 - SYMPTOMS OF THE CRISIS IN EUROPE

Chapter 1

Introduction and analytical approach

Just a decade ago, we would have said that the intention we pursued with our book was to prevent Europe from being drawn into a new war, or being driven into it. In the fall of 2024, as we write this introduction, we will be too late with this appeal against war. Europe has entered into an open war again since 2022. This is not a "Cold War", as it is still offered to the public by the media. Since February 2022, probably close to one million soldiers and civilians have already died in this war. Millions are on the move and fleeing the war zone and its borderlands.

How could this happen? Cynically, one could answer: because the 14,000 Russian-speaking residents in the Luhansk and Donetsk regions, killed in their own country by the Ukrainian government since 2014, after the "Euro-Maidan", were not counted. In German, they say that they "did not count", i.e. they were not worth being counted. Cynical? It's wartime again!

Behind this concealment of the terrorization and killing of its own population by the Ukrainian government, however, there was intention, one may assume "bad intention".

In 2015, the Minsk Agreement was signed in a binding manner under international law, and Germany, France, Russia and Ukraine pretended to take responsibility for its implementation. The main focus was on the observance of a ceasefire and the negotiation of an autonomous status for the two Russian-speaking regions of Luhansk and Donetsk.

However, as it turned out, there was no manifest intention on the part of Ukraine and the Western states that had signed the Minsk agreement to implement this agreement. As the former German Chancellor Angela Merkel publicly stated in 2023, the main intention of the Minsk agreement was to "buy Ukraine time"[16]. Time for doing what? Since 2015, Ukraine has been massively armed by NATO to prepare for an

---

[16] As an example, from the Tagesspiegel of December 9, 2022, where we read: "The former Chancellor described the Minsk Peace Agreement of 2014 as an attempt to give Ukraine time".

imminent war with Russia. That had been the intention behind the staging of the Euro Maidan. In order to spread fog and give Russia hope, in the years from 2018 to 2020, new fragile ceasefire agreements were reached on average every three months by the Trilateral Contact Group for Ukraine, consisting of Russia, Ukraine and the OSCE[17].

Today, it is obvious that NATO's preparations for a war with Russia have been in full swing since 2015 at the latest. The Ukrainian army has been massively upgraded, equipped with weapons and military material, and supported by European and American military advisers.

Russia put an end to this false and nasty game in February 2022, with its military intervention in Ukraine. In terms of its own self-defense, Russia

---

[17] OSCE stands for the Organization for Security and Co-operation in Europe. The OSCE emerged as an international institution from the negotiations on "Security and Co-operation in Europe", which ended in 1975 with the Helsinki Final Act. We cite this to show that 50 years ago, there was a will for peaceful cooperation in Europe. This initiative has been completely destroyed since 1990, with the end of the Soviet Union. The will to war has regained the upper hand. OSCE has become an organ of NATO and US interests, i.e. a transatlantic institution.

found herself in a situation, in which the country had no other choice.

What can be achieved with this book in such a situation? Why do we address it to the public?

One of the principal questions we want to ask ourselves is: What were the reasons for the sabotage of the Minsk agreement by the Western powers and NATO? What were the intentions behind the preparation of the war against Russia? After all, as we know today, Germany and France were only proxies for the "global West", i.e. for NATO and US interests, in this tactical game.

Methodologically, we want to advance from the perception of symptoms to the understanding of reality in order to answer this question. The answer to our questions is hidden behind *the veil of symptoms*[18] that only show us a semblance of reality through false mirror images of reality that want to fool us. The most important instrument we will apply for understanding reality will be thinking, and the most important prerequisite is

---

[18] In his lectures of 1919 on the *symptomatology of history*, Rudolf Steiner challenges us to see the reality behind the symptoms, the truth behind the events. Refer to the lectures of Steiner in GA 185:
https://anthrowiki.at/Geschichtliche_Symptomatologie.

our own fearlessness to face the often terrible (un)truths and lies, for which some of our fellow humans and their nations are responsible. If we courageously face reality in this sense, then we will increasingly come to an understanding of the "spiritual driving forces" that are effectively driving the behavior of some of the key political and economic actors behind the veil of symptoms. In the course of our analytical description, we will provide important insights into these processes of geopolitics and the mechanisms that are deployed in the struggle for global hegemonic power that is going on behind this veil of symptoms.

For those who want to face reality, the facts are not so difficult to understand. Of course, one must be willing not to be blinded or satisfied with the "colorful reflections"[19] of reality, which the media, our political leaders and the power elites are diffusing everywhere.

Intelligent and honest political analysts, such as Noam Chomsky, have been telling us what is going on behind the veil of symptoms for decades. In an interview in the *New Left Review* (No. 57, September/October 1969), which was

---

[19] A winged saying that Goethe puts into the mouth of his Faust; see Faust II, Act One.

published in Germany in the appendix *Linguistics and Politics* to the book *Language and Spirit*, Chomsky said: "The goal of creating an integrated world economy dominated by American capital ranks first for the elite that governs the United States. It's not just about having safe areas for American investment, markets, and control over raw materials, as important as they may be. It is also necessary to keep defense-spending, i.e. ultimately the costs of war, at a high level. This is the most important Keynesian mechanism for maintaining what is called a healthy economy". This is a clear statement: high spending on a war economy is seen by US power elites as an important mechanism for maintaining a healthy economy. We will have to come back to this point when we talk about the war economy, into which the EU and her various member states have been forced since 2023 by the hegemonic policies of the USA. As Eckart Conze writes: "Research rightly and almost unanimously considers the USA to be the hegemonic power of the Western world since 1945"[20].

[20] Eckart Conze; Hegemonie durch Integration: Die amerikanische Europapolitik und ihre Herausforderung durch de Gaulle, in: Institute für Zeitgeschichte, Vierteljahreshefte für Zeitgeschichte, Jahrgang 43 (1995), Heft 2.

By taking away the veil that is covering the reality behind the symptoms, their historical origin and root causes, we want to show a way to come to an in-depth understanding of important political and economic processes and contexts in our time. This kind of "analytical and symptomatologic history" should then provide the basis for making a diagnosis, which we see as a prerequisite for showing possible future solutions to eventually eliminate the root causes of the evils we have identified.

With our symptomatologic look at history, we pretend not to remain at the symptomatic level with the analysis we are undertaking, but we intend to explore this question of reasons and intentions behind the veil of historical symptoms. In this, we will shed light on the reality of events and processes from different angles and aspects in order to understand how Europe got on the path to its self-destruction and its imminent apocalypse.

At the conclusion of this brief analytical and intellectual process we will go through in this book, it should become clear what the situation in Europe is today and where the path taken will consequently lead in the coming years and decades. It should have become obvious that we don't want to write a war reportage, nor do we want to indulge in the diplomatic backstabbing in detail, as it has been and still is presented in the media every hour for years now. Our goal is to come to an understanding of the root causes and drivers of these processes that currently shape our lives in Europe.

We also do not intend to write a comprehensive scientific treatise, in which the relationships and interdependencies of politics, economics and society are explained in detail. Rather, we are concerned with creating evidence for the driving forces, as well as the relationships and interdependencies behind the events and facts, bringing them to light and making them more and more obvious. Following this line of reasoning requires us to bring in the courage to face the facts and not be afraid of the consequences of an impending catastrophe, towards which we are heading with our eyes wide open. It is our conviction that this catastrophe can no longer be prevented. In the fall of 2024, it has become obvious that we are already moving into its very center. Europe is rapidly heading toward its own apocalypse at a breathtaking pace in a dynamic process of self-destruction.[21]

Through our academic training and research on history and political economy, we have learned that there are forces at work in history, good and bad, that cannot always be precisely named and do not follow any "logic". In our book, we will repeatedly refer to benevolent actors and good forces, too, who are trying to counteract this impending European catastrophe. As long as these actors and forces exist, we should not give up hope completely.

However, we are convinced that Europe and the so-called "West" will find it very difficult to find their way out of this catastrophe on their own.

With this book, we will limit ourselves to the period of the past century until today. These have been the decisive one hundred plus years for this path to catastrophe that Europe has

---

[21] We are not the first or the only ones to have come to such an understanding. Emmanuel Todd, who has published several books on the subject, is one of the examples. Available in German are: World Power USA: An Obituary, from 2003; available in French: La Défaite de l'Occident, from 2024. However, we have developed our own line of argumentation that starts with historical processes in order to then argue consistently in the sense of political economy.

traveled. So we start in the time shortly before the First World War, when Diaghilev and Stravinsky staged their "Ballet Russe" and "Le Sacre du Printemps" (the "Rites of Spring") in Paris, when Oswald Spengler published the first drafts for his "Decline of the West", when Thomas Mann wrote his "Death in Venice" and was inspired to write his "Magic Mountain", and when C. G. Jung had his visions of the blood flowing all over the European continent.[22] These visions were the impulse for C. G. Jung to start working on his Red Book, which finally led him to the development of Analytical Psychology.

This example of C. G. Jung provides us with a good example of a personal crisis being transformed into a highly creative intellectual and spiritual process. Reading the personal history of R. Buckminster Fuller, we witness a similar situation as a starting point for personal transformation. In the case of Buckminster Fuller, this happened to him at the age of 32, when his first daughter had died just one year after her birth, while his professional career was at its lowest and he was broke. He went deeply into himself and started a new life, in the lifelong

---

[22] It is worth reading the 1989 book "Rites of Spring: The Great War and the Birth of the Modern Age", by the Latvian-Canadian historian Modris Eksteins.

company of his wife and family, to serve humanity with the best of his capabilities. It seems that these two examples of highly developed persons provide us with a model for self-transformation, coming out of a deep crisis, to open the way for creative and inspirational energies. At the level of a federation of nations, these examples might also inspire Europe to find a way out of her deep crisis.

PART 1

SYMPTOMS OF THE CRISIS IN EUROPE

Chapter 2

Lack of Political Will and Strategic Thinking in Europe

This world means something to the capable and is not mute to the brave. Why does he need to roam eternity! Let him grasp what firm reality is.

> Goethe, Faust.
> The Tragedy, Second Part, 1832. Act 5

In his important historical work on the "Decline of the West, A Morphology of World History", Oswald Spengler presented[23] a comparative analysis and philosophy for the understanding of the classical Greek man and spirit (the Apollonian type) compared with the modern, scientific-technically educated man and spirit (the Faustian type). As an attentive observer of

---

[23] Spengler says he found the idea for this book in 1913. The first volume was published in 1918, and the second volume was published in 1922.

world political events, one may feel reminded of these thoughts in the current situation.

To be honest, one cannot help but marvel at the American political will, i.e. the "Faustian will", to assert its interests. It almost arouses a feeling of admiration to see the courage and determination with which the USA has driven the Europeans into the current global conflicts in Iraq, Syria, Libya, Sudan and Yemen, to finally drive them in 2022 into the new open war against Russia combined with the conversion of their civil industries into a war industry as an extension of the American military-industrial complex.

Even if this strategic cold-bloodedness may have grown partly out of a courage of desperation, we honestly cannot avoid admitting that such vehement determination, which is the prerequisite for great wars and major crimes alike[24], has been completely lost in Europe. Looking at the present European leaders and power elites, such an attitude must today be considered downright unthinkable.

---

[24] In the chapter "Law of Aggression" in his book "The Laws of Human Nature" (2021), Robert Greene cites very convincing examples. This is perhaps even more true of his book "The Laws of Power" (1998).

European political leaders are much more likely to radiate a melancholic nostalgia, as we know it from the "Knight of the Rueful Countenance".[25] Big words and impressive gestures are at best dared in the American slipstream. Independent, sovereign action can no longer be expected. Europe has dwarfed itself politically in her political and other public personalities and follows the example of the small Baltic EU member states, who borrow their importance solely from their bigger brother on the other side of the Atlantic and their older siblings from "Brussels".

To be honest, we must also acknowledge that, on the face of it and according to the impression given by the leaders at the global political level, it is the Russian and Chinese role players who are most likely to exude sovereignty on the big stage of world politics that can compete with the United States.

This appearance and our perceptual observation are supported by the fact that, apart from the three large nations mentioned, no nation or confederation of states can define similarly clear

---

[25] Don Quixote, the "hero" from Miguel de Cervantes' novel, gave himself this nickname on the advice of his squire.

geopolitical goals and would also be able to deploy the courage to enforce them in an independent and sovereign way.

Since the admission of the Eastern European countries to the EU and NATO in 1990, and the accession of France to NATO in 2009, Europe and the EU have definitely lined up in order behind the American hegemon.

Apart from the USA, it is only China that, with its *Road and Belt Initiative (RBI)*, the founding of the *Shanghai Cooperation Organization (SCO)*, and the associated large Interbank Consortium, has set the clear geopolitical goal of building an alternative to the Bretton Woods institutions and the Western world. This is China's offer to the Global South and to all the states and nations of the world in search of their independent development.

Under Putin's leadership, Russia has managed to pull the ripcord in time and prevent the sell-off of its natural resources under stress and in difficult times, with great courage and considerable effort. Russia was woken up, due to the war with Ukraine, and is now forced to increasingly build and shape its own political profile at the global level against the combined power of the entire West. The military potential and efficient war technology, in combination with its wealth of natural resources, are the important factors in Russia's ambition to make the Eurasian north and the Central Asian heartlands spheres in which it will be recognized for its leading role.

PART 1

SYMPTOMS OF THE CRISIS IN EUROPE

Chapter 3

Overview of the EU's foreign policy role

Within the framework of this study, we cannot attempt to reconstruct the historical evolution of the European Union, or to offer an overall overview of the institutions and status of the European Union. Nevertheless, we want to create a picture in order to put the theses and considerations that we will present in this book into a meaningful framework. In doing so, we will be guided by our personal experience that we have been able to gain in professional practice as organizational consultant with various European institutions since 1995, especially in our work with and for the European Commission.

The first point that we would like to emphasize is that the European Union is not a democratic project[26]. It has clearly been pushed forward by

[26] In the political discussions on the EU and the European Commission, the "democratic deficit" is repeatedly pointed out, rightly in our view. For an overview: https://de.wikipedia.org/wiki/Demokratiedefizit_der_Europ%C3%A4ischen_Union#:~:text=Das

European political leaders and power elites as a joint European initiative. The European Economic Community (EEC) was founded in 1957 with the "Treaties of Rome". The primary goal at that time was to reassure each other that the future in Europe should be shaped without further wars. The subject of these EEC treaties was limited to certain sub-areas and took into account the early realization that a political or even military union could not be achieved immediately. Priority was therefore given to the economy and peace building. This had already been decided earlier by representatives of European power elites at the Bilderberg conferences[27] related to the preparation of the European community. It is also important to note that Great Britain is not one of the founding members. The United Kingdom, together with

---

%20Demokratiedefizit%20oder%20Europ%C3%A4ischen %20Union,Wirken%20nicht%20ausreichend %20demokratisch%20legitimiert.

[27] The Bilderberg Conferences are informal meetings of influential people from Europe from business, politics, the media, academia, the high nobility and secret services, where thoughts on current political, economic and social issues are exchanged and agreements are made. The Bilderberg Group is not a formal organization. The first Bilderberg Conference was held in 1954 at the invitation of Prince Bernhard of the Netherlands at his Hotel Bilderberg.

Denmark and Ireland, did not join the European Communities until January 1973.

When we point out this elitist character of the EU, it seems very important to us to emphasize that the EU's most successful and popular program is probably "Europe of the Regions". This program emerged after 1980 as a political concept intended to promote geographical and historical regions within Europe independently of the direct influence of the EU member states and to support them in their regional independence. It is a kind of integration model in which individual geographical and historical regions in Europe are to be given more sovereignty and strengthened in accordance with the principle of subsidiarity. In this federal system approach, citizens are to be more involved in decision-making. The "Europe of the Regions" program promotes cooperation through joint projects and initiatives that are implemented across countries. They can affect economic, cultural or ecological regions as well as promote joint projects. We mention this program because it shows that cooperation between the people in the regions, historical settlement areas and cities concerned in Europe can effectively bring fruitful results and experiences. From this perspective, the evils and problems of the European Union seem to stem more from the power elites in the member states. The Treaty of Maastricht, which came into force in 1993, i.e. under Jacques Delors as head of the European Commission, established the Committee of the Regions as an advisory body of the European Union.

Overall, it must be understood and also positively emphasized that the European Union was created and constantly developed in a constructive process between the member states. So there was no secret plan, or blueprint. Thus, in 1993, the EEC was renamed the European Union by the Treaty of Maastricht. New institutions have also been created again and again, such as the European Court of Justice, to take on common tasks. In 2009, the Treaty of Lisbon established a common set of rules for the functioning and management of the European Union. However, this Treaty of Lisbon, which was originally presented in 2005, with the ambition of a European Constitution, was not adopted by all parliaments[28]. Nevertheless, it has retained its validity as the European Treaty.

---

[28] In fact, what has been ambitiously planned by the European power elites to be become a "European Constitution", has been rejected in 2005 by the voting population in France and the Netherlands.

Obviously, this Treaty is a project of the European power elites, with deliberate exclusion and without the direct participation of the European population.

An important topic that we would like to address briefly here concerns European foreign policy. Even if the creation of the EEC were to have primal significance for Europe's internal affairs, i.e., the economic and political relations of the European Member States, it must not be overlooked that the founding of the EEC and the European Union was also to have foreign policy significance from the outset. This is already evident in the quite contrasting discussions of the groups that formed early on around the two "founding fathers", Jean Monnet and Robert Schumann. While Jean Monnet had envisaged a European federal state based on the model of the USA from the beginning, Schumann clearly favored a confederation of states in the spirit of Charles de Gaulle's policy, i.e. the so-called "Europe of the Fatherlands".[29] This area of

---

[29] In his book "Inventing a Nation", Gore Vidal informs us in his highly elucidating style that this polarity between the centralist Unitarian nation state on the one side, and the federalist construction of a nation with a certain autonomy of the individual states, was also characteristic during the era of the creation of the USA. This polarity has

tension basically continues to this day, although it must be said that, at the latest since the reign of the German Chancellor Angela Merkel, from 2005 to 2021, the creation of the European Unitarian central nation state based on the model of the USA has progressively taken shape. This irreversibility of the European integration process from the perspective of a European Unitarian central nation state is very convincingly demonstrated in the studies and books of Charles B. Blankart. In 2007, Blankart published his knowledgeable and profound study on *Federalism in Germany and Europe* in the series "New Studies on Political Economy", published by the Nomos Verlag. Based on his scientific analysis of the "financial constitution" of the EU, Blankart shows (on p. 14) how the "paradigm shift in Europe, especially in Germany, against federalism after the First World War" prevailed. From this time on, it had become clear that federalism in its initial form would no longer have a future within the European Union.[30] Today, the Unitarian central

been characteristic of the political situation in the USA until today. Republicans clearly prefer the federalist nation, while the Democrats prefer the Unitarian centralist nation state.

[30] The standard work by Charles B. Blankart: "Public Finance in Democracy: An Introduction to Public Finance",

nation state has already become a reality. This development has definitely taken root under Commission President Ursula von der Leyen, first under the pretext of the measures taken during the so-called Corona pandemic and finally in the period after 2022, during the war in Ukraine. We suppose that these roots cannot be eradicated anymore.

In this context, it is also important to understand that the complex institutional structure of the European Union that has emerged, has largely been created on the model of the French bureaucracy. The main administrative and bureaucratic structures of the EU were put in place during the reign of French President Mitterrand and under the leadership of European Commissioner Jacques Delors. This is certainly one of the reasons why the entire structure of the EU has been strongly modeled on the French centralist presidential system. This centralized structure has subsequently also led to the European Commission (EC), as the central institution, acquiring more and more additional powers. This process of "delegation of powers" to the European Commission has been promoted, at least indirectly but steadily, by

---

Hardcover, 2017.

European governments, because it has repeatedly enabled European governments to make decisions in "Brussels" that would have been difficult to defend at home in front of their own parliaments. If such "proposals" come from "Brussels", then they are usually just nodded off by the parliaments at home. One thinks of the "Euro rescue". It is still true today that the effects of the EU and its institutions, as well as their political and social consequences, are not understood in their real scope by the people or even by most politicians in the member states. This understanding exists, if at all, for the most part in the European Parliament, because the parliamentarians there are operating closer to the actual events and to the proceedings and decision-making processes in "Brussels". However, the European Parliament has still remained largely powerless in the face of the European Commission (EC) and the Council of the European Union, which represents the governments of the Member States. Nor is it a parliament that would adequately represent the European population, as the number of members does not correspond to the respective populations of the member states. Although it also has a so-called "direct democratic legitimacy", it has hardly any decision-making powers, and in particular, it has no budget responsibility.

An important event in the short history of the EU can shed some more light on this institutional scenario and institutional network of the EU, which is often accused of a "democratic deficit". The event we are referring to took place during the term of office of Commission President Jacques Santer, who was in office from 1995 to 1999 and immediately followed the third Commission of Jacques Delors. At that time, the European Court of Auditors received information from the press, which it diligently investigated. Irregularities were uncovered as having been committed by French Commissioner Edith Cresson, a former French prime minister under Mitterrand, which were stigmatized as corruption. Edith Cresson was responsible for the important Commissariat for Science, Research and Development. Due to the intervention of the European Court of Auditors, the entire Commission under Santer had to resign after the European Parliament threatened a motion of censure. It is important for us to note here that the European Court of Auditors has largely lost its influence since this incident. Despite numerous serious irregularities, including in budget management and administration, there have never been consistent results from the work of the European Court of Auditors since 1999. Its reports are practically never discussed or presented to the public in the European public or by the parliaments of the member states. This example shows how important processes of political governance are increasingly faded out of the light of the democratic public. We are not aware of a single one of the many cases reported by the European Court of Auditors since 1999 that would have been taken up by the European public or parliaments in order to investigate them more closely and perhaps even draw conclusions from them. If anything, so-called "democratic deficits" are pointed out by the EC in member states such as Hungary, Poland or Slovakia to justify questionable disciplinary measures against "dissenters from the majority opinion". Progressively and without democratic control by the people, the European central state has submitted to a tendency towards an authoritarian, unitary and coercive state, as it became known in antiquity with the late Roman Empire[31].

---

[31] The historical development of the Roman Empire towards an authoritarian, Unitarian and coercive state is superbly described by the historians Theodor Mommsen in

A very important step in the formation of institutions within the EU was initiated in 1993 with the creation of the Common Foreign and Security Policy (CFSP) of the European Union. The main objectives of this CFSP are officially "to preserve peace, strengthen international security, promote international cooperation and develop and consolidate democracy, the rule of law and respect for human rights and fundamental freedoms[32]". It was not until 1999 that the European Council introduced[33] the post of High Representative for the CFSP, i.e. a kind of European Foreign Commissioner. With a further decision of the European Council in 2001, the Political and Security Committee (PSC) was created with the intention of assuming political control and strategic orientation for the management of international crises.

"The History of Rome", and Edward Gibbon in "The History and Decline of the Roman Empire".
[32]

https://www.europarl.europa.eu/factsheets/de/sheet/158/eu-au%C3%9Fenpolitik-ziele-mechanismen-und-ergebnisse

[33] The European Council is the body of the heads of state or government of the European Union. At least twice every six months, the Council meets for a meeting, also known as an EU summit.

We would like to make a few important comments on this topic of Common Foreign and Security Policy that are important for understanding the EU's self-image and must be taken into account when reading the following chapters in this book. We want to refer to some very important developments that are practically unknown to the European public. These developments have taken place in recent decades and should be well understood to better appreciate the role of the EU as an actor on the international stage and in the context of global developments.

Starting from its original focus on European domestic policy, i.e. the focus on economic and political relations between the member states of the EEC, a European Union has progressively emerged that is increasingly intended to play a role on the stage of international politics and within the international political and economic decision-making processes.

This new role was consciously and strategically developed by Mitterrand and Delors, who had a strong influence on the EU during their periods of government and activity, mainly from 1985 to 1994. France wanted to pursue policies to promote the importance and influence of France as the "Grande Nation" and, if possible, to strengthen its role, i.e. to play off the influence of the "Grande Nation" through the EU with a potentiated power, so to speak. Historically and at the institutional level, European foreign policy arose from the centralization of the European development policy[34], which put the EU in a position to act confidently and effectively as a global actor with relatively generous resources at a very early stage.

Promoted mainly by France, and in the spirit of the European transfer of financial and economic power from the "wealthier" to the less prosperous states, the European Investment Bank (EIB) was founded as early as 1958 with the task of promoting European economic policy by lending with its own capital resources "in order to contribute to a balanced and smooth

---

[34] The development policy institutions of the member states were not abolished after 1993. But the vast majority of development funding has been handed over to the EU for use in accordance with EU rules. Originally, most of the funds went to the ACP (African-Caribbean-Pacific) countries. After 1990, extensive programs for the economic development of the countries of Central and Eastern Europe were launched and financed by the EBRD – European Bank for Reconstruction and Development, under its French president, Jacques Attali, a personal friend of Mitterrand.

development of the internal market in the interest of the Union"[35]. After 1990, i.e. after the dissolution of the Soviet Union, the EBRD (European Bank for Reconstruction and Development)[36] was another important instrument created primarily to finance the construction of infrastructure in the new and future member states of the EU in Central, Eastern and Southeastern Europe.

At this point, we would like to note that the creation and development of the EU have been observed internationally with great interest and often even with applause and admiration. A unique and exemplary process seemed to have been set in motion to bring states together peacefully and in mutual interest. In this way, the EU has become a model for many international and regional alliances and associations of states in Asia, Africa and Latin

---

[35] We will see later that this first centralized European instrument has been created to cover the requirements for managing the Marshall Fund. Ref. to our footnotes on the Marshall Fund and the studies and books by Hans-Werner Sinn and Werner Abelshauser.

[36] The first president of the EBRD was Jacques Attali, a long-time advisor to Mitterrand. For a long time, Attali was considered one of the most influential personalities, globally. He has also published many books on various topics.

America. So it is no wonder that at this time there has been talk of a multipolar world, with the EU as an important and exemplary new "non-aligned" actor. The most important principle promoted by the EU's foreign and development policy, from 1960 to about 2000, has been "partnership" between equal and sovereign partners. The EU has offered its partnership to countries and nations around the world with the purpose of working together to create and shape a better, more peaceful, and more prosperous world.

However, after the event of 9/11 in 2001, i.e. the destruction of the Twin Towers of the World Trade Center, this orientation of European foreign policy was to change fundamentally. As late as 2003, there was still considerable resistance from Europe to the imperialist policy of the USA[37], which was forcefully demonstrated by the wars in Iraq and Afghanistan. However, this resistance did not last long, and the EU was increasingly drawn into the orbit of US foreign policy interests. The principle of partnership ultimately gave rise to "association agreements" and other legal structures, with which the previous EU partners were forced to exercise

[37] We refer here to the corresponding chapters in the book "Colossus" by Niall Ferguson.

political obedience and adopt a neoliberal economic policy course. Only under these conditions did the EU allocate financial resources to the partner countries. Freedom of choice was increasingly restricted for the partner countries.

An authoritarian style then increasingly prevailed within the European Commission. Opposition to the policy of "association agreements" in line with the economic and political interests of the EU, and in harmony with the USA, was not tolerated anymore. In the meantime, in 2009, France also joined NATO. Increasingly, the economic and political interests of the EU have been linked to the military interests of NATO. As we will show in the relevant chapters here in our book, Europe has completely lost its sovereignty over a creeping political process spanning over a hundred years. This is arguably one of the biggest event for Europe since the French Revolution. At that time, the hope for freedom-equality-fraternity arose in Europe. After 2001, times have changed, and we in Europe have once again entered the dark age of ideological polarization and armed conflicts, civil wars and wars, which we had believed to be over after 1945 and with the creation of the European Union as a 'peace project'. It seems fateful for Europe, as if the evil demon of discord, strife and war does not want to let us escape from its claws.

PART 1

SYMPTOMS OF THE CRISIS IN EUROPE

Chapter 4

Europe the "common home" – Russia the eternal enemy

We drafted this chapter with the intention to contrast the various problems that are coming out of our analytical description of the European integration process with a more positive perspective on Europe and the EU. Unfortunately, this positive perspective and creative vision for Europe is not shared by the United States, because it obviously contradicts its interests concerning global hegemony and dominance over Europe.

The first Secretary General of NATO, Lord Hastings Lionel Ismay, already made the remark that Russia should be kept out, the Americans should be in, and the Germans should be kept down[38]. It should be noted that this statement

---

[38] Quoted from https://www.
NATO.int/cps/en/NATOhq/declassified_137930.htm. Lord Hastings Lionel Ismay was NATO's first Secretary General, a position he was initially reluctant to accept. By the end of his tenure, however, Ismay had become the biggest

was not only about NATO, but also about Europe as a geopolitical entity. In an interview, Jacques Baud, a graduate in international security at the Graduate Institute of International Relations in Geneva, former colonel in the Swiss Army, and employee of the Swiss Strategic Intelligence Service, expresses himself on this subject in a clear way as follows: "The policy of the United States has always been to prevent Germany and Russia from working more closely together."[39] This point of view is common knowledge in US-European studies and is presented in many relevant books.[40]

The positive perspective and vision that we want to present in this chapter refer to the concept of the so-called Greater Europe, which includes the rapprochement and gradual integration of

advocate of the organization he had famously said earlier on in his political career: "It was created to keep the Soviet Union out, the Americans in, and the Germans down."

[39] Interview recorded on 05.04.22, by Thomas Kaiser for Current Affairs in Focus. Quoted in Presenza – International Press Agency: https://www.pressenza.com/2022/04.

[40] Refer to Eckart Conze; Die gaullistische Herausforderung. Die deutsch-französischen Beziehungen in der amerikanischen Europapolitik 1958–1963, Munich, 1995; oder auch vom selben Autor: Die große Illusion. Versailles 1919 und die Neuordnung der Welt, 2018.

Russia and European countries. As is well known, French President Charles de Gaulle famously spoke out in 1959 in[41] favor of an alliance from the Atlantic to the Urals, which "will decide the fate of the world". This idea was taken up again in 1985 by Mikhail Gorbachev, then General Secretary of the Central Committee of the Communist Party of the Soviet Union (CPSU).[42] He turned this into a call to see Europe as the "common home".[43] Remarkably, this idea was taken up and developed after 1990 by the governments of Russia, jointly with the European Union and its main member states. The Partnership and Cooperation Agreement between the EU and Russia was signed as early

---

[41] Le voyage présidentiel en Alsace, 1959.

[42] The visit of the General Secretary of the CPSU Central Committee, Mikhail Gorbachev, to France in 1985.

[43] Anyone who wants to devalue such an initiative for cooperation with the use of the term "Eurasianism" only makes it clear that he is concerned with defamation, but not with finding modalities for peaceful cooperation.

In the title of the essay "Rule from Lisbon to Vladivostok", by Robert Hahn, to which we refer here, "rule" is also in the foreground. There is no talk of cooperation here. An "obscure ideology" is suspected behind this proposal of European cooperation, which has mutated into a fascist battle cry for "Russian exiled intellectuals". Yes, in this way, you can refuse dialogue.

as 1994.[44] The focus here was still limited to economic cooperation and the creation of the necessary conditions for the future establishment of a free trade area.

We should point out here that such partnership agreements have been concluded by the EU with many states on all continents. So this is in no way about a special privilege for Russia.[45] In order to make the partnership agreement with

---

[44] Agreement on partnership and cooperation establishing a partnership between the European Communities and their Member States, of one part, and the Russian Federation, of the other part, 1994.

[45] For the unbiased reader, we should also note that the EU also offers so-called association agreements. These are to be classified higher than partnership agreements. These association agreements are international treaties that the European Union concludes with third countries in order to establish special relations with each other. The priorities of stabilization and association agreements between the EU and third countries differ. Depending on the structure, the associated partner is granted different mutual rights and obligations. These association agreements between the EU and third countries serve to bring the EU closer together on the way to a possible later accession to the EU, such as the agreements with Turkey and the Western Balkan states. However, association agreements have also been concluded with countries such as Tunisia, Israel, Morocco, Jordan, Egypt and Algeria. Such agreements with these countries primarily serve trade policy, but also migration and security policy.

Russia more concrete, a group was convened in 2001, with the support of the President of the European Commission, Romano Prodi, to develop a project for a common European economic area.[46] In the same year, Russian President Vladimir Putin declared the importance of close trade and economic relations between Russia and the EU as a common goal in a landmark speech in Germany to the Bundestag.[47] This was followed by the adoption of the *roadmap* for the common economic area in 2005.[48] In 2010, Putin proposed *the creation of a free trade zone from Lisbon to Vladivostok* in an article in the Süddeutsche Zeitung.[49] This idea was increasingly understood and finally adopted as part of Russia's foreign

---

[46] Joint Statement on the Energy Dialogue by President of the Russian Federation Vladimir Putin, President of the European Council Guy Verhofstadt, with the assistance of the Secretary General of the Council of the EU/High Representative for the Common Foreign and Security Policy Javier Solana, and President of the European Commission Romano Prodi, 2001.

[47] From the protocol of Vladimir Putin's speech in the German Bundestag, 2001.

[48] EU and Russia: A roadmap for the Common Economic Space (CES), 2005.

[49] Putin, 2010.

policy.[50] The harmonization and development of European and Eurasian integration were formulated as strategic tasks in relation to the EU. The creation of a common economic and humanitarian space from the Atlantic to the Pacific has thus been declared an important goal of Russian foreign policy.[51]

In contrast, Russia was increasingly critical of its political relations with the United States. In his speech at the 2007 Munich Conference on Security Policy, Putin criticized the monopolistic dominance of the United States in global relations, claiming that the United States was displaying an "almost unrestrained use of hyper-force in international relations." He went on to say that the result is that "no one feels safe! ... Of course, such a policy promotes an arms race."[52] In an interview in January 2007, Putin declared that Russia was in favor of a democratic, multipolar world and the strengthening of the international legal system.[53] In his speech in 2008, at the celebration of "Victory Day" against

[50] Foreign Policy Concept of the Russian Federation, 2013.

[51] Foreign Policy Concept of the Russian Federation, 2016.

[52] You can find it in the reports on the 43rd Security Conference in Munich.

[53] Indian Television Channel Doordarshan and Press Trust of India News Agency, 18 January 2007.

Nazi Germany, Putin warned with regret that "the threats are not diminishing, but merely changing and appearing in a new guise. These new threats follow the same contempt for human life and the same efforts to establish exclusive domination over the whole world."[54] At the 33rd G8 summit in June 2007, Putin said to the USA: "We do not want confrontation; rather, we want to offer ourselves for dialogue. However, we demand that this dialogue recognize the equality of the interests of both sides." However, Russia saw its security interests increasingly called into question. NATO expanded eastward in further steps by accepting the former countries of the Eastern Bloc as members. Missiles were stationed in the countries of Eastern Europe, and NATO was getting closer and closer to Russia's borders in a threatening way.

Parallel to these increasingly tense developments on the political side, the rapprochement on the economic side was nevertheless pushed forward.[55] There were still

[54] Transcript of the speech in the Kremlin archives, March 5, 2008.

[55] In Germany, this policy of economic relations with Russia under the government of Willy Brandt was described by the slogan "Change through Trade".

forces within the EU that did not want to give up the economic advantages of relations with Russia. In February 2017, the German *economic research institute IFO* published an article in which it considered the free trade zone from Lisbon to Vladivostok not only feasible, but also beneficial for both sides.[56] In June 2019, an important delegation of representatives of the EU and the Eurasian Economic Commission met for a meeting. The aim of the meeting was to promote dialogue on the technical aspects of trade policy, technical regulation, customs legislation, and digitalization, as well as the exchange of information on the regulatory framework of mutual interest.[57] In the summer of 2019, after a meeting with Russian President Putin, French President Emmanuel Macron published a post via social media in which he pretended that he "considers Russia to be a deeply European country and believes in a Europe that stretches from Lisbon to Vladivostok".[58]

---

[56] Felbermayr, G., & Gröschl, J., 2017.
[57] Eurasian Economic Commission and European Commission are building technical dialogue, 2019.
[58] Blogging on Facebook in Russian, Macron notes progress in ties with Moscow, 2019.

It will not have escaped our notice that these encouraging diplomatic initiatives, notes and remarks by the EU and its member states took place at a time when the implementation of the Minsk agreements of 2015 was actively obstructed by the same European states, obviously in agreement with the USA. During these years, the Ukrainian government bombed and maltreated the two Russian-speaking regions of Luhansk and Donetsk on a daily basis, with an estimated 14,000 people falling victim to these military attacks, which were carried out by its own Ukrainian government and covered by the European states and the USA. So it is only understandable that the Russian government must have asked itself more and more what exactly had to be done to end this situation.

During these talks and negotiations on cooperation between the EU and Russia, the lack of common values was repeatedly and critically emphasized in the statements of Western political leaders. At the same time, it was repeatedly emphasized that Russia's relations with the western part of Europe should "normalize" and that the Russian leadership must recognize that Russia is ultimately a

European and not a Eurasian state.[59] For Russia, acceding to this demand of the Western states would have meant giving up an important part of its identity and history. This identity of Russia includes historical relations with the Central Asian peoples, as well as the peculiarity of its geographical location as the central northern part of the Euro-Asian continent. This demand from Western Europe was and is therefore ultimately unrealistic and neither historically nor geographically justified.[60]

---

[59] Bratersky, 2017.

[60] One of many sources: The Cambridge History of Russia, edited by Dominic Lieven, 2005. An overview with references to the history of Russia can be found on Wikipedia.

PART 1

SYMPTOMS OF THE CRISIS IN EUROPE

Chapter 5

The New World Order after the Treaty of Versailles

"The question is, how can we get away from the rules, within which we... since the Treaty of Versailles, are proceeding politically. The challenge is to change the rules..."

"Ecology of the Mind,
Part VI, Crises in the Ecology of the Mind",
1966 lecture "From Versailles to Cybernetics",
Gregory Bateson

FOREWORD

Only a few people in 1919 could have imagined how important the political decisions after the First World War would be for the future coexistence on our planet. After the end of the British Empire, the European monarchies and the classical bourgeoisie, the age of democracies, globalization and US hegemony was heralded.

Even if the lives of people, on a large as well as on a small scale, do not follow a plan, it is nevertheless astonishing to see how a red thread runs through the history of mankind over the last hundred years.

LIFE IN A CRISIS MODE - SYMPTOMS OF GLOBAL POLITICAL STRUCTURES

A hundred years ago, American President Woodrow Wilson established a foreign policy doctrine that was, in his understanding, intended to avoid future global conflicts and secure US interests through the worldwide spread of a market economy and democracy and, in cases of emergency, through military interventions in trouble spots.[61] The term Wilsonianism was coined when Wilson presented his 14-point program "for eternal peace" in Europe in 1918, even before the

---

[61] There is a vast amount of literature on the subject of the Treaty of Versailles, the negotiations, and its significance. For a quick access and to clarify the significance for American hegemonic politics, we recommend: "Colossus: The Rise and Fall of the American Empire", 2004, by Niall Ferguson. A summary, worth reading, with a bibliography can be found on Wikipedia:
https://de.wikipedia.org/wiki/Friedensvertrag_von_Versaill es

negotiations on the Treaty of Versailles had been launched at the end of the First World War[62]. Wilsonianism had thus set itself the goal of showing the world the way out of a "global" crisis[63]. Wilson is considered in the USA a president who personally represented high and noble standards and also initiated some

---

[62] With the arguments summarized in the 14-point program of the then President Wilson of 1918, he had already justified the entry of the USA into the First World War before the US Congress and the American public. Also compare the anthology by Jens Heisterkamp (ed.), Die Jahrhundertillusion. Wilson's Right of Self-Determination of Peoples, Steiner's Critique and the Question of the National Minorities of Today, Frankfurt/Main, 2002. This anthology was very competently reviewed in the journal Perseus, der Europäer, Vol. 6 No. 8, June 2002, by Andreas Bracher, under the title "Völkische Selbstbestimmung und Dreigliederung".

[63] Compare, among others, the British economist John Maynard Keynes, who attended the negotiations on behalf of the British government at the time and already clearly named the nonsense of Clemenceau's French negotiating position at the time. An important source is also the essay "From Versailles to Cybernetics" by Gregory Bateson, published in: Ecology of the Mind, Suhrkamp Wissenschaft 571, Frankfurt 1985, which unfortunately was never published, but provides important insights into the process of the Versailles negotiations. Important points for us here: (a) The Treaty of Versailles, also sometimes called the Dictate of Versailles, was the

meaningful initiatives.[64] However, two points were decisive in this historically important moment: on the one hand, the USA claimed the right for themselves, it even considered it its duty to ensure peace in the future, mainly in Europe, but finally, at a global stage, if necessary, by force of arms. The second important point concerns the fact that he allowed the revanchist claims of France and Britain against Germany to pass without objection in the Treaty of Versailles. As a result, Europe finally moved in the direction of the catastrophe of the Second World War that was already lurking. Instead of looking for a constructive way out of the dilemma, Europe had finally continued on the path that would lead to the destruction of its own historical significance in the future. The result was that the

starting point for the Second World War, which led Europe, including the Soviet Union, under the Nazis and fascists led by Hitler into another catastrophe. Wilsonianism, which was launched at the same time, was the beginning of Pax Americana, i.e. the claim of the Americans to bring "peace and democracy" to the world under their leadership.

[64] See Lesson 62: "World War I – The Road to Intervention" and Lesson 63: "World War I – Versailles and Wilson's Gambit" from the book "The History of the United States", 2nd Edition, 2003, by C. Guelzo, Gary Gallagher, and Patrick N. Allitt.

USA had become the big winner of the First World War.[65]

No one has analyzed more prophetically than John Maynard Keynes, why the Treaty of Versailles had to trigger a new war and political conflicts that are still smoldering today.[66] Keynes' polemical essay contains a clear reference to the not regained level of wealth that Europe had enjoyed before 1914, and the bleak outlook on the less than hopeful post-war period. No one else has described so vividly and with analytical mockery, how peace was gambled away in 1919 and incalculable damage was inflicted on Europe. In doing so, he offers at the same time important insights into the psychology and behavior, as well as the particular interests of Woodrow Wilson, Lloyd George and Georges Clemenceau, the negotiators on the American, British and French sides[67]. Thus, shortly after the "primordial

---

[65] We should not mention here that the United States insisted on repaying the loans it had lent to France and Great Britain during the war years, even before it joined the war.

[66] War and Peace. The Economic Consequences of the Treaty of Versailles, 1920, John Maynard Keynes.

[67] Keynes refrained from commenting on David Lloyd George, the British negotiator. Obviously, he didn't want to make enemies at home.

catastrophe"[68] and the brief regain of a spirit of optimism in the "wild" 20s, Europe soon switched back into crisis mode, from which we have not been able to get out to this day, even though we have created great material wealth in the meantime through strong economic growth after 1949. Apart from brief breathers in the 1920s and from 1950 to 1970, which gave cause for optimism, the splendor of the European world powers was rapidly fading, and the age of European global dominance was inexorably approaching its historic end.

We still live and develop today in this apparent mode of a steadily increasing crisis in Europe. So we should not be surprised if our media and political leaders make us believe that we in Europe have been constantly threatened by a whole series of crises since 2007. This is how we read on Wikipedia about the crises that were emerging and ongoing since this time: *The world*

---

[68] Historians refer to the First World War as a "primordial catastrophe". This designation goes back to the American historian and diplomat George F. Kennan, who characterized the war in 1979 as "the great seminal catastrophe of this century". A differentiated interpretation will appreciate the war as a cipher for the end of the bourgeoisie and for the "crisis of classical modernity".

economic crisis from 2007 onwards was triggered by the bursting of a real estate bubble (in the USA; our note), with the accompanying financial crisis and banking crisis, which was later followed by sovereign debt crises, and sometimes state crises, as in Greece.

A number of years have passed since 2007. At that time, as we have seen, the world was in the midst of a major economic crisis, accompanied by other important crises. The real estate price bubble in the USA, also called the sub-prime bubble, had burst. We were all affected in Europe by the so-called Lehman banking crisis.

Obviously, we should be afraid for our money, for our livelihoods and for our way of life. Not yet for our lives. That's what we were told, and we reacted accordingly and were ready, if not to accept everything, then at least ready to bear burdens "without alternative".

Since then, we have been living in crisis mode, which has intensified in the past decade. This mood is led by the media, by politicians and scientists of all stripes, who try to offer us explanations for everything that has just happened and is happening again and again. They all offered their stories and steered the world with this consistency of public mood. In the European Union (EU), the so-called sovereign debt crisis was soon added to this scenario. The euro crisis was then still an additional gift to politicians. In this way, they were able to make it clear to all of us: we could only do as well as before, if we made more effort and were willing to make more sacrifices. We were told to listen to our politicians and the responsible power elites — they certainly would know what to do and what is best for all of us[69].

Oh yes, and elsewhere there were other and more crises; new crises arose again and again. In Syria, Iraq and Afghanistan, war has been waged on a large scale. The Arab Spring broke out in the Northern African states in 2011, with massive unrest and civil war-like conditions in some cases. It didn't take long before Yemen was also heavily bombed. Saudi Arabia obviously had a great interest in finally being able to use its air force with the opportunity to deploy the expensive American bombers, while the USA also had a great interest in doing so, because they had to provide training, for adequate payment, of course, and supply the

---

[69] In the media, even at the highest level, we are informed that the "state quota" has been rising steadily since then. This points to increasing centralization and the strengthening of the unitary state.

ammunition, as well as secure supplies for destroyed or shot down aircraft. We all became witnesses to an old philosophy saying that every crisis provides opportunities to make comfortable profits.

Clearly, there has been a lot going on in the world over the past years and decades.

We should not forget the various color revolutions, or should we say attempted *coups d'etat*, some non-violent protests, as in the case of Georgia, some not successful, as in the case Belarus and Kyrgyzstan, others leading to the outbreak of a war with the deployment of NATO aircraft and nuclear ammunition, as it has been the case in former Yugoslavia. From today's perspective, it is very important to mention the "spring revolution" of 2014 on the Maidan in Kyiv, with the subsequent coup in Ukraine and the Crimean crisis. In addition, there is the constant and increasingly felt threat, albeit mostly promoted by our media, from China, whose economy threatens to buy up all of us here in Europe, and which, as a state in Asia, threatens and wants to colonize not only a few atolls, but the entire Pacific world and is now in a "trade war" with the whole world[70]. We take all this from our media every day, and are called upon by modern methods of "framing" to believe our "responsible" elites and their noble representatives and to follow them faithfully.

And let us also remember the other European crises that we were able to "experience" during this time. We are constantly threatened by immigrants, some have been invited and then uninvited again. Europe is progressively splitting up. Great Britain has split off from the EU in a Brexit, and the Eastern European member states of the EU allow themselves to express their own positions in different areas and do not want to continue being patronized by the Western European member states, such as France and Germany.

Reality is complex, and it is not always easy to understand the processes and make them

---

[70] This geopolitical situation is also the reason for the "Achberg Peace Initiative", as it was initiated by Herbert Schliffka and associated friends as a consequence of the "Achberg Impulse for Freedom, Direct Democracy and Global Solidarity in Economic Life" (https://kulturzentrum-achberg.de/). Schliffka provides the framework for this initiative in the essay "Geopolitical Strategies: Dangers for a Self-Determined Europe? – Achberger Beiträge für ein "gemeinsames Haus Europa" im 21. Jahrhundert.

understandable[71]. However, that is what we intend to do here in our book, at least to some extent.

THE ULTIMATE CRISIS: WAR

In our understanding, the Mises Institute of the USA[72] is the principal economic institution in the US that upholds a highly informed and critical spirit about the role of the US Federal Reserve Bank (FED) as a tool of government and associated financial cartels in their role in creating wars. We highlight this point here to draw attention to a particular factor in the creation of a distorted public opinion.

This factor, we wish to point out, became virulent and particularly visible in the years following the so-called financial crisis in and after 2008. We relate here mainly to the situation in Germany, because that is the country, where we have been living during that time. However, what we say about Germany

---

[71] In his lectures of 1919 on the symptomatology of history, Rudolf Steiner challenges us to see the reality behind the symptoms, the truth behind the events.

[72] https://mises.org/

applies in the same way to other European countries, as well as the USA.

We are talking here about the fact that the economists and financial analysts that have been commenting on the financial crisis after 2008, have generally been talking of a crisis, or an impending and threatening crash, limited to the finance industry. For Germany, we briefly refer to three authors and researchers: Max Otte, Dirk Mueller and Thomas Meyer, former Chief Economist of Deutsche Bank, who, after 2007, published a series of articles in the FAZ newspaper and also drafted a number of highly informed books on the topic[73].

Max Otte published in 2019 the book "Weltsystemcrash: Krisen, Unruhen und die Geburt einer neuen Weltordnung". This book has been a long term bestseller in Germany. The title translated by us is: "World System Crash: Crises, Unrest and the Birth of a New World Order". Dirk Mueller has published in 2018 „Machtbeben: Die Welt vor der grössten Wirtschaftskrise aller Zeiten". The title translated by us is: "Power Quakes: The World before the Biggest Economic Crisis of All Time".

---

[73] Ref. to "Europe's unfinished Currency. The Political Economics of the Euro", 2013, Thomas Meyer.

It is remarkable that these authors, and many more that we might quote, have always and still do not dare to think their analyses through to the very end. The most important reason for this is that they limit themselves essentially to the fields of economics and finance. Their main intention is to provide advice to investors. This is legitimate, but it is not enough for ordinary people in Germany or Europe. Why? Because it is fading out an important part of reality, and we would dare to say, the more important part, i.e. the truth about the financial crisis and its final consequences.

These authors, and we could certainly expand the list with Holger Stelzner, Prof. Sinn and many others, prefer to limit themselves essentially to the fields of economics and finance. Why? Because the "whole truth" would probably be shocking to most ordinary people, and to investors in particular. The authors, conceal a part of reality because they are afraid of being sanctioned by the government and becoming accused by the mainstream media of spreading conspiracy theories. This would, of course, damage their reputation and credibility as financial advisors and academics.

All these authors, consciously or unconsciously, avoid using the word "war". Imagine Dirk Mueller talking about "war", instead of using the words power quake, crash, or showdown. Then that would become a completely different story. Or if Max Otte were to rename his book "World System Crash" to "Global System Crash and Total War". What would people think of it? And how would the media have reacted to this?

The most recent example that came our way is the interview given in the NZZ (Neue Zürcher Zeitung), on 13 August 2024, by the economist Daniel Stelter, who is running a highly informative website ("beyond the obvious" – bto). Stelter has been interviewed in the follow-up to the recent mini-meltdown of the stock markets that happened in August 2024. In this interview he was talking about "fear of crashes" (Crash Angst), without mentioning with one word the ongoing war in Ukraine and the impending war industry in Europe. These examples show, how supposedly smart and honest persons with a rather high level of social responsibility, are in fact misleading the public.

With our book, we are taking a different stance and position. We believe that, in most cases, it is to the advantage of people to be told the truth.

It usually helps people to know what is going on in the world and to have a good understanding of reality. Psychology supposes a direct link between knowledge concerning understanding one's own reality and the growth of consciousness. Therefore, we would have preferred, if the aforementioned analyses of these economists and financial advisors had been thought through to the end and if "the child would also have been called by its name". A better understanding of reality could become the starting point of the journey to a progressive transformation of our societies.

It is our conviction that understanding reality, supplemented with the courage to take responsibility, are the two most essential prerequisites for the urgently required transformation of our societies in Europe and of a paradigm shift that is leading to the way out of the permanent crises in Europe.

Only by facing reality with courage will people be ready to look out for options to emerge from the current Europe- and US-driven and globally effective crisis as unscathed as possible and with a positive new approach. People have to find the courage to ask themselves: How can we transform Europe away from the old paradigm of crises and relentless wars? What are the alternatives to the world system crash and to global and total war?

People increasingly understand that they are only put off and often simply lied to. The fraud of the global political and power elite is increasingly being seen through. It slowly dawns on people, and they increasingly understand that humanity as a whole is moving on a downward trend. Reality shimmers through the stories of the mainstream media. The belief in a better future is fading. Trust in the power elites is being eaten up more and more.

The various economists mentioned know that the current financial and monetary system has no future, it no longer works[74] to the benefit of the people and their nations. Important basic rules and principles have already been undermined. Economists are seriously pondering the question concerning the financial system of the future. Currently, the big financial players, the Anglo-American cartels, are "buying time"[75], while they are making huge benefits in funding the war machine the US and NATO are

[74] Among the specialists mentioned, it is Thomas Meyer, who has continued with his warnings and even presented a whole series of books showing the way out of the financial and currency crisis. Ref. to Wikipedia.

running at an ever-increasing scale. That is the essence hidden behind the symptoms of the current geopolitical events, as we have shown in our book "War & Business", published in 2024, demonstrating the functioning of the American Business Model for hegemony.

We would highly appreciate these high-caliber economists discussing with us alternative options for the "world system crash" or the "global and total war". What would be a way for Europe and the world to get out of the global crisis? What could we in Europe do, and which paths could humanity take?

THE NEW WORLD ORDER WAS HERALDED BY THE USA IN 1919

When the present series of the so-called crisis started in 2007, it was only one step on the way. The 20th century has been an "age of extremes"[76], and it ended in crises that found their "natural" continuation in the 21st century.

---

[75] We refer here to the book "Gekaufte Zeit: die Vertagte Krise des demokratischen Kapitalismus", 2013, Wolfgang Streeck. (our translation of the title: "Bought time: the postponed crisis of democratic capitalism").

[76] The Age of Extremes, World History of the 20th Century, 1995, Eric Hobsbawm.

As early as the beginning of the 20th century, more precisely towards the end of the First World War, Europe and the world were to be finally, if not saved, then eventually put on the right track. This was to be achieved first, through the entry of the USA into the war, and then through the implementation of US President Wilson's 14-Points Program. It was "Wilsonianism" that had been launched by the USA as a by-product of the Treaty of Versailles, together with the initiation of the League of Nations. What France and England would negotiate with the defeated Germany was not so decisive from the point of view of the USA. Much more important was the new doctrine of the American foreign policy, which, in a decisive turn, set itself apart from the previous policy of non-interference in European affairs and separation of global spheres of influence[77]. In the future, the USA would not limit itself anymore to the American hemisphere but would bring peace all over the world, if necessary, also by force and

[77] It should not go unmentioned that this policy of hegemony was not initially implemented by the United States, since domestic politics tended to be limited to the American hemisphere. The hegemonic claim of the USA was ultimately a consequence of the Second World War and was only finally initiated by the then President Roosevelt.

through wars. The League of Nations, which the US has never joined, was supposed to provide a diplomatic platform for international dialogue on the basis of American rules. Its major purpose was to facilitate the management of global public opinion and to secure the dominance of the USA in the international arena. This was the core of Wilsonianism, which provided the model for the United Nations (UN) and the Security Council to this day, and justifies every war led by the USA and its allies in NATO, from Vietnam to Afghanistan, then from Iraq to Syria, Libya and Yemen, and today in Ukraine[78].

As we know, wars, the most important instrument of American foreign policy, alongside diplomacy, must also be financed[79]. For this

---

[78] For example, Wilsonianism could be used to justify Turkey's invasion of Syria from 2017 to 2018.

[79] Three important sources should suffice here to underline the pragmatic intelligence of the Americans. The first US Secretary of the Treasury, Alexander Hamilton, understood "financing" as a crucial means of shaping policy and created important instruments for this purpose. Some historians therefore call the USA "Hamilton's Republic".

The Ascent of Money: A Financial History of the World, 2008, Niall Ferguson. In this book, Ferguson shows that the most important political importance of banks, both private and central banks, is the financing of wars.

purpose, the USA created the American central bank, the Federal Reserve Bank (FED), in 1913. As we will see in further detail, this was the critical step towards the implementation of the American hegemonic policy, because it provided the financial basis and enabled covering up for the increasing needs for funding of wars. The US Government has now been equipped to function as an empire through a steadily increasing amount of loans and debt that have grown to exorbitant dimensions to this day.[80]

The Federal Reserve System: its origin and growth; reflections and recollections; 2 volumes, New York, 1930, Paul Moritz Warburg. Paul M. Warburg, a banker from Hamburg, is considered the main initiator of the US central bank FED, which was founded in 1913. In 1921, Paul M. Warburg became the founding chairman of the Council on Foreign Relations (CFR), the most important institution for the coordination of American policy by its elites, with a focus on international relations.

The Creature from Jekyll Island, 1994, George Edward Griffin.

[80] A very good overview with impressive graphs of the historical development and current perspective of the debt of the USA can be found in an article by the Kantonalbank Zürich. Sources: Zürcher Kantonalbank, CBO, Census, OMB.
https://www.zkb.ch/de/blog/anlegen/us-staatsverschuldung-rekordkurs.html.

When American banks stumbled in 2007, because the repayment of cheap mortgages and loans was no longer guaranteed, the then US President George W. Bush was asked whether he wanted to save Lehmann Bank at the expense of the taxpayers. That was the moment, when this courageous and determined president, following the advice of his high-profile Wall Street-hardened financial and economic advisers, said that he didn't want that. The result was that Lehman Brothers Bank had to file for bankruptcy. The financial bubble burst. This opened the way for rapid write-downs and a quick and expedient way out of the crisis for the financial cartels and banks of the USA. New opportunities would also arise out of this crisis.

EVERYTHING HAS ITS PRICE, ESPECIALLY FOR GERMANY

The stupid thing for the Europeans was, that most of these largely unsecured American mortgages and loans - so-called sub-prime credits-had been passed on from American to European banks, including Deutsche Bank, Commerzbank, and also to some big Irish banks[81]. Therefore, in the end, due to the decisions of the eminent European leaders, especially the French and German power elite, their politicians and central bankers, the European taxpayers had to pay back the bad loans of the American banks. Thus, Europe already contributed to a large extent to the financing of the American economy, its armaments industry and the war machine. As we all know, cost and risk sharing within NATO has always been an important issue from the point of view of the USA.

At the same time, as a result of the financial crisis in the USA, the euro crisis suddenly arose in Europe, triggered by the so-called sovereign debt crisis.[82] After all, the banks and their

---

[81] Incidentally, this has also contributed to the further decline of Deutsche Bank and Commerzbank, which, by international standards, have become insignificant financial institutes.

[82] In an article by the State Agency for Civic Education in Baden-Württemberg, it says: "The euro crisis has been a crisis within the European Union that has been going on since 2009. It combines aspects of a sovereign debt crisis, a banking crisis and a financial crisis. In some EU countries, increased borrowing led to high inflation. This could no longer be regulated by a national fiscal policy, so that permanent current account deficits led to high national debt."

owners and investors wanted their money back, if possible, with a good return on investment. The norm was the 25 percent return, which Deutsche Bank regularly set as a target at that time, but which is often exceeded by the Anglo-Saxon banks and funds to this day[83].

The German government, in close cooperation with France and the European Central Bank (ECB), did what it was asked to do and financed all claims, both, those of the banks, and those of the EU Member States. The parliament in Germany, as the formal representative of the voters and taxpayers, approved all payments without exception. There was no alternative, at least that's what the then President of the ECB, Jean-Claude Trichet, said, and so the Chancellor and the German government repeated it.

It should only be briefly noted here that the debt of the states has continued to grow steadily since that time. No one has seen a "proper" way out for a long time. With seeing eyes, the world, at least the "Western" world, is heading more and more towards the abyss.

[83] "The 25 percent is not set in stone, but it is a benchmark that the best in the world have achieved," said top banker Josef Ackermann, head of Deutsche Bank, from 2006 to 2012, about his goal of achieving a return on equity of 25 percent before taxes.

What actually happened in these years of the euro crisis and during the so-called global and European structural adjustment, should not surprise us anymore. These "structural adjustments" have been led by the FED and the ECB, not more than a subsidiary of the FED, which have been assisted by the Bretton Woods institutions. Tacitly and without the public being aware of it, the definitive takeover of the European industries and finance institutions was gaining pace again. It has been consistently implemented in just a few years by the Anglo-American capital and their funding institutions, banks and financial cartels. The last remnants of resistance were overcome non-violently. For the Americans, it was like a fairy tale, similar to the "Fall of the Wall" for the Germans, because everything happened without violence. Europe had capitulated non-violently and given away all their assets.

Consequently, everyone was happy. The people in Europe, that it had not gotten worse, and the US investors, because they were able to take over Europe's economy and the management of European capital and the European economy to a maximum extent and on favorable terms without much effort[84]. With the purpose of further smoothing these processes, the EU installed a former Goldman Sachs executive as president of the European Central Bank (ECB). In the US, the leading role of the financial institutions in government is an old tradition. More recently, Bill Clinton engaged under his administration Robert Rubin, a seasoned banker and businessman. In the US, the Treasury Department has continuously been firmly in the

---

[84] The investment funds are now majority owners of entire sectors in the Dax. This means that they not only own majorities in individual companies, but also banks. Rather, they are majority-owned by entire industries, which they can then control more or less at will. It is no longer the individual company or the individual bank that determines its policies, prices and wages. The corporate policy and, thus, the socially relevant decisions are made by the investment funds. These are therefore approaching the capacity for economic OVERALL CONTROL. Perhaps they already have this capacity for the most important key industries — in Germany, mechanical engineering and vehicle construction, together with the defense industry, including robotics and other high-tech companies, the chemical industry — and the banks, which have now become "operationally" irrelevant and no longer operate independently. Compare: Has everything been done yet? Focus Magazine, No. 8, 2009, Who Owns Germany?
In 2024, there is not a single company in the DAX in which Black Rock would not have a stake.

hands of Goldman Sachs, or other leaders of Wall Street and the financial cartels.

In the US, the crisis of 2007/08 was therefore only a kind of new start, while in Europe it led to a strong and final shift in the historical claims to national power and to the end of financial and economic autonomy. European industry, together with banks and financial institutions, was henceforth firmly in the grip of Anglo-American banks, financial institutions and financial cartels. After the crisis of 2007/08, they didn't have to get up and back on their feet, but thanks to their global, huge and liquid investment funds, they were immediately and always ready to continue financing the course of the world. After all, business had to go on, because we all wanted to continue to do our, more or less, important business.

The Anglo-American investment funds thus took advantage of this time, when money was scarce in Europe, and companies and banks were often at their limits, especially in the EU's Southern member states. They helped Europe by making numerous strategic investments and taking over many "struggling" companies, often directly, but mostly by taking over majorities through their investment funds. In the meantime, the DAX companies listed on the German stock exchange are under the ownership of Anglo-Saxon capital by more than 50 percent[85]. In addition, in the years after 2008, a large number of medium-sized companies in Europe were also bought up by American companies and by Anglo-American capital. This clear trend intensified again to an incredible level after 2022, when the German government exposed their principal industries, such as car and machine production, as well as tool making, to progressive deindustrialization and increasing economic and political dependence on the US. In the meantime, even the large electrical power grids in Europe are being taken over by US companies, such as Westinghouse, and by other international investors. So, one cannot actually speak of energy security in Europe anymore. Rather, we must confirm a new and even more exclusive and consolidating dependence through incorporation by the US. This relentless trend now encompasses France and most of the other important countries in Europe, such as Italy,

---

[85] Report of the FAZ, "Many American investors, The Dax is firmly in foreign hands", by Daniel Mohr, JANUARY 26, 2017. – These statistics do not include cross-ownership, i.e. if Deutsche Bank owns a share in a company, then this is attributed to Deutsche Bank. Meanwhile, Deutsche Bank is already majority-owned by foreigners.

Spain, Poland and the Netherlands.[86] These processes confirm that Europe has already given herself up voluntarily.

The transfer to these global Anglo-American investment funds of the most important real estate assets in Germany and throughout Europe corresponds to another takeover of European assets. What in the past belonged mainly to municipalities, trade union associations or state institutions has now often gone to global investment funds, which adorn themselves with German or European names in order to present themselves as nice German and European companies, demonstrating, how close they are to the citizen. We have just received news reporting how a US hedge fund is buying up a Spanish municipality by taking over its debts. Returns on this investment are not publicly discussed. We do not want to go into detail here about the debts of German and European municipalities, including those with

---

[86] The Chair of Energy for Society at the de Grenoble Ecole de Management (GEM) of the University of Grenoble is now asking itself "how Europe can prevent its blindness in the field of energy policy (Politiques énergétiques : comment éviter une dystopie européenne?) and at the same time warns against selling off to Anglo-American and Chinese investors.

foreign investors, which they have taken on to finance their investments and operations[87]. The policy of the USA therefore does not serve "to ward off EU competition" on the world markets, i.e. as an industry location policy. Rather, the policy of the USA represents the ever-consolidating incorporation of Europe and its states as vassals.[88]

We were all so happy that the economies in Europe were humming again after 2009. We were told that we should all be happy about it. Even though a large number of temporary jobs have now been introduced, which are subsequently and over time leading to increasingly precarious living conditions and the threat of poverty in old age. Even the employees of the prisons in Bavaria are now forced to pursue additional gainful activities in order to be able to finance their livelihoods[89]. The media

[87] The German Association of Cities commented: "At the end of 2022, the municipalities and associations of municipalities, including their shareholdings, were indebted to the non-public sector with 313.9 billion euros, according to a model calculation by the statistical offices of the federal and state governments. This corresponded to a debt of 4,034 euros per capita.

[88] Refer to cit. Brzezinski, op. cit..

[89] FAZ, from January 2, 2018, Bavaria, First the prison, then the part-time job.

report daily on the poor situation of most employees in the "nursing professions". Nevertheless, we should all be happy that there is enough work for everyone, which ostensibly gives us cause for great happiness every day. In all this, the EU had managed, albeit at an immense economic and political cost, to hold Europe together. Truly, a remarkable result.

EUROPE: BRIDGE BETWEEN EAST AND WEST, OR OUTPOST OF US HEGEMONY?

Foreword

When the EU created the European External Action Service (EEAS) as a direct outflow of its Common Foreign Security Policy (CFSP) at the beginning of the 21st century, it was supposed to become a "service for peace, security and conflict resolution". How is it then that Europe is increasingly affected by crises and threatened by wars and becomes directly and indirectly involved in them, as in Syria, Libya, Iraq, Afghanistan, Sudan, Yemen and now Ukraine? Can it be that someone does not do its job right? Or is it the case that the EEAS has a very special understanding of what its job is? Will these political and military actions help us to realize the European peace project[90]? Will Europe regain the position of a promoter of peace, if it pursues the further development of the European Union into a global political and military "power", acting as a strong partner of NATO and as a "powerful" actor in world politics in the future? Please be reminded that, driven by the US and NATO, this policy of the "powerful actor" is officially being sought by the EU under the leadership of France and Germany, and strongly supported by increasingly belligerent member states, such as Poland and the Baltic countries. Italy, Spain, the Netherlands and the Belgium have never put into question their role as loyal vassals to the US. Their economic incorporation by the US has been consolidated quietly since World War II.

As we have already mentioned above, in order to answer these questions concerning the "nature" of European integration, we must *move from the perception of symptoms to the understanding of reality*. This reality is hidden behind the veil of

---

[90] It is not only on the website of the German government that the EU is called a peace project:
https://www.bundesregierung.de/breg-de/schwerpunkte/e uropa/fragen-und-antworten-zu-frieden-in-europa-448742

symptoms, which only show us a semblance of reality. We know reality is complex, but that shouldn't stop us from trying to understand it[91]. But how can that work? What can be an effective analytical method to attain an adequate understanding of reality? As we have already

---

[91] We quote Gerd Weidenhausen in Die Drei, No. 5., from a review by Wolfgang Bittner, "The Conquest of Europe by the USA", Mainz 2015, to illustrate how the European bourgeois middle-class still falls due to its own fear, and wants to present the matter as if the EU still had a choice, as if it still wanted to have a choice. It must be acknowledged: "The self-interest of the EU is the benefit of the USA". However, in our understanding, this is "over". It's done! The Europeans, especially the German intellectuals (the French are often still more courageous), instead of "acknowledging what is", still lose themselves in subjunctives out of fear. To put it clearly: The EU no longer pursues an independent policy, as any German Chancellor and Foreign Minister could confirm to us if he wanted to be honest. So here is the typical quote, in which it is pretended that the EU still has all options: "the tendency to appease the role of EU policy, which evolves in the wake of US policy: In its supposedly so noble democratization ambitions, the latter was not only thwarted or even betrayed by targeted US interventions within the framework of its "Eastern Neighborhood Policy", which has been practiced for some time, rather, it pursued very selfish economic and political interests from the outset, which made it forget to bring Russia on board in the negotiations on the EU Association Agreement with Ukraine. The mess that spread in the wake of this blatant

said, the most important instrument for understanding is thinking, and the most important prerequisite is fearlessness. Combined. These two factors will enable us to face the facts and the often terrible events, for which we humans in Europe are responsible[92]. Of course, officially, nobody in Europe will take responsibility. Following the official reading and propaganda, the cause of the evil deeds are the actions of "the others". Today, the others are the Russians, the Chinese, the Shiite Muslims, the Cubans, or other left-wing and deviant partisans. These are the people who are not willing to obey and follow the invitation for the application of rules and values promoted single-handedly by Europe and the US.

In view of this situation, we want to name, at this stage, only one single fact that wants to hide behind the veil of symptoms and behind our fear of facing reality and seeing things as they are.

---

omission was therefore, to a large extent, self-inflicted. Despite all the competition for influence and power, EU-Europe and the USA are pursuing a policy of division of labor with pre-distributed roles ...".

[92] This is how C. G. Jung expressed himself in his biography when he remarked, looking back on National Socialism and its consequences for Europe and the world: "If people had had the courage to look evil in the face and call it by its name, it could have been prevented".

What is this single fact that is hiding behind the war against Russia, which is only a symptom of driving forces that are effective behind the veil? - If one honestly reflects on the fact that China, measured by its large population, is a comparatively small country in terms of area and relatively poor in raw materials, then the thrust of the USA, with NATO as a transmission belt, quickly becomes apparent. This supposes, however, to think and to have the courage to look behind the veil of symptoms and to face reality as it is. More on this in the next chapter.

THE APPROPRIATION OF RUSSIA'S RAW MATERIALS IS THE PREREQUISITE FOR POWER OVER CHINA[93]

The US pursues clear goals and long-term, strategic interests. You can't blame them for that. The long-term strategic goal of the American hegemonic strategy is to dominate the Chinese market and shape it according to

---

[93] Already in the Asia-Pacific-Forum of December 31, 2012, Noam Chomsky expressed himself on this topic in a clear and plausible way in an annual outlook. There he speaks of a "Revenge Of History: Chomsky On Japan, China, The United States, And The Threat of Conflict in Asia", i.e. of events that show how historical events can take revenge.

Western rules and "values". For the USA, however, the path to dominance over China leads through the conquest of and dominance over Russia. The US will therefore do everything it can to appropriate Russia's raw materials and natural resources via Europe.[94] Accepting this fact, we got to the root cause of the war in Ukraine, as well as the attempted regime changes and relentlessly provoked unrest in Georgia and Armenia, as well as other Caucasian countries.

Under the then Russian President Yeltsin[95], the USA already saw itself very close to its goal. They wanted to flood Russia with their capital, i.e. "invest" in Russia, buy up the country and its resources, and take it over "peacefully". Russia could have remained politically "independent", just like Germany and Europe. The economy and

---

[94] Numerous analyses on the strategic orientation of American China policy can be found on the website of the Council on Foreign Relations (CFR), https://www.cfr.org/future-us-china-relations. Noam Chomsky also expressed himself in the spirit of our argumentation in a conversation with C. J. Polychroniou on the topic "Why China, not Russia, threatens the US-dominated world order". Published in German on July 9, 2022, in Telepolis; Original in Truthout.

[95] From 1991 to 1999, Boris Yeltsin was the first president of Russia after the end of the Soviet Union.

the financial industry dominating the country, however, would have been owned by and in the hands of Anglo-American capital and operated by it according to its rules.[96] Nor should it surprise anyone that the so-called "Russian crisis" that threatened the country in 1998 and 1999 was a debt crisis, the so-called "ruble crisis".[97] This debt would have provided an opportunity for foreign financial institutions and the Anglo-American financial cartels to take over the country's economy on favorable terms.[98] Local or regional investors in Russia,

---

[96] This was a kind of "Rockefeller" capitalism that the US wanted to implement, regardless of the losses for Russia, and with a clear goal. During this time, the large private conglomerates of the oligarchs emerged. After 1999, Russia took back control over the most important conglomerates that were aiming to run the Russian economy, i.e. oil and gas companies, as well as the banks according to their own rules, and placed them under national supervision again. The trial against the oligarch Khodorkovsky was the last sensational act in this process so far.

[97] It is not unimportant to note here that the "Russian crisis" as an economic crisis began shortly after the beginning of the "Asian crisis". So it's a good time for global investors.

[98] Niall Ferguson shows in his book "Colossus" how the British already used the debt of states during their empire, examples are Iraq and Egypt, in order to be rewarded for their "effort" and to bind the colonized states

who had become nervous, sold their stocks, bonds and ruble holdings at low prices out of fear and transferred the proceeds to countries that seemed particularly safe, especially the UK and the USA. Russia was on the verge of bankruptcy.

The principle based and "natural" interest of US policy towards Russia at that time was obvious. The aim was the complete takeover of its economic and natural resources, and this at the lowest possible price. The rest, areas such as culture and society, would not have been bothered by the USA. Culture in the USA has since long been run by "media". In the long term, the Russians and their allies would also have watched mainly Hollywood films and communicated exclusively via the social media channels of American companies.

If the US had succeeded in taking over Russia's economy and natural resources at that time, China's essential access to natural resources and raw materials would have been blocked in the future. The path to future growth would have been difficult, if not hindered, for the Chinese

---

economically and financially to the British "motherland".
Let's call this the "debt trap" set by the empire.

economy.[99] Without a reliable economic partnership with Russia, China would not have had the chance to match the American hegemon in the long term, or at least to fend it off. China would have had to pay the Anglo-American financial groups for the Russian raw materials. This is the "circular economy", the foreign policy and foreign trade "business model" that are guiding US hegemonic policy[100]. The United States, in possession of Russia's natural resources, would have become a hegemon without competition. It is exactly this hegemony that the United States is aiming for in the geopolitical global game of chess, an endeavor that has intensified since the end of the Cold War, as has been openly stated by Zbigniew Brzeziński, the advisor to several American

---

[99] There is often talk about China's investments on the African continent. From this perspective, it should be clear that this is also primarily about raw materials and sales markets. From this point of view, the importance of Australia for China can also be understood. Australia has a relatively small population, but is in possession of large deposits of raw materials on its continent.

[100] So it is not out of pure suspicion to claim, that the US also earns money, when Saudi Arabia sells oil to China. This is a result of the still prevailing situation of the US-dominated global economic trade policy and geopolitics in . Details on this are given in our book on "War and Business", published in 2024 .

presidents and governments[101]. So this is "the crux of the matter". This is what the great global American strategy has been about since 1919, with Wilson's 14-Points Program for global peace, and with new intensity since 2001, with the "war against terror".

The growing intensity of this hegemonic striving is therefore essentially fed by two sources: on the one hand, from the increasing pressure from the exorbitantly growing and unsustainable American debt, and on the other hand, from the rise of China, as the first serious economic and political competitor that is considered by the USA as a future threat to their hegemonic position. This is the background to all the wars that have been waged recently by the United States and also by its proxies, from Afghanistan, as Pakistan's important neighbor, through Iran, Iraq, and from Syria over Libya to the poor country of Yemen, as guardian at the southern access to the Red Sea and the Suez Canal. In addition, since 2014, the USA and NATO have intensified the rearmament of Ukraine, with the clear goal of attacking Russia militarily and conquering it. The open war, which has been going on since 2022, must be considered a

---

[101] The Grand Chessboard: American Primacy and its Geostrategic Imperatives, by Zbigniew Brzezinski.

consequence and outflow of the American hegemonic strategy. The smaller skirmishes, such as in Georgia and Armenia, we mention here only in passing. We also want to refrain from geopolitically important initiatives pushed forward by the USA and NATO in the Pacific, as we want to concentrate on Europe in this book.

So this is what is at stake on the chessboard of the American industry and capital: free access to raw materials and markets according to US rules and at the most favorable terms. These are the essential strategic elements. The African continent, as another large reservoir of raw materials, has a similar role to that of Russia, both overall and in the long term. However, the geostrategic pressure to act there is not yet so great.

For the USA, China is the great competitor that it wants to limit or, better said, "dominate" through Europe and the possession of Russia's raw materials and natural resources.

The industrial production capacities of Europe certainly also play an important role in this global strategy for hegemonic power, and could, of course, have played a role as an important collateral for the European countries. Germany and other European countries, still have good and very useful technical and industrial facilities. As we have seen, they already belong to a large extent to American owners, who can dispose of them at their will, if it really matters. In the event of war, as has been the case since the war against Russia and as we are witnessing it in the context of the "war economy", that has been launched in Europe since 2023, the European countries finally have to put their entire production capacities at the service of NATO, and thus at the service of the American geopolitical strategy. No German government has ever really left any doubt about the fact of the unconditional "West-orientation" of the country. Even the Green Foreign Minister Joschka Fischer was very diligent and sneaky in paving the way for the USA and NATO to southeastern Europe and the forceful destruction of Yugoslavia.[102] One of the largest US military bases in Europe today is in Kosovo — which is not yet a nation, but is already an important pillar of the bridge to Eastern Europe, and is going to become, in the near future and

---

[102] Joschka Fischer's speech on the NATO mission in Kosovo and Serbia:
https://de.wikipedia.org/wiki/
Rede_Joschka_Fischers_zum_NATO-Einsatz_im_Kosovo.

for strategic geopolitical reasons, a full member of the EU and NATO.

Just a small step further, one comes to the following statement: the EU and NATO are the political and military bridge pillars of the USA in an easterly direction on the Eurasian continent in its struggle for global hegemony. In the west, i.e. the Pacific region, it is Japan and South Korea that had to take on the role of the US bridge pillars. The USA has not been pursuing an industrial location policy in Europe for a long time, but it is creating geostrategic facts to assert its own interests in the sense of the hegemony of Anglo-American capital and political power[103].

Since 1945 at the latest, Europe has progressively been incorporated by the US and has no longer been considered a competitor to it, but an integral part of a global strategy for US

---

[103] On the close relationship between capital and war, see Niall Ferguson's books, for example: The Cash Nexus. Money and Power in the Modern World, 1700–2000, London: Allen Lane/Penguin Press, 2001; or: War of the World. History's Age of Hatred, 1914–1989, Allen Lane, 2006. Niall Ferguson is certainly not a "revolutionary," but he is courageous, usually honest and extremely intelligent — a historian who can help us see the reality behind the symptoms. His specialty is the monetary and financial economy.

world domination. Already in the early writings of Brzezinski, the European states are logically called "vassals".

SUMMARY: THE REORGANIZATION OF THE WORLD AFTER VERSAILLES

Human history does not proceed like a mechanical construct, the world is too complex for that. And yet to the well-trained historian a certain direction and consistency in historical development become visible. Thus, we understand that certain decisions made in 1919 by the victorious powers of the First World War led to a new world order.

Looking at and analyzing the underlying principles that have been guiding the political decision-makers, as well as the economic and financial managers in charge, provide us with a clear understanding of the processes that led to subsequent and current political and economic events and actions. The same principles and rules that underpinned the decisions of that time during the "peace negotiations" during the Treaty of Versailles in 1919 can be seen at work during the processes of the shaping of power and domination that we have observed during the following century until today. This analytical work of the political and economic-trained historian is our way of recognizing a structure in the supposed chaos around us. Thus, our intention becomes evident that, with our book, we want to serve the process of learning from history.

The insights we have gained so far encourage us to take a close look again and again, when political decisions are made. We must face this challenge with attention and the awareness that the consequences of such decisions will have to be borne not only by the currently living, but often even more so by the future inhabitants of this planet.

Chapter 6

How Europe Lost Her Identity

Introduction

It is not our intention to present here a study on the integration process of the European Union (EU). We rather pursue the purpose to show, on the basis of critical points and events, how this process has proceeded and to which important results it has led. The relationship between France and Germany after the Second World War in 1945, and since the reunification of Germany and Europe after 1990, is at the heart of the process of European integration. We will show how the relationship between the two economically and politically most important nations in Europe, with the EU as the decisive shaping framework, has developed.

It is important for us to take a pan-European view, i.e. to see, in the end, how Europe as a whole has developed geopolitically, and what scenario it presents to us today. At the same time, our attention is focused on the role of the USA, as the decisive co-shaping actor of the EU and as a critical influencing factor in the history of its emergence and specific organizational structuring.

BROTHERS UNDER ARMS 2019 – THE MEDIA WARNING SHOT

It was an article in the FAZ[104], on the French National Day on July 14, 2019, that triggered us writing this section of our book. Please be reminded that this was exactly one hundred years after the signing of the Treaty of Versailles in 1919. In this article, the FAZ correspondent in France praised the new "brotherhood under arms" and underlined this importance with a picture showing French and German soldiers together at the parade in Paris on the Champs-Élysées. We were immediately shocked by the presentation of this event, the joint parade of soldiers, as the most important symbol of German-French friendship in our time. The enthusiastic German comment on the picture reminded us of the public mood as it had been built up by political leaders in each of the two

---

[104] Frankfurter Allgemeine Zeitung (FAZ), the only German international daily newspaper.

countries at the time of the "sleepwalkers"[105], i.e. right before the First World War. "Brothers to arms!" was the slogan in both countries before the outbreak of the First World War.[106] The title "Brothers under Arms!" is only minimally more nuanced.

If we had been shown a picture of German and French, as well as other European citizens, celebrating together on the Champs-Élysées on July 14, it could have made us happy, as a sign of international understanding and friendship. As it was, however, this lead story in the FAZ of 2019 was more like a media warning shot.

So we want to take this picture and the commentary in the FAZ as an opportunity to ask ourselves in which direction the process of European integration has moved over the past decades after the Second World War. We will take the EU as a kind of overarching political framework to draw the lessons from these

---

[105] "The Sleepwalkers" is the title of a book published in 2012 by the British historian Christopher Clark, on the events leading to WW I.

[106] At the same time, France has also financed the armament of Russia and Serbia through its banks, especially Rothschild, in order to prepare the two-front war. see "The Sleepwalkers: How Europe Went into the First World War", Christopher Clark, DVA, 2013.

developments insofar as they had a significant impact on the present situation of Europe as a whole.

THE FOUNDING YEARS OF THE EU: CENTRAL STATE OR COMMUNITY OF FATHERLANDS?

The starting point for the establishment of a European community has been the principle agreement by the six founding nations[107] to draw lessons from the past, considered as an era of wars, to shape the future within a European institutional framework. The first concrete steps were taken in the early 1950s, with the foundation of the European Coal and Steel Community (ECSC). A process of building trust through cooperation has thus been set in motion, leading to the Treaties of Rome, which were signed in 1957, eventually establishing the European Economic Community (EEC). The long way towards the foundation of the European Union in 1991 had been started. The USA had lobbied early for European integration and emphatically supported this process of European unification from the very beginning.

---

[107] The six founding countries are France, Germany, Italy, Belgium, the Netherlands and Luxembourg.

It is remarkable, however, that two fundamentally different political tendencies became noticeable right from the start. On the one hand, there was France, which is considered in Europe to be the first historically grown central state[108], and which did not want to give up its role as a "Grande Nation", strove for a confederation of nation-states. In contrast, the USA, which took its own federal state as the most appropriate model, has supported the formation of a European central unitary state since the first years of European unification.[109] The creation of such a federal state, based on the American model, would have meant that the previously sovereign European nation states relinquish their sovereignty and delegate most of their sovereign power to the European central

---

[108] On this by Fernand Braudel, l'Identité de la France. Published in German as "France, Volume 1: Space and History / Volume 2: The People and the Things / Volume 3: The Things and the People, 2009, Fernand Braudel.

[109] It is remarkable that the same polarity between a federation of nations and the centralized federal state was characteristic for the opposition between Republicans and Democrats during the founding years of the USA.

state.[110] This was the model that France openly opposed.

In a third group, Switzerland, England, Norway, Sweden, Austria, Portugal and Denmark founded the European Free Trade Association (EFTA) in 1960, which from the outset was explicitly and essentially limited to the freedom of trade and the movement of goods, but left the political sovereign power of action to the individual countries as independent nations.

So there was an obvious contradiction, on the one hand, between the model of a European central unitary state in line with the aspirations of the USA and, on the other hand, the model of a federalist confederation of states, as it is still implemented today by EFTA.[111]

In concrete terms, this historic European integration process showed very early on that the USA, as a kind of regulatory power, was pursuing very concrete goals in Europe.[112] Thus,

[110] We will mention here only one book by Frederic Bozo that deals with this issue, "Deux stratégies pour l'Europe", Paris, 1996.

[111] The European Free Trade Area, founded in 1960, currently comprises only the four states of Iceland, Liechtenstein, Norway and Switzerland.

[112] We refer the reader for more details on these processes and the determining role of the USA to Eckart Conze; Die

under pressure from the USA and through the skills of their French lobbyist, Jean Monnet, the USA succeeded early on in limiting the effectiveness and scope of EFTA. The EFTA founding states, England, Austria, Denmark and Sweden, were soon forced, under pressure from the USA, to switch to the camp of the EEC and the later EU.[113] In this way, the US achieved a greater uniformity to facilitate their political, economic and trade relations with the EU and, in their eyes, make it more efficient. More importantly, however, the US saw the EU as an integral part of NATO from the outset. The US wished that its economic and military zones of influence in Europe would be centralized in a coherent manner in the long term.[114] This showed very early that in the US, political power

---

gaullistische Herausforderung. Die deutsch-französischen Beziehungen in der amerikanischen Europapolitik 1958–1963, Munich 1995.

[113] Of course, we have to see the Brexit of 2020 in this context. In the long run, England does not want to be integrated into a centralist confederation of states in order to give up its sovereignty there.

[114] At this point, we should not forget that the European states, especially the victorious powers England and France, but also Italy, were heavily dependent on the USA and had to repay loans they had taken out during the war years in the first decades to lead the fight against the Nazi regime.

is always seen as being part of economic power. In their eyes, both are intrinsically functioning together.

This centralist approach of the EU, demanded by the United States and skillfully promoted by Jean Monnet at the political level, was soon opposed in France by General de Gaulle. He had been elected the first president of the Fifth Republic in 1959, under the constitutional reform formulated under his leadership. De Gaulle, as President of France, had successively granted independence to the French colonies and ended the war in Algeria in 1963. De Gaulle was personally convinced of the necessity of building the process of European unification on the basis of the identity of historically grown cultural, social and political individual European countries. Only through a healthy national and cultural identity of the nations in Europe could, in his understanding, a freely willed union of the European states function in the long term.

This first phase of European integration after 1945 and up to 1963 has been analyzed in detail

---

The Marshall Plan was launched for Germany, which very quickly and successfully strengthened economic relations between Germany and the USA and led to close integration of the two economies at an early stage, with Germany as the junior partner.

by the German historian Eckart Conze and presented in various studies and books. Conze presented a first detailed study of the American policy towards German-French relations in the period of 1949 to 1963, under the title "The Gaullist Challenge", as early as 1995[115]. In it, Conze writes in the first lines of Chapter II: "Research rightly and almost unanimously considers the USA to be the hegemonic power of the Western world since 1945", and further down he adds "The Second World War had a catalytic function for the emergence of American hegemony". Conze also confirms that the American striving for hegemony had a "triple interest in European unification", because although it was "primarily economic", it was also "thought through from the beginning, militarily and politically". In our context, Conze's assessment is that "the supranational integration approach of the Treaties of Rome ... also aimed at the establishment of supranational political structures" in the medium term. He goes on to explain that "de Gaulle's conception of Europe, the center of which was the national

---

[115] Eckart Conze: Hegemony through Integration: The American European Policy and its Challenge by de Gaulle, in: Institut für Zeitgeschichte, Vierteljahreshefte für Zeitgeschichte, Volume 43 (1995), Issue 2.

sovereignty of the individual states", contradicted this.

General de Gaulle was considered by all sides undoubtedly a convinced European. He vigorously pursued, from the onset, reconciliation with the newly formed Federal Republic of Germany. This was in line with the great importance he attached to the sovereignty of the nation-states in Europe. In 1963, de Gaulle and Adenauer signed the Élysée Treaty in Paris, the so-called Franco-German Friendship Treaty, which since then has promoted relations between the two countries, building on regular consultations and various measures to strengthen mutual trust and cooperation. De Gaulle wanted to recognize Germany's national sovereignty through this act and give it special emphasis. Only sovereign nations, in de Gaulle's eyes, could be sovereign political and economic partners.

In this sense, France under President de Gaulle soon changed its policy towards NATO. From the outset, the US had rejected the French proposal for a European army under French leadership and with the inclusion of Germany. After France had succeeded in rapidly building up its nuclear force, *Force de frappe,* since 1960, and especially after de Gaulle's re-election in 1965, France intensified her efforts to form a European defense policy independent of the United States. France wanted to continue to play an active role in shaping NATO, but with an independent European defense alliance, as part of NATO. In line with this thinking, NATO was to be brought under European command in Europe, and the American and Canadian troops were to be placed under European command. The US categorically rejected this request, whereupon de Gaulle demanded the withdrawal of Allied troops and NATO headquarters from France. Since 1966 at the latest, de Gaulle justified this attitude with a clear political assessment, announcing that "France is now striving for the full exercise of its sovereignty, which cannot be guaranteed by the stationing of foreign forces on its soil".[116] At the same time, de Gaulle declared the withdrawal of French troops from NATO, where they were under American command. The 30,000 NATO soldiers had to leave France, and the various NATO military

---

[116] We read about this in Der Spiegel, 14.03.1966, "France – US bases – ground, sky, sea - In 1944 the Americans came to liberate de Gaulle's France. In 1966, de Gaulle wants to liberate France from the Americans."

quarters and command centers were moved to Belgium, the Netherlands and Germany.

As we have seen, there were two fundamentally different ideas and visions for the European Union and about its future political design. The first, and prioritized idea, was favored by the Americans and, in the person of Jean Monnet, promoted[117] within the power structures in Europe to further the American incorporation of Europe. This concept of the structure and organization of the EU worked towards a federal state, as a centralized unitary state, in which individual nations would gradually transfer their national powers to the EU and delegate them to her responsibility. The second vision is closely linked to the person of General de Gaulle, who vigorously defended this position and the

---

[117] We refer here to the excellent analysis by Werner Wüthrich, who dealt in detail with the topic of "European integration" in the Swiss magazine "Zeit-Fragen" from 2011 to 2012. There he also presents the "Monnet method" as the key to understanding the Euro crisis. In other articles, he shows in a historical context the two fundamentally different approaches to organizing the countries of Europe – the concept of the European Community and that of EFTA, the European Free Trade Association. In doing so, he also works very well on the underlying political principles of these two concepts, one of which is more centralist and the other federalist.

political ideas associated with it. This idea is based on the emphasis on a strong position of the sovereign nations and strives for a confederation of states of the "fatherlands". According to this model, nations should agree on common goals, such as the creation of a common market and a common defense. However, the basis and principal actors of cooperation should always be the individual, sovereign nation states. [118]

On paper, i.e. according to the theory, this organizational structure of the EU, as a confederation of states, was valid for a long time. In principle, it still is today. The European Commission is the "guardian of the Treaties" and, in principle, has no executive function. In principle, it must follow the guidelines and implement the decisions of the national governments, the Council of the European Union. In reality, these intentions could not prevail. This is shown very convincingly by Charles B. Blankart in his studies and books, in which he refers to the importance of the

---

[118] In an interview published in GlobalBridge on May 21, 2024, British historian and Russia expert Richard Sakwa also takes this position, calling himself a "Gaullist." We are at the funeral of the old school of diplomacy", on May 21, 2024.

"financial constitution" in the European Union, i.e. the power over the finances of the EU structures. He emphatically shows, how the "paradigm shift in European, especially in German federalism after the First World War", prevailed. Blankart makes it clear that federalism in its current form no longer has a future within the European Union.

So the unitary and central state of the EU has already become a reality. Under Commission President Ursula von der Leyen, this development has finally become rooted in the practice of cooperation between the EU institutions, first under the pretext of the measures taken during the so-called Corona pandemic and finally in the post-2022 period, since the war in Ukraine. Already under the reign of the German Chancellor Angela Merkel, competences and functions were increasingly and systematically delegated to the European Commission. The German Chancellor benefited from the fact that during her long reign[119], in France the French presidency was held by Nicola Sarkozy, Francois Holland and Emmanuel Macron, rather weak or even insignificant political figures. With the current presidency of

---

[119] She was Chancellor from 22 November 2005 to 8 December 2021.

the European Commission, Ursula von der Leyen, a politician protégé of Merkel came into play in 2019, who vehemently represents the absolute and exclusive Western orientation of European politics, and is willing to enforce this for the entire EU without any restraint. [120]

This principle based attitude of closely aligning the EU with US policy had increasingly become evident during the Corona policy, when the Commission President awarded large contracts to US pharmaceutical companies "freehand".[121] Recently, this unilateral position of the EU has deepened, not least under the uncompromising commitment to NATO policy and the massive provision of arms and financial resources to Ukraine. Effective, or even critical control by the member states, is being perceived less and less, and in some cases, as in the case of Hungary,

---

[120] This process has been documented in detail in the book "EL AÑO 2024: Ucrania y Eurasia en la crisis del declive occidental Fuente" (English: The Year 2024: Ukraine and Eurasia in the crisis of the Decline of the West), published in 2024 by Rafael Poch-de-Feliu, professor at Universitat Pompeu Fabra (UPF) in Barcelona and for the Universidad Nacional de Educación a Distancia (UNED).

[121] To this end, lawsuits, including by EU member states, were filed in European courts against Ms von der Leyen's behavior in May 2024. The hearings were then adjourned by Belgian courts for unknown reasons.

even sanctioned. The member states were brought into line. The docile behavior of Member States that have persisting serious economic and financial problems, such as Italy, France and Greece, has been ensured by the creation of new instruments facilitating the generous allocation of enormous financial resources to graciously honor their political alignment and support with economic and financial boons. In addition, the massive and targeted provision of funding for public relations and the media is targeted to ensure general approval among the public in Europe. Critical voices are increasingly prevented by laws, decrees and regulations that are classified as "endangering the system" or anti-democratic[122]. The European Commission (EC) has thus put itself in a position, in which it has "ruled through" since the Corona policy and the war in Ukraine[123],

---

[122] There is now a "Democracy Promotion Act" in the EU. Regarding the laws, if you issue orders to prevent public opinion, it is sufficient to obtain information from the press reports on the control of social media and the public media (ÖRR). Censorship by so-called "Correctiv" institutes, which are funded by the state, speak for themselves.

[123] "Governing through" was a wish formula of the German Chancellor for the design of political processes; i.e. governing without obstacles. In the daily newspaper "Die

i.e. without perceptible control by the populations of the member states. The EC is announcing its decisions or pushing them through according to its ideas and those of the leaders in the most important member states. In the same line, the EC has managed to get the right to leverage financial resources by taking debt on its own, i.e. by bringing its own bonds onto the market, controlled by institutions under the supervision of the European Commission and secured by the member states[124]. Even a brief critical look at these processes will show any observer that these processes of institutionalization and centralization of the EU have become irreversible. They are run without any democratic control or effective oversight.

At the end of this brief analytical overview, we have attained a good understanding of the current situation and see with the required clarity, where Europe stands today in this process of European unification.[125] We have

_____

Welt" of 07.04.2010, the report "Merkel says goodbye to "governing through". Was that the case?

[124] Prof. Hans-Werner Sinn, former director of the Ifo Institute in Munich, has followed these developments most consistently.

[125] For more details, the reader may refer to our book "Europe lost her Sovereignty", 2024, Georg von Goldbach.

identified the principal outcome and consequences of the European unification process. This will put us in a better position to finally ask, what possible options for shaping politics in Europe still exist in the future.[126]

We will in the following paragraphs look at some of the highlights and major events of European unification to indicate the major impact these processes have brought for Europe and her waning sovereignty.

THE "EUROPEAN AXIAL AGE" OF 1985-95 UNDER DELORS AND MITTERRAND

The period after 1985, when Jacques Delors began to serve as President of the European Commission, started still during the period of the EEC, before the formal establishment of the EU. This period is considered to be the decisive

---

[126] At this point, we will not go into the Marshall Plan, the economic importance of which is usually greatly overestimated. Its main importance lies in its promotion of European integration in accordance with the will of the United States. S. h. Hans-Werner Sinn: Der Mythos vom Marshall-Plan; as well as the economic historian Werner Abelshauser, who in his books on the "Myth of the Economic Miracle" also refutes the thesis of the "initial spark" by the Marshall Plan.

phase in the shaping of the EU. Delors had been promoted to this post by the French President François Mitterrand, where he gave proof of his exceptional political expertise from 1985 to 1995. Delors had represented France in the European Parliament early on, and then distinguished himself as an outstanding and loyal politician in several governments under Mitterrand's presidency. This period of European integration under the Mitterrand-Delors axis constituted, in retrospect and in several respects, the "European Axial Period", during which the policies of European unification and integration, as well as France's role in Europe and as a global power, had changed fundamentally. As we will see, both events are again strongly related to the parallel expansion of American dominance in Europe.

In the literature on this topic, reference is usually made to the fact that since the 1980s and then also through the new constellation after the reunification of the two German states and the collapse of the Soviet confederation, Delors had strived for and promoted an ever greater deepening of the integration of the European states in the EU. This indicates, it is assumed, that Delors and Mitterrand worked towards the European, centralist federal state. Superficially, this assumption is certainly correct and overall indisputable. However, this assumption deserves a more nuanced consideration. This view does not automatically mean that Delors and Mitterrand also sought the realization of the European federal state under US hegemony. On the contrary, the intention was driven by a strong primacy for European interests. Neither Mitterrand nor Delors would deny this; rather, this attitude has been at the core of their political life. We must not overlook the fact that France's goal was to establish her role as a major European power through the EU and, if possible, to promote this role even further.

For both politicians, France's Gaullist claim to recognition as an equal partner of the great nations was non-negotiable. In this sense, Mitterrand and Delors were staunch nationalists and Gaullists. In this sense, European integration was to be primarily oriented towards the interests of France and the EU was to be shaped according to the still prevailing statist ideas of the French bureaucracy. Under these premises, both politicians strove for a European Union that would become a mixture of a centralist-federalist state, but at the same time be able to assert its claims on the international stage in a sovereign manner vis-à-vis foreign powers, especially the United States. It is in this spirit that all of Delors' work as President of the European Commission should be understood.

As early as 1986, under Delors as President of the EEC, the Treaty of Rome of 1957 was sustainably reformed for the first time and the foundations for the European internal market were laid. To this end, the "Delors Commission", created for this purpose, developed the mechanism of the European legislative process, which has remained the valid "benchmark" and formal guide to this day, in an extended form via the "acquis communautaire"[127], for the proceedings for integration and association of other member and partner countries. Since then, this formal integration process does not only concern the structuring of the internal market, but all areas of public life are included without exception, from the rule of law, trade, economic rules and laws, as well as social norms and the media, and not to forget migration and foreign policy. This far-reaching process of legal and regulatory unification of the countries of Europe and the associated states had been legally adopted by 1992 and the results had become legally valid from 1993 onwards as part

---

[127] In legal jargon, this is called the "EU acquis".

of the mutual obligations of the member states. The EU was thus finally established as a construct based on the rule of law.[128] This must be highlighted as the first major achievement of the European Commission under Delors.

In parallel with this process, and in consistent complement to it, Delors presented a three-stage plan for the establishment of the Economic and Monetary Union in 1989. He had asked the European Council, i.e. the European member states, to provide him with the mandate for this initiative, which he had initiated, as early as 1988. The work of the Delors Commission was presented to the European Council in a report which then became the basis for the development of Economic and Monetary Union through the Maastricht Treaty[129], which is now regarded as the founding act of the European Union. This result from 1993

---

[128]This process is fully documented and described on the official website of the EU under https://Europa.eu/.
[129] It should be noted here that the most important demand of France, represented by Mitterrand, during the negotiations on German reunification, was the abandonment of the Deutsche Mark and the adoption of the Euro as the future European currency. France thus saw itself as an active participant in Germany's economic potential.

is considered the outstanding achievement under the EU Commission of Delors.

THE TURNING POINT IN THE PROCESS OF EUROPEAN INTEGRATION

However, here we come to a crucial point in our argumentation. For, what at first glance looks like a great moment for the future of France and her European, but also her global political claims, ultimately becomes the decisive turning point in French as well as European history. In the sense *of an irony of history*[130], the end of the "Grande Nation" is looming from this point on. The key to this understanding can be found, if we take a closer look at the role of the United States in this process.

We should not assume that the US played with hidden cards during this time. Rather, it seemed to have been a game with an open outcome. Measured against the hegemonic importance that the USA had achieved economically and militarily after the Second World War, however,

---

[130] In the social sciences and humanities, the principle of "unintended consequences" or "unintended effects" has been known for a long time.
https://de.wikipedia.org/wiki/Unbeabsichtigte_Folgen#cite_note-1.

the outcome should no longer be surprising. As we shall see, the process of European integration led to the result that the United States has sought from the beginning. European integration followed along the lines the United States has wished and worked for since 1945, and, ironically, it also provoked the end of France as the "Grande Nation".

French politics has reached a point, from which it would only have made progress on the desired nationalist path through a consistent continuation of politics in the sense of the Gaullist-formulated interests of the French nation. However, history wanted it differently, and the course of history led to a different result. Delors and Mitterrand retired in 1994 and 1995 as key figures in shaping French and EU policies[131]. This did not ensure a consistent continuation on the federalist path initiated by the EU under the leadership of France and was ultimately gambled away for France, as we will briefly show here in the following part of our descriptive analysis.

---

[131] Mitterrand stepped down from the French political scene in 1995 after his second mandate. He died in 1996 and ended his EU presidency in 1994 after three terms in office.

At first glance, it looks as if France has obviously taken on the dominant role in the policy of European integration during the three terms of Delors' EU presidency. It seemed as if France had been able to clearly defend her interests and achieve her major goals. It seemed quite clear that with the implementation of the 3-step plan of the European Commission under the leadership of Delors and under the Treaty of Maastricht, the European Union would finally have a French face, a French structure and a French intellectual and political leadership. But this appearance is deceptive.

The preservation and consistent enforcement of French interests would have required, at the same time, a defense against the Americanization of European politics[132]. However, it turned out that even great political leaders like Mitterrand and Delors were not up to the challenge in the end. The reason for this is very easy to find in Germany's particular geopolitical position. American policy toward European unification has been consistent and unambiguous. The position of Germany, which

---

[132] For an introduction to the topic, we recommend the book by Anselm Doering-Manteuffel, "Amerikanisierung und Westernisierung", Version: 2.0, in: Docupedia-Zeitgeschichte, 19.08.2019.

was economically integrated and dominated by the USA from the beginning, and was severely limited in its political maneuverability as a nation by its unconditional loyalty to the USA and NATO, was decisive for the achievement of American political goals in Europe. In Europe, France was thus largely alone with its original policy of centralist-federalist confederation of states, according to Gaullist ideas and under French leadership, in contrast to the model of the centralist federal state promoted by the USA.[133]

Mitterrand and Delors were always realistic enough to assume that the European integration

---

[133] The USA knew very early on how to bring England, Austria and Denmark into line, i.e. away from EFTA and towards the emerging EU.

Werner Wüthrich shows this process in great detail and convincingly in a series of several articles in the Swiss magazine "Zeit-Fragen" under the title "European Integration".

There he also goes into great detail and knowledge of the different roles of Jean Monnet and de Gaulle.

A convincing analysis of the influence of the USA on the process of European unification was presented by the German historian Andreas Bracher in his book "Europe in the American World System, Fragments of an Unwritten History of the 20th Century", 2001.

process would largely follow Monnet[134]'s ideas and would follow the example of the USA towards a European federal state. Mitterrand was an excellent realpolitiker who consistently pursued his goals and, at the same time, did not refuse to accept political constraints and facts. Mitterrand and Delors therefore knew that, in the end, they could not assume that the United States would allow the trump cards it had in the form of dominance over Germany and NATO to be taken out of their hands.

But, as staunch Gaullists, they did everything in their power and hoped to the end that this centralist European federal state would ultimately be under the clear leadership of France. France was to play the leading role in preserving European sovereignty and the power

---

[134] Let us remind you that Jean Monnet and Robert Schumann are usually referred to together as the founding fathers of the European Union. It is usually not mentioned that the positions of the two politicians were very different. Monnet clearly pursued the policy of forming a European nation-state, while Schumann favored the Gaullist "Europe of the Fatherlands".

to shape[135] European politics.[136] That is why we have applied here this paradoxical designation of Mitterrand and Delors as "Gaullists", while both belonged to the French Socialist Party and were not formally classified as Gaullists in France[137]. In their politics, however, both were convinced Gaullists, i.e. French nationalists. When we speak here of French leadership and political

---

[135] The article by Günther Hellmann in the series "From Politics and Contemporary History" on the topic "Between creative power and hegemony trap". It is worth reading concerning the latest debate on a "new German foreign policy". It should be noted here that in these discussions, a distinction is made between decision-making power and creative power.

[136] In this context, it is important to point out that in 2010, Delors was instrumental in the creation of the "Spinelli Group", which was founded as an initiative of the European Parliament to promote efforts within the EU to create a federalist confederation.
It should also not be forgotten that Delors was probably the last president in the EU who convincingly represented the principle of "subsidiarity" and emphasized its importance for shaping European policy.

[137] In the "normal" French understanding of politics, socialist politicians are not Gaullists, because according to this understanding they should belong to the conservative party.
But we call Mitterrand and Delors Gaullists here because they represented de Gaulle's policy, that is, a policy that always keeps an eye on France's national interests as a "Grande Nation" and must never give up.

creative power, we mean spiritual orientation and political leadership by the national genius of France[138]. This leadership of France in Europe was not going to be realized. Europe had finally become prey to the American hunger for power and money, the key ingredients for its struggle for global hegemony. What started after 1945 as hegemonic power over the "West", would progressively strive to cover the entire planet, as we have shown in our book "War and Business. The American Success Story of the Past Century", published in 2024.

To achieve this goal of French supremacy over Germany and over Europe, France saw the need for the German economic capacities and resources to be transferred to the EU. Hence, Mitterrand's *bon mot* was, that he did not desire anything from the Germans as much as the Deutsche Mark and the Deutsche Bundesbank. In fact, France, under Mitterrand, prevailed in the negotiations for German unity after 1989, and had the Euro fixed as the new currency unit, as the equivalent for its approval of German reunification. These results of the negotiations on reunification were then consistently implemented in the Maastricht Treaty under the

---

[138] https://fr.wikipedia.org/wiki/G%C3%A9nie_fran%C3%A7ais

leadership of Delors. Politically, of course, the Bundesbank has nothing directly to do with German unity. Strategically, however, the takeover of the Deutsche Bundesbank by abandoning the Deutsche Mark and introducing the Euro was the decisive step in transferring control of the country's economic capacities and financial resources to the EU under French leadership. From the point of view of Mitterrand and Delors, this was tantamount to placing the German industrial capacities and resources under French supervision and control within the EU. [139]

In summary, we have to say that Mitterrand's policy was always very realistic, but at the same time strategically clever and long-term. In doing so, he always kept in mind that it must be the goal of French politics to secure the "Grande Nation" its legitimate place among the nations. However, Mitterrand could not overlook the fact

---

[139] This was a decisive step forward in the complete takeover of Germany by France, as it had been pursued and claimed in the Treaty of Versailles under Clemenceau. For part of the German public, this result of European integration is also called "Versailles 2.0".
The article in Telepolis, "Complete, legal expropriation by law", by Marc Friedrich and Matthias Weik, 2019, is worth reading.

that the United States, as a consequence of the outcome of the Second World War, was striving for a hegemony through the creation of a new world order, which was based on the institutions of Bretton Woods and the UN Security Council. In the eyes of Mitterand, the European policy of the US with their predominant influence in Europe could have been contained by a united Europe, with France and Germany at the center. According to this understanding, France needed the EU, with Germany as the dominant economic power, in order to be able to assert her place as the "Grande Nation" against the hegemony of the USA. Mitterrand took over this claim of France's important role from de Gaulle.[140] According to France's ideas, i.e. the ideas of Mitterrand, the basic structure of the EU was to be shaped in such a way that, in conjunction with Germany's economic power, it would play a sovereign role in world politics. In this sense, France and her policy under Mitterrand and Delors was the final attempt to establish the bulwark against US hegemony in

---

[140] Refer to "François Mitterrand; socialiste Gaullien, T. Desjardins, Paris, Hachette 1978 ; or the biography "C'était François Mitterrand", by Jacques Attali, Paris, 2007, a long-time companion and confidant of Mitterand.

Europe. As we understand today, this bulwark has completely collapsed.

France has to admit that since 2022 at the latest, with Ukraine and Europe's proxy war against Russia, the US has emerged as the clear winner from these European developments for integration. The big loser in particular is France, which has finally been downgraded to the second rank of the nations. Certainly, there have always been other EU states that would have liked to see an independent and sovereign European policy, such as Denmark, Austria, the Netherlands or the Czech Republic. However, Germany in particular could not and did not want to free itself from the economic and security clutches of the USA and NATO. Realistically, it was practically impossible for Germany to achieve a truly sovereign status after 1949.[141]

The Treaty of Maastricht, signed in 1993, thus created the EU as the decisive stage in the realization of an "ever closer union of the peoples of Europe", as the treaty itself says. France had not succeeded in consolidating its dominance in Europe, because the crucial

---

[141] It is known that the victorious powers of the Second World War have not yet offered Germany a peace treaty.

partner France needed for this model of a sovereign EU had long since ceased to be independent. Germany was, to put it in the language of the United States, a loyal vassal on the great chessboard of American hegemonic claim in Europe.[142]

And yet, we may ask ourselves: why should we not want to live under this constellation in Europe? After all, it is true that since 1949, we have been able to lead a largely peaceful life in Europe, which has gone hand in hand with unprecedented prosperity and wealth. Isn't this call for European sovereignty a nostalgic undertaking, without concrete, urgent justification and ultimately directed against the interests of the EU itself? – These questions are certainly justified and deserve analytical consideration in the sense of a current assessment. We would like to make a contribution to this deepening analysis in the following paragraphs.

---

[142] This assessment is consistently used in the publications of the Foreign Policy Research Institute in the United States and is supported by the book "The Grand Chessboard: American Primacy and its Geostrategic Imperatives", by Zbigniew Brzezinski, New York, Basic Books, 1997.

EUROPE IS LOSING HER WAY - GOING ASTRAY ON AMERICAN PATHS

We agree that this image of the "brothers in arms" marching in 2019 together on the Champs-Élysées is not the only one that is symptomatic of the EU and the process of European integration. We do not overlook the most valuable circumstances of an open border policy and the results of economic integration by the EU. However, the question must be asked without reluctance or fear, as to who determines the rules, according to which we Europeans are shaping life in Europe. This is, if you like, the 'primal question' that the then president of France, Charles de Gaulle, posed in 1959 very clearly and emphatically, and which we should ask ourselves in our own interest. After all, the demands of the Declaration of Human Rights for freedom, equality and fraternity do not only apply to individuals; they must also apply to nations and countries, where this is called the "right of self-determination" or sovereignty. Countries and the people who live in them must have the right to self-determination and to the self-determined shaping of their respective communities.[143]

In an open contrast to this "right of self-determination" or sovereignty, which we claim, the US, under its President Wilson, has introduced since 1919 the international doctrine of interference in the affairs of foreign nations on the world stage as a legitimate instrument of power in global politics. Since then, the US has taken the right to punish

---

[143] We subliminally ask about the "raison d'être", a term that is kept directly out of all discussions in Germany with reference to the Basic Law.

We, on the other hand, are of the opinion that the "raison d'état", i.e. the question of the meaning of our state, must be asked anew.

The ruling parties obviously see the reason of the state in gaining ever greater international prestige and greater power by generating more and more funds, which are then available for "international tasks" in the sense of NATO, the EU and the UN, as well as to raise the egoistic profile of the international power elites.

It is time to fundamentally change this understanding of raison d'être, which was essentially coined by Machiavelli and other contemporaries during the Renaissance.

We see the fundamental raison d'être in securing and, if possible, expanding prosperity and quality of life for the population. "Power" is only the decisive factor in a hostile environment. In a world of cooperation, "power" becomes secondary.

countries by means of violence and war, or by economic sanctions, if it is of the opinion that a country does not abide by rules set by the USA and their allies.[144] This Wilsonianism, is not primarily about a contest for better ideas, but it derives its "right" and even its "duty" to interfere, with the American self-image, that is, the way the American people sees its "missionary" destiny. In this sense, NATO has become an "alliance of values", [145]i.e. a military instrument to put the "missionary" destiny of the USA into practice. This missionary "value imperialism"[146] explicitly involves the interference and violent correction of the political behavior of countries, today officially called "regime change," as well as the

---

[144] Niall Ferguson described and traced this "imperialism" in great detail in its historical development and in its various shades in his book "Colossus: The Rise and Fall of the American Empire", 2004.
From a self-critical American perspective, Gore Vidal has summarized his observations in "Perpetual War for Perpetual Peace: How We Got to Be So Hated", first published in 2002.

[145] In line with our argumentation, Sevim Dağdelen has recently published a comprehensive book "NATO: A Reckoning with the Alliance of Values", 2024.

[146] We also refer here to the "Series: Dresden Collected Comments on Security Policy – dgksp discussion papers – of April 14, 2021.

instrument of sanctions, which have become a popular tool of American and European politics today.[147] It has turned out for the USA that this instrument of sanctions, due to the exclusive American power of disposal over powerful instruments for financial transactions,[148] together with its dominant role as an economic power, can be used in a targeted and effective

---

[147] Refer to "Extraterritorial US sanctions", by Sascha Lohmann, in SWP-Aktuell 2019/A 31, May 2019. - In it, he writes: "Since the founding of the Republic, the US government has been expanding its authority beyond its own borders to pursue economic, foreign and security policy goals. The extraterritorial application of U.S. law to natural and legal persons, assets and actions outside one's own territory is favored by three factors: First, an ideological obligation to a natural right, which is expressed in a commitment to the inviolability of inalienable rights that are considered valid even beyond one's own borders. Secondly, by a legal culture that is characterized by the experience of constant territorial expansion and domination – initially as a former settler society and later as an occupying power after the Second World War. And third, through an independent judiciary that has a wide margin of discretion to interpret the geographic scope of U.S. law and its enforcement by administrative authorities."

[148] Refer to the excellent article "The Super Weapon of Mr. Glaser, Sanctions against Russia and Iran: How American Tax Officials Become Economic Warriors", by Kerstin Kohlenberg and Mark Schieritz, on October 23, 2014, in DIE ZEIT No. 44/2014.

manner for the interests of the USA[149]. Such sanctions are increasingly applied by the US jointly with their partners from the EU, Canada and Japan in order to interfere in the economic well-being of entire countries and their populations in a targeted manner and also to hit them economically by force.[150]

By contrast, the European Union was originally founded as a peace project that wanted to serve as a model for the world with its innovative model of an explicitly voluntary union of nations. Wars and other coercive

---

[149] In the war against Russia that is currently being waged in Ukraine, it has become clear that the US is using the sanctions policy against Russia for its own interests. In the case of Nord Stream 2, this went so far that an important infrastructure for Europe's energy supply was blown up in order to promote the American energy industry.

[150] As we write this text, hundreds of sanctions are being applied by the US, particularly against North Korea, Iran, Syria, Venezuela, Russia, China, and even against Europe and individual countries within Europe. In many cases, the EU itself imposes sanctions under pressure from the US, even if they violate its own interests. Euphemistically, this is called "economic war". Not infrequently, however, these sanctions also have deadly consequences, as in the case of countries into which war has been brought, such as Syria, where a population in war is additionally punished with sanctions because the "regime" is not acceptable to the USA and Europe.

means were initially not part of the political toolkit of the EU. The early slogan with which the EU offered its model worldwide was "partnership". This policy is seemingly to be continued to this day with the "Partnership and Cooperation Agreements" (PCA), which are offered and negotiated worldwide.[151] However, reality provides us with a different picture.

As recent events in Ukraine, but also in North African states such as Egypt, Lebanon, Libya and Syria, as well as in Turkey and Georgia, show, this instrument of "partnership agreements" is increasingly being used by the EU as an instrument of power to "get states on track" or to keep them in line with the EU's interests. Based on this experience of the partner countries, the EU is increasingly

---

[151] The author of this essay has been involved in the implementation of these partnership agreements and association agreements for several decades as an advisor to the EU and various partner countries in several regions of the world. He has therefore had the opportunity to help shape these negotiations and the reform processes since the presidency of Delors. The author has thus seen these political processes from both sides and has played a supporting role in them. It was always important to him to represent the "Europe of Partnership". The Europe of power in the sense of US hegemony was never his intention.

perceived worldwide as a growing political power that aims at political and economic "dominance", and is largely subordinate to the goals of the USA as the global hegemonic power.

Since the wars against Yugoslavia and Libya, this image of the EU partnership has experienced very obvious cracks in the eyes of many partner countries. In addition, there are the current wars in Syria[152], Iraq, Afghanistan and Yemen, all within a few hours' flight of Europe's capitals, in which NATO and some of its important European members are directly involved and actively engaged with armed forces.[153]

---

[152] In Syria, as in Iraq, American forces are still "occupation forces" against the will of the respective governments of these countries. Syria is also suffering unspeakably from the sanctions regimes of the USA and the EU.
See also "Syria Crisis and EU: Catastrophic Poverty and Emigration as a Last Resort", 22 February 2024, Thomas Pany. The same applies to "Syria – The Never-Ending Story (of lies)", February 20, 2020, by Tobias Riegel.

[153] To illustrate the role that Germany is taking on in Syria and as a member of NATO, here are just two examples: one is that "Germany finances Erdoğan's resettlement policy in northern and eastern Syria", from January 24, 2020, by Elke Dangeleit, and the other one is "Turkey: Merkel's breaking of civilizational taboos", from January 25, 2020, by Tomasz Konicz; both articles have been

In addition to the constantly expanding "peace missions" in North, West and Central Africa, new areas of operation and "peace missions" in Asia and on all the world's oceans are being considered, and already being implemented. We can assume that these ambitions will be perceived both in Latin America, where they currently affect countries such as Bolivia, Chile, Ecuador, Colombia, Peru and Venezuela, as well as in Asia, where, in addition to the nuclear powers China, India and Pakistan, the large countries and important nations, such as Indonesia, Malaysia and the Philippines, are keeping a close eye on the EU's policy of interests and political ambitions. The European power elites want to present it to us as a sign of strength and sovereignty, when France and Germany, in alliance with other European states such as Spain, Italy and the UK, join forces to form and build a large and comprehensive industrial-military complex in Europe, following the role model of the USA.[154] In their external view, the affected countries from the "Global South" tend to view these

published in the online magazine Telepolis.

[154] Refer to Peter Carstens in the FAZ of January 21, 2020, "German-French Project" - A Fighter Aircraft for 100 Billion Euros".

clear military ambitions of Europe and the EU with suspicion. The priority of issues to be tackled by geopolitics in the Global South is different from the primarily warmongering politics of the US and EU, driven by NATO. Nobody can close their eyes to the fact, that the US and EU have driven the world into politics of military buildup, violent conflicts and war. What a waste of resources and energy! Nobody can seriously take this as rational politics serving humanity.

Aren't these global events of geopolitical initiatives and activities, symptoms of a change of direction in geopolitics? Does this new approach promoted in Europe not represent a serious change and massive expansion of the mandates of the EU and NATO? If we have this suspicion, then we should also ask ourselves whether this is what we want in Europe. Would it not be time for Europe to start determining its own geopolitical processes and initiatives that concern its interests and well-being? Should Europe not step back into the role of sovereign designer of its own political destiny?

Unfortunately, the indications point into the opposite direction. Europe finds herself in a contemporary political maelstrom, in which

Europe and her nations are no longer able to control their fate. They have to an ever greater extent given up the political will to shape their future destiny.

Nowadays, the European policies of increasing armament and the further expansion and development of a European military-industrial complex are celebrated in grand attire.[155] It is deliberately overlooked that the industrial-military complex in Europe, as well as the entire rest of its economic capacities, are already largely controlled by the American-dominated financial corporations and their instruments.[156] As a consequence, this means that we are witnessing the expansion of the American industrial-military complex on the territory of the EU and are enthusiastically celebrating this outcome of US hegemonic

[155] As one of many other examples, the article in the FAZ of January 21, 2020, "German-French project" - A fighter aircraft for 100 billion Euros, should be mentioned here. This rearmament and its public celebration also affect all other branches of arms, such as the establishment of a joint fleet for use on the world's oceans, but especially in Asia directed against China.

[156] As one of the more recent sources, we quote Jens Berger, "Who protects the world from the financial corporations?", Frankfurt, 2020.

strive, as if they are in our own interest.[157] The rest of the word, in the Global South as well as in Russia and China, is considering these hegemonic policies as frightening. They consider it highly troubling to see the EU deliberately joining the hegemonic politics of the US.

Concerning the economic definition of a war economy, we refer to the book of Andreas Forner "Wirtschaft und Krieg. Verhältnis von Ökonomie und Politik in Krisenzeiten" (our translation: "Economy and War. The Relationship between Economy and Times of Crises"), where he is covering this subject from an economist's point of view. In a recent publication in WeltTrends 199, Hubert Thielicke / Lutz Kleinwächter (eds.), Potsdam 2023, Forner presents a scientific essay concerning the criteria to apply for an economy of war related to the different parties engaged in the war in Ukraine.[158]

---

[157] Very informative is the article by Werner Rügemer in the online magazine "Nachdenkseiten" of April 23, 2019, "USA in decline? – But in the EU, it is more powerful than ever before". By the same author, "The Capitalists of the 21st Century. Generally understandable notes on the rise of the new financial players", Cologne, 2018.

However, in our view, this scientific analysis of Andreas Forner has only limited value, and for different reasons. For example, the analysis does not take into account that NATO is promoting this war with a cumulated budget coming from its 32 member states, while Russia has to bring up its budget by her own forces. Therefore, not one single NATO member is operating under a war economy, while together they are funding and equipping Ukraine, a nation in war. In addition, the huge financial and material support to the Ukrainian state budget coming from NATO member states and the EU is not appropriately taken into account in its impact on the Ukrainian war budget. If these two points had been considered, then the picture developed by Forner concerning the war economies and related industries in the US, Europe, Ukraine and Russia would look very different. This example shows that NATO is for the USA and the West the perfect war machine. It allows leading wars through the accumulated budgets of 32 industrialized nations, without burdening

---

[158] Refer to Andreas Forner, "Ein ordnungspolitischer Ausnahmestatus. Klare Maßstäbe statt Inflationierung", in WeltTrends 199, Hubert Thielicke / Lutz Kleinwächter (eds.), Potsdam 2023.

the budgets of the individual nations excessively. Hence, the European nations, as well as the US, are not leading wars, but they are promoting and funding wars, not only in Ukraine, but also in Palestine, Lebanon, Yemen and Syria. The combined economic forces of the 32 NATO member states provide the perfect camouflage for their real intentions and the violent actions and wars they promote globally.

An example will help us to illustrate these US driven policies that are promoted through NATO. Since 2014, the US has progressively built up Ukraine to prepare for a proxy war against Russia. Since 2022 the war have been opened. This has led to a situation, where Europe increasingly finds herself in s backdrop of a worrying security situation. The German government felt therefore in need to present in 2022 a *National Security Strategy*, for the first time in the history of Germany after 1945. This document is intended to "provide more orientation" and was subsequently followed by a China strategy and updated defense policy guidelines for Germany. The editors of the WeltTrends 199 publication summarize their analysis of various aspects of Germany's *National Security Strategy* of 2022, with the clear statement that it "(a) amounts to the militarization of the state and society, and (b) is basically aimed at hostility to Russia, (c) systemic confrontation with China, and (d) vassal loyalty to the United States. The two percent target is fixed and thus a long-term military armament".

The editors of the WeltTrends 199 publication continue their comments, saying that "anyone who had hoped for an independent role of the economically strongest state in the center of Europe, aimed at mediation and effective arms control, had to be deceived. Germany obediently aligned itself with the line set by the other side of the Atlantic".

In this sense, we saw in the enthusiasm of the FAZ, Germany's only international liberal-conservative daily newspaper, when on July 14, 2019, it "saw the Franco-German brothers marching under arms on the Elysian fields", the symptom of an emerging crisis, that we would have done better to avoid. Unfortunately, this crisis has become real with the war in Ukraine that has intensified massively over the past years. Even worse, we may assume that this alliance of war between the EU, the USA and NATO has also poured into formal institutional structures and informal power relations among the EU and NATO. Getting out of the crisis will for Europe not be an easy job.

This title and the picture in the FAZ take up the situation in Europe before the First World War, at least through the spirit, if not with words. In 1914, the French and the Germans were equally enthusiastic, and in the war that followed, they paid dearly, with enormous human sacrifices on both sides. The Second World War followed, less violent for France, because German troops led their war mainly to Eastern Europe and against Russia, in search of "living space", for raw materials and natural resources. Today, in the 21st century, Europe has entered into a war with the same purpose, i.e. to conquer free access to raw materials and natural resources in Russia. This may be justified by hegemonistic aspirations. However, it does not qualify Europe for moral or value-driven global leadership.

After the Second World War, France had finally become a member of the United Nations Security Council as one of the winners and had equipped itself with its own arsenal of nuclear weapons. France wanted to remain the "Grande Nation" and play a leadership role in

Europe. In 2024, we must admit that these political intentions have largely failed. France, together with Europe, has definitely taken over the role of vassals in the service of the American hegemon and its NATO. France has been the last bulwark in Europe, but it finally had to succumb and give up.

Politically, Mitterrand was indeed the last Gaullist, who wanted to defend the interests of France and Europe in the face of American power. France, as a nation of great cultural power, was the last bastion of conscious resistance against the Americanization of Europe.[159] With the French defeat, Europe has also given in to the forced adoption of the one-sided, scientific and technically limited concept of progress of the USA, as well as its hegemonic political claims in Europe and on a global level. Since then, France and Europe have gradually withdrawn from this position of resistance to cultural, economic and political incorporation by the USA. They have in fact begun to transform their national and European identities in favor of gradual

---

[159] On this topic, we refer to the article on "Americanization and Westernization", by Anselm Doering-Manteuffel, in: Docupedia-Zeitgeschichte, 18.1.2011.

incorporation into the American hegemonic empire.

This is consistently demonstrated by the event that France joined NATO again in 2009, to become a full member. This is even more corroborated by the fact that US capital currently controls more than 50% of the assets, industries and financial institutions in Germany and other important European countries, with an upward trend.[160]

So, if we look back at the current situation and the joint parade of the French and German armed forces on the Champs-Élysées in 2019, we should understand that the wars that Europe will fight in the future are the imperialist wars of the United States. France and Germany, and thus Europe, have become direct and unconditional allies and vassals of the political, military-industrial and financial hegemonic forces of the United States.

The submission to the interests of the USA and the dissolution of Europe's sovereignty seem to have been decided for the time being and will only be corrected in the foreseeable future by drastic measures and a geopolitical

---

[160] As one of many possible sources, we refer to Werner Rügemer, "The Capitalist of the 21st Century", 2019.

realignment of European foreign policy. Membership in NATO is the critical factor and plays the paramount role here. The uncritical integration of NATO's policy into the geopolitics of the EU has meant the end of the sovereign creative power of its foreign policy. This has also led to Europe definitely turning from a peace project into a global warmonger that is currently waging a proxy war against Russia for the very interests of the USA and within the framework of NATO. For possible corrections of the relations with the USA, an assessment of Europe's membership in NATO must therefore be the first step to take. As a starting point for the establishment of political relations among sovereign partners, Europe will have to return to the positions of Charles de Gaulle.

PRELUDE TO THE WAR AGAINST RUSSIA: THE AMERICAN "CORDON SANITAIRE" FROM THE BALTIC TO THE BLACK SEA

Since the Maastricht Treaty of 1993, and accelerated after the financial and debt crises of 2007–08, the EU has succeeded, first, in successfully gaining access to German financial and economic resources through European integration. This process has then been consolidated and even gradually expanded[161] with the transfer of the German resources through the various financial "crisis instruments," most of them established by the EU as a consequence of the so-called Euro crisis. Since that time, Germany has willingly submitted to the policies of the EU and the European Central Bank (ECB), which have used the common European resources to buy up the ultimately uncovered government bonds of the countries from the south of the EU. Likewise, through the ECB's mechanisms, huge liabilities on the Target balance sheet have accumulated to secure economic liquidity in the southern European member states.[162] These target liabilities are secured mainly through German assets, without any control exerted by

---

[161] To understand this rapid development of financial instruments, a glance at the official website of the EU is enough. The sovereignty of the member states is no longer given and depends on the "purse" of the EU: https://www.Europarl.Europa.eu/factsheets/de/sheet/91/finanzielle-unterstutzung-der-eu-mitgliedstaaten

[162] Prof. Hans-Werner Sinn has critically analyzed the mechanisms of these transfers of German assets to the Southern European countries. Various reports are on his website: https://www.hanswernersinn.de/de
Dr. Daniel Stelter is following in these footsteps: https://think-beyondtheobvious.com/

Germany.[163] In addition, the European Stabilization Mechanism (ESM) was created without setting a limit to its volume, or establishing rules for consistently holding the benefiting countries accountable.[164] Likewise, the EU banking union will lead to the general and mutual liability of the member states, with the more "generous" paying the bills for those member states that prefer to keep their assets at home. The EU, as a platform for the transfer of virtually all financial and economic resources and unlimited mutual liability for all obligations, has become a reality. Germany has virtually ceded the power to dispose of its assets and all its economic resources to the EU.[165] This picture fits in with the fact that, according to the latest reports, Germany wants

---

[163] Details on these mechanisms, processes and their results have been presented in "Target Balances and the German Financial Account in Light of the European Balance-of-Payments Crisis" in the CESIFO WORKING PAPER NO. 4051 CATEGORY 7: MONETARY POLICY AND INTERNATIONAL FINANCE DECEMBER 2012, by Hans-Werner Sinn and Timo Wollmershäuser. Prof. Sinn has published various analytical documents related to these issues.

[164] These developments in the financial and economic sectors of the EU have been most consistently critically followed by Prof. Hans-Werner Sinn: https://www.hanswernersinn.de/de.

to transfer the command of its army to NATO, and that means to the USA. This was announced by the German Minister of Defense in his speech on May 10, 2024, at *Johns Hopkins University's School of Advanced International Studies*.

These processes lead to fatal consequences for Europe as a whole that are overlooked by most of the commentators, either deliberately or by lack of competence. The particularly fatal issue about this situation is, that the United States has become the big winner through the European "communalization" of German and European resources. Due to the strong dominance of the US financial sector and Anglo-American cartels over German industry and the entire German economy[166], which includes a large part of the banks as well as the

---

[165] Prof. Dieter Spethmann commented on this relatively early when he publicly and empathically warned that "Germany is giving away its prosperity", on January 19, 2011, in the FAZ.

Nowadays, Prof. Sinn, former director of the IFO-Institute in Munich, is probably the most prominent voice to speak out very clearly in public.

But also in the FAZ, the then co-publisher Volker Stelzner, as well as Thomas Mayer, former chief economist of Deutsche Bank, warned urgently against these results for many years.

German real estate industry, and since 2022, the entire energy sector as well, this US dominance over Germany has eventually been transferred to the entire European economy as a whole. Thus, the French-German-British-Spanish military-industrial complex finally becomes an American-dominated industrial complex of gigantic proportions, and this on European territory and with European engineering and funding. If we assume, rather conservatively[167], that about currently 50% of the world's arms production[168] comes from the United States, then we must be impressed by the fact that the military dominance of the United States and NATO will still be considerably increased by the direct access to the European economy in general, and the military-industrial complex in particular. Thus,

---

[166] Economic analyses for countries such as Greece, Spain or Italy would certainly confirm these statements. In the years following the Lehman crisis, this trend has intensified, as US-dominated financial instruments have used this period of European weakness to buy up *available* European assets, primarily industrial companies, banks and service providers, cheaply.

[167] We refer here mainly to publicly available figures, such as those from SIPRI.

[168] All information can be found on the website of SIPRI – Stockholm International Peace Research Institute. https://www.sipri.org/databases/armstransfers.

NATO has become the perfect tool for the American global war machine, which we have analyzed in our book, of 2024, "War and Business: The American Success Story of the Past Century".

In our understanding, this massive process of intensified armament is not a good sign, because weapons are not primarily built for deterrence, but their primary purpose is to be used in wars, even if it is in so-called "defensive wars".

Yet another fatal result has come to light through the strong focus of European integration on the West under US hegemonic dominance.

This strong geographical and geopolitical orientation of the EU towards the West has led to the Central and Eastern European states being severely neglected by EU politics. Even smaller initiatives such as the "Weimar Triangle" with Germany, France and Poland cannot hide this. No one will deny that it has become a reflex to look at the French-German partners first and usually exclusively with every problem and challenge in the EU. The spirit of the German policy of reconciliation, which had been initiated in an impressive way under Willy

Brandt, was never understood, neither in Germany nor in Europe, in its essence and significance. It is regrettable to see how, since the open war against Russia, the policy of détente[169] has been ideologically ostracized in Germany and Europe as well, since 2022.

The consequences of this revisionist and one-sided orientation of European foreign policy are fatal. In the course of the first decades of the 21st century, the USA succeeded in successively forming a "cordon sanitaire", i.e. a "buffer zone", in the eastern rear of Europe within the framework of NATO. These new "borderlands" are strategically consistent and explicitly aligned against Russia.[170] The Baltic States, together with Poland, Kosovo, Bulgaria

---

[169] See Willy Brandt's biography "Securing Peace and Overcoming Walls – Ost- und Deutschlandpolitik 1955–1989". https://www.willy-brandt-biografie.de/politik/ost-und-deutschlandpolitik/

[170] We do not think it is a good sign that US policy today is once again resorting to a concept that was first an instrument of European policy in the period before the First World War. It seems to us like an indication that Europe cannot break away from its past. If we were to fall back into the European politics of wars, which have shaped the continent for many centuries, then that would be fatal.

and Romania,[171] have been contractually bound by the USA and NATO and supported militarily with equipment paid with American loans. Today, these states willingly form the new frontline states of NATO and the US hegemonic policy directed against Russia.

For the Europeans and the EU, this means once again being faced with a *fait accompli* and having to accept a policy on the European continent that they themselves have not shaped as sovereign nations. As we have had to learn since 2022, this "cordon sanitaire" prepared, to our deep chagrin, the ground for the next big war on the territory of Europe. We have already shown that, from the point of view of the US, the priority objective of its hegemonic policy must be to gain free access to the resources that lie on Russian territory. From the US point of view, this is the decisive means of effectively curbing the growth of the Chinese economy and limiting the expansion of China's geopolitical importance and power for all time to come.[172] In the perspective of the

---

[171] Since 2014 at the latest, Ukraine has also been included here. Ukraine is neither in the EU nor in NATO, but it has been built up by the US and Great Britain to become the new frontline state against Russia.

USA, the prerequisite for power over China[173] is the appropriation of Russia's natural resources and raw materials. It appears that the US is fully successful with its global strategy through the economic incorporation of the European economy and its military-industrial complex. Europe has accepted its complete political submission to the US hegemonic strategy and, in 2024, completed the military integration of the European armies into NATO.

THE USA AT THE THRESHOLD OF DOMINANCE OVER THE EURASIAN CONTINENT

The US pursues clear goals and long-term, strategic interests. You can't blame them for

---

[172] In the Pacific region, the US is pursuing its ASEAN policy, which has been actively and skillfully pursued since Clinton's first term in office, with the goal of integrating as many Asian countries as possible economically and militarily in order to bring them into vassal status, as the US has successfully succeeded in doing with the European states.

[173] Already in the Asia-Pacific Forum of December 31, 2012, Noam Chomsky expressed himself on this topic in a clear and plausible way in an annual outlook. There he speaks of a "Revenge Of History: Chomsky On Japan, China, The United States, And The Threat of Conflict in Asia", i.e. of events that show how historical events can take revenge.

that. The next step and strategic goal in the long-term American hegemonic strategy, is to dominate the Chinese market, i.e. to shape it according to its own rules and "values". For the USA, the path to dominance over China leads through the conquest of Russia. The US will therefore do everything it can to annex Russia's raw materials and natural resources via Europe.[174] Accepting this symptomatic fact, we reached an understanding of the driving forces behind the war in Ukraine, as well as the attempted and repeated regime changes and unrest in Georgia, Armenia, and other Caucasian countries. The aim of this US policy is to destabilize the region and eventually attack Russia.

Under the then Russian President Yeltsin[175], the USA already saw itself very close to its goal.

---

[174] Numerous analyses on the strategic orientation of American China policy can be found on the website of the Council on Foreign Relations (CFR), https://www.cfr.org/future-us-china-relations.
Noam Chomsky also expressed himself in the spirit of our argumentation in a conversation with C. J. Polychroniou on the topic "Why China, not Russia, threatens the US-dominated world order". Published in German on July 9, 2022, in Telepolis; Original in Truthout.

[175] From 1991 to 1999, Boris Yeltsin was the first president of Russia after the end of the Soviet Union.

They wanted to flood Russia with their capital, buy up the country and its resources, and take it over "peacefully". Russia could have remained politically "independent", just like Germany and Europe. The economy and the financial industry dominating the country, however, would have been owned by and in the hands of Anglo-American capital and operated by it according to its rules.[176] Nor should it surprise anyone that the so-called "Russian crisis" that threatened the country in 1998 and 1999 was a debt crisis, the so-called "ruble crisis."[177] This debt would have provided an opportunity for foreign financial institutions and the Anglo-American financial cartels to take over the country's economy on

---

[176] This was a kind of "Rockefeller" capitalism that the US wanted to implement, regardless of the losses for Russia, and with a clear goal. During this time, the large private conglomerates of the oligarchs emerged. After 1999, Russia took back control over the most important conglomerates that were aiming to run the Russian economy, i.e. oil and gas companies, as well as the banks according to their own rules, and placed them under national supervision again. The trial against the oligarch Khodorkovsky was the last sensational act in this process so far.

[177] It is not unimportant to note here that the "Russian crisis" as an economic crisis began shortly after the beginning of the "Asian crisis". So it's a good time for global investors.

favorable terms.[178] Local or regional investors in Russia, who had become nervous, sold their stocks, bonds and ruble holdings at low prices out of fear and transferred the proceeds to countries that seemed particularly safe, especially the UK and the USA. Russia was on the verge of bankruptcy.

The principle-based and "natural" interest of US policy towards Russia at that time was therefore the complete takeover of its economic and natural resources, and this at the lowest possible price. The rest, areas such as culture and society, would not have been bothered by the USA. Culture in the USA has long been run by "media". In the long term, the Russians and their allies would have been "Westernized" and would also have watched mainly Hollywood movies and communicated exclusively via the social media channels of American companies.

If the US had succeeded in taking over Russia's economy and natural resources at that time, China's essential access to natural resources and

---

[178] Niall Ferguson shows very well in his book "Colossus" how the British already used the debt of states during their empire, examples are Iraq and Egypt, in order to be rewarded for their "effort", and to bind the colonized states economically and financially to the British "motherland".

raw materials would have been blocked in the future. The path to future growth would have been difficult, if not hindered, for the Chinese economy.[179] Without a reliable economic partnership with Russia, China would not have had the chance to match the American hegemony in the long term, or at least to fend it off. China would have had to pay the Anglo-American financial groups for the Russian raw materials. This is the "circular economy", the foreign policy, and the foreign trade "business model" that are guiding US hegemonic policy[180]. The United States, in possession of Russia's natural resources, would have become a hegemon without competition. It is exactly this hegemony that the United States is aiming for in the geopolitical global game of chess, an

---

[179] There is often talk about China's investments on the African continent. From this perspective, it should be clear that this is also primarily about raw materials and sales markets. From this point of view, the importance of Australia for China can also be understood. Australia has a relatively small population, but is in possession of large deposits of raw materials on its continent.

[180] So it is not out of pure suspicion to claim, that the US also earns money, when Saudi Arabia sells oil to China. This is a result of the still-prevailing situation of the US-dominated global economic trade policy and geopolitics. Details on this are given in our book on "War and Business", published in 2024.

endeavor that has intensified since the end of the Cold War, as has been openly stated by Zbigniew Brzeziński, the advisor to several American presidents[181]. So this is "the crux of the matter". This is what the great global American strategy has been about since 1919, with Wilson's 14-Points program for global peace, and has been promoted with new intensity since 2001, with the "war against terror".

The growing intensity of this hegemonic striving is therefore essentially fed by two sources: on the one hand, the increasing pressure from the exorbitantly growing and unsustainable American debt, and on the other hand, the rise of China, as the first serious economic and political competitor that is considered by the USA as a future threat to their hegemonic position. This is the background to all the wars that have been waged recently by the United States and also by its proxies, from Afghanistan, as Pakistan's important neighbor, through Iran, Iraq, and from Syria over Libya to the poor country of Yemen, as guardian at the southern access to the Red Sea and the Suez Canal. In addition, since 2014, the USA and NATO have intensified the rearmament of Ukraine, with the

[181] The Grand Chessboard: American Primacy and its Geostrategic Imperatives, by Zbigniew Brzezinski.

clear goal of attacking Russia militarily. The open war that has been going on since 2022 can only be seen as a consequence of these developments. The smaller skirmishes, such as in Georgia and Armenia, we mention here only in passing. We also want to refrain from geopolitically important initiatives pushed forward by the USA and NATO in the Pacific, as we want to concentrate on Europe in this book.

So this is what is at stake on the chessboard for the American industry and capital: free access to raw materials and markets according to US rules and at favorable terms. These are the essential strategic elements. The African continent, as another large reservoir of raw materials, has a similar role to that of Russia, both overall and in the long term. However, the pressure to act there is not yet so great geostrategic.

For the USA, China is the great competitor that it wants to limit, or even better, to "dominate" through Europe's interventions and the possession of Russia's raw materials and natural resources.

The industrial production capacities of Europe certainly also play an important role in this global strategy for hegemonic power. They could, of course, have played a role as an important collateral to be brought to a virtual negotiation table by the European countries and the EU. Europe still disposes of good infrastructure and useful technical and industrial facilities, which, as we have seen, already belong to the Anglo-American financial cartels, who can dispose of them largely at their will. In the event of war, as we are witnessing it in the context of the "war economy" that has been launched in Europe since 2023, Europe will finally have to put its entire production capacities at the service of NATO, and thus at the service of the American geopolitical strategy.

Obviously, we are not following Forner[182], with its definition of "war economy" that is exclusively linked to the part of the GDP directed to the military. Through the NATO approach, war can be led against countries, as is the case with the war against Russia, where each of the NATO partners brings in his contribution, while

---

[182] Ref. to Andreas Forner, published in his book "Wirtschaft und Krieg. Verhältnis von Ökonomie und Politik in Krisenzeiten" (our translation: Economy and War. The Relationship between Economy and Times of Crises"). In a recent publication in WeltTrends 199, Hubert Thielicke / Lutz Kleinwächter (eds.), Potsdam 2023, Forner presents a scientific essay concerning the application of the BIP criteria for an economy of war to the different parties engaged in the war in Ukraine.

not one of the NATO members is formally in war against Russia. This "NATO partnership approach" finally leads to the result that Ukraine is able to lead a proxy war on behalf of NATO with a military as well as the public budget, not only completely funded by US and European sources, but funded far beyond the real capacities of Ukraine. Thus, the notion of a "war economy" has entered a completely new dimension.

Following the officially declared downfall of the Soviet empire in 1991, Europe has been consistently submissive and diligently paved the way for the USA and NATO to southeastern Europe through the forceful destruction of Yugoslavia.[183] One of the largest US military bases in Europe today is in Kosovo — which is not yet a nation, but is already an important pillar of the bridge to Eastern Europe and will, in the near future, for strategic geopolitical reasons, probably become a full member of the EU and NATO.

---

[183] Refer to the speech of the then German Minister of Foreign Affairs, Joschka Fischer, on the NATO mission in Kosovo and Serbia:
https://de.wikipedia.org/wiki/Rede_Joschka_Fischers_zum _NATO-Einsatz_im_Kosovo.

Just a small step further, one comes to the following statement: the EU and NATO are the bridge pillars of the USA in an easterly direction on the Eurasian continent in the struggle for global hegemony. In the West, i.e. the Pacific region, it is Japan and South Korea that have had to take on the role of the US bridge pillars. The USA has not been pursuing an industrial location policy in Europe for a long time, but it is creating geostrategic facts to assert its own interests in the sense of the hegemony of Anglo-American capital and political power[184].

Since 1945 at the latest, Europe has progressively been incorporated by the US and has no longer been considered a competitor, but an integral part of its global strategy for world domination. Already in the writings of Brzezinski, the European states are logically called "vassals".

---

[184] On the close relationship between capital and war, see Niall Ferguson's books, for example: The Cash Nexus. Money and Power in the Modern World, 1700–2000, London: Allen Lane/Penguin Press, 2001; or: War of the World. History's Age of Hatred, 1914–1989, Allen Lane, 2006. Niall Ferguson is certainly not a "revolutionary," but he is courageous, usually honest and extremely intelligent — a historian who can help us see the reality behind the symptoms. His specialty is the monetary and financial economy.

Europe has given up her sovereignty

The EU and practically all European countries have thus definitely and unequivocally given up their sovereignty and independence since the 21st century.

Whether Europe can and wants to regain its sovereignty cannot be answered conclusively. With the analytical description we conducted in the previous chapters, we have sketched out this process, through which the whole of Europe lost the sovereign power to shape their countries and decide on their political destiny. Such clarification is needed in Europe today. Only on the basis of this awareness, which we intend to bring to light, will the people in Europe be able to ask themselves whether they can and want to change the given situation. In any case, it has become obvious that the developments around the process of European integration over the past decades have unhinged the basic rules for a functioning democracy in Europe. The people in Europe can no longer decide for themselves about the actions to be taken to shape their lives and destiny. On the contrary, important decisions are made by external institutions and foreign nations according to foreign interests. This means that there can no longer be any talk of democracy. Even the concepts of "multi-level governance", which are very popular within the EU and its institutions, cannot help overcoming this lack of direct democratic participation.[185] Obviously, decisions on the destiny of Europe are taken in Washington and New York, not in Paris, Berlin, or Brussels.

The aim of this chapter has been to show the profound transformation that has taken place

---

[185] There is extensive literature, discussions and one could almost say a "movement" within the EU on "multi-level governance". We just want to note here that, in our view, this prominent concept is diametrically opposed to the claims of "democracy". The practice of "multi-level governance" is ultimately undemocratic and anti-federalist. "Multi-level Governance" as it is practiced by the EU means essentially, and this statement is based on ample evidence, that (a) everybody may do as he or she deems appropriate, (b) at the end nobody is responsible for any consequences, and (c) nobody will be held accountable for any outcome.

The structures of an ESM correspond exactly to this concept. It is explicitly stated in the statutes that the responsibility of the acting person is to be excluded in any case and forever. Nobody can be held accountable for anything.

In our understanding, however, democracy and responsibility belong inseparably together.

in Europe since the end of the Second World War. Only through an understanding of the deeper causes, the interdependencies of the actors, and the historical background will it be possible for us to find orientation, bringing us to a situation where we might be able to take up the challenges of the future. Only by overcoming the obstacles of this deep and persistent crisis, in which Europe currently finds herself, can new forces emerge in order to open up new paths and opportunities for the sovereign, peaceful and sustainable design of our living environments and the shaping of our societies.

SUMMARY PART ONE

In Part One of the book, we have been looking at the Symptoms of the Crisis in Europe. The application of the scientific method of historical reconstruction and analytical description of the relevant processes and events has led us to present a clear picture of the political economy, which is characteristic of Europe today. The critical result of the historical development of Europe's political economy over the past decades is its increasing involvement and even promotion of wars on the continent and beyond.

The fact that the current war in Ukraine has seemingly grown out of nowhere, is, in our view, the principal symptom of the crisis in Europe. The almost tacit and hidden processes of the emergence of the recent war against Russia are an evident symptom of the fact that this war is, at its origin, not a European war. This war has its origins outside of Europe, in the US. Ukraine and Europe are used as US proxies. We have provided clear evidence and brought to light the constituent role and driving force of the USA, which is at the economic and political level, at the origin of this primordial symptom of Europe's crisis.

In the first part of the book, we have taken an evidence-based approach and have been looking at the most important symptoms of the crisis in Europe. Now, as we have a sufficiently well understood the symptoms, we will dedicate the second part of the book to the analytical description of the root causes of the crisis in Europe.

PART TWO

THE ROOT CAUSES OF THE CRISIS IN EUROPE

Chapter 1

Linear solutions: the Overdue Paradigm Shift

„... how do I show the fly the way out of the fly-bottle?"

Wittgenstein, Philosophical Investigations, §309

FOREWORD

In Part Two of the book, we will focus our evidence-based approach on the descriptive analysis of the root causes of the *Crisis in Europe*. We aim for a deep epistemological understanding of the root causes of this crisis. Historians do agree that modern man in Europe has its origin in the era between the 13th and 15th century, the time concluding the Middle Ages in

Europe. This implies for us that we will describe and analyze the principal historical events and cultural factors that have shaped Europe and the social and economic life in her societies since the Renaissance. The origins of the historical memory and of modern Europe's self-image and consciousness in the 15th and 16th century will thus been brought to light. This will eventually lead us to a thorough understanding of the principal elements and their systemic interdependencies that are characteristic for the mind-set and mental framework for modern man in Europe. This understanding is required for the identification of the principal root causes that are underlying the Crisis in Europe.

Our examination will lead us deeply into the historical and cultural context of modern-time Europe. Our questions in this second part of the book will be complex. We will understand that the possible answers and potential solutions will be challenging for Europe on her way into the future of our globalizing world.

The scientific tool we are applying is a historical reconstruction of the creation of modern Europe from the Renaissance until today. Not only will the origins of the historical memory and of modern Europe's self-image and consciousness be brought to light. We will also provide evidence for their impact on life in Europe and on a global scale. We assume that the *modus operandi* of Europe, the way it functions internally and internationally, has its origin in the historical memory and self-image of modern Europe. This hypothesis will be examined in Part Two of the book, and evidence for its reasonable justification be provided.

We start this second part of the book with a short chapter to present our research interest and the methodology applied to examine our hypothesis. Three critical areas will be in the focus of our approach.

In chapter two of part two of the present book, we take a detailed look at the current Global Governance system as a result of the growing Western economic and political dominance since the Renaissance.

In the third chapter of Part Two, we will present a deep analytical description of the critical and constituent elements that are characteristic of the mindset of Europe and its people. These three constitutional elements are (a) the growing individual consciousness and the role played by the individual in society; (b) the specific view modern Europe and its people have developed with regard to "progress"; and (c) the third constitutional element for the specific mindset of Europe and its people is "growth" and the specific way it is seen. The critical role of Europe in the development of modern science is analyzed throughout the chapters of this part of the book. It is functioning as a "basic melody" during the entire analysis.

These three elements are considered constitutional to the specific mindset of Europe and its people. Combined, they are constituting a complex that is at the root of the Western model of capitalist development. This specific mindset, in its combination, is also representing the paradigm that is directing the actions of Europe in its international relations. This specific view on the three elements of this constitutional mindset is, in its combination, considered the principal root cause of the economic, financial and environmental crises in Europe, as well as its global impact. Specific attention is drawn in our analysis to the rapid demographic growth that has taken place since the 15th century, and in particular since the rapid industrialization in the 19th and 20th centuries. This rapid demographic growth is a root cause for the globally growing stream of migration, as well as for increasing tensions, violent confrontations and wars inside and between countries. This rapid demographic growth is at the same time considered a root cause for the disturbances concerning social and political cohesion that are characterizing our societies in Europe and beyond. Rapid demographic growth is finally perceived as the root cause of the destructive pressure on the living environment in most countries on earth.

In summary, Part 2 of the book will provide convincing evidence for the negative impact of the European social, economic and political model on global well-being and peace. In fact, the implementation of this specific European capitalist development model has brought life on earth to a threshold. This applies to the political level, where European-driven development has led to the creation of an ever-increasing arsenal of nuclear weapons that are not inspiring confidence in the sustainability of European and Western politics. In parallel, the world has obviously also reached a threshold through its exceeding pressure on the living environment on earth. Through the unique approach we are applying, systemic interdependencies between the principal root causes (a) the role the individual is playing in society, (b) the specific European view on progress, and (c) the unique European view on growth, will become visible. The presentation of the interdependencies between the principal root causes and their impact will bring us into a position, where we can provide evidence for humanity being a self-regulating system on earth.

Obviously, all these root causes for the crisis in Europe have spread through the process of globalization and are exerting their impact globally. As a result, the crisis in Europe and the Western-dominated world has led to a crisis that has a global scope. At the same time, there is an existing lack of globally valid rules for governance that would enable the nations and international institutions to effectively cope with the crisis. Geopolitics in the age of hegemonic strive is mainly occupied with the building up of the war machines and armies to drive violent confrontations and wars. The forces that are working out of Europe's collective memory[186]

---

[186] We refer with the notion of "collective memory" to the work presented in 1925 by the French philosopher and sociologist Maurice Halbwachs in his book "Les cadres sociaux de la mémoire". Since then, this concept of the collective memory has been further analyzed and advanced. As an example, refer to "On the Cultural Constitution of Collective Memory", 2008, Qi Wang, a researcher in psychology at Cornell University.

and its specific mind-set obviously have difficulties to cope with the ongoing paradigm shift that is characteristic for the present era, in which long term existing structures are breaking up. The geopolitical initiatives to manage humanity's actions concerning a globally overheating economy, an exponential demographic growth rate, and a generalized destructive pressure on the living environment on earth are lacking efficiency and power. The suggestions and actions of the Western power elites are not convincing the Global South, and they find ever fewer followers. Sustainable solutions to the globally existing problems, which have taken their origin in Europe, are not found. Trust in the Western capabilities to successfully face the various challenges does not build up. Europe and its Western allies are losing steam and are getting out of breath. The Global South, representing the vast majority of the populations and nations on earth, does not consider Europe to be an honest broker anymore. We observe increasing evidence that Europe and the West are losing their last battle. Hence, it is high time for Europe and the Western nations, and they would be well advised to look for an honorable and peaceful outcome.

INTRODUCTION

The wider public has been talking about New Thinking for years. The media talk and write that we need "new minds". Even the "New Man", and, of course, the "New Woman", are called upon again and again. Others speak of the "new image of man".[187] To us, these wishes and demands seem to be fundamentally right and good, because we need new skills in a rapidly changing world and have to adapt our behavior to rapidly changing circumstances. But we also know that the New Man or Woman, or "right" and "different" thinking, cannot be prescribed. The physical person is constantly renewing herself, but a new spiritual person is formed either through spiritual revolutions, as in the Renaissance, or through experiences in lengthy personal learning and transformation processes. For the individual, this usually requires lifelong learning processes, spiritual renewals or personal transformations. It becomes

---

[187] In 1968, Arthur Koestler and J. R. Smythies published the volume "Revolutionization of the Sciences of Life, The New Image of Man", as a result of the Alpbach Symposium at that time.

increasingly evident that the "renewal" of people will be at the origin of a new world order.

So we want to ask ourselves how we Europeans, as part of humanity, can find our way to such a "renewal" and to correspondingly new thinking and actions. What can and do we in Europe have to do to become a creative part of the change and the ongoing global paradigm shift?

In today's specialist literature on this topic, it is often assumed that there is a difference, or contrast, between linear (convergent) and lateral (divergent) thinking[188]. Mostly, however, these remain philosophical or epistemological considerations. The question of the conditions and prerequisites of how to get from a certain way of thinking, an intellectual or spiritual attitude, to a specific action, is usually ignored. So the critical question usually remains unmentioned, or is not dealt with in these discussions: How do we get from "right" or better thinking to "good" and increasingly better action? In the context of our topic, which is about the crisis in Europe and its geopolitical implications, this step, from theory to practice, is of course critical. Because it is right here that the

---

[188] Psychologist J. P. Guilford introduced the terms "convergent thinking" and "divergent thinking" in 1956.

question of power comes into play. In politics, it is the question of power that must be asked in order to really attain a level, where changes and innovations may be induced, including the formulation of "new rules". In politics, the egoistic strive for power is the critical hurdle between talking and action that is to be overcome. And then it gets very exciting again, and we are moving right back into the center of our topic. The question of power is challenging the way I deal with my own interests in relation to the interests of others. Am I ready to acknowledge the interests of others as equal to my own? Or is it about setting the rules of the game in such a way that my own interests are always prime and have absolute priority, or even exclusivity in a one-sided way, as in a zero-sum game?

In this part of the book, we will not enter into a discussion about theories and philosophies. It is our aim to provide evidence showing that, in our understanding, "new thinking" will in the long term lead to "different actions" and to new attitudes and behaviors, even in politics or geopolitics. We want to be careful here and therefore do not speak of "right action". For, a single human being cannot judge ethical or moral issues in an absolute way, as Immanuel

Kant showed already some 250 years ago in his treatises on the Categorical Imperative and Practical Reason. On the other side, Kant insisted on the possible ranking of ethical ideas and moral values, albeit within the limits of acknowledged moral principles. Today, we presume that such moral principles will have to be mutually recognized among people. It is about the search for the better ideas. In consequence of this argumentation, we do not shy away from our social and political responsibility and remain committed to intellectual honesty. Hence, we will present our opinion in an open and transparent way, providing clear indications of what we consider to be "better ways and more sensible actions".

We assume that a fundamental change in the way people think and act in our European societies would lead to a social paradigm shift[189].

---

[189] The term paradigm shift was coined by Thomas S. Kuhn in 1962 and refers to "the change of fundamental framework conditions", whereby Kuhn in his work primarily refers to the scientific-theoretical and scientific-historical context by tracing and analyzing the process of change in fundamental framework conditions for individual scientific theories. In his book, he showed how paradigm shifts take place in the scientific field, what laws such a paradigm shift of rethinking and other actions follows. Since that time, the term has been used in many

Change will not remain superficial, but will eventually go to the roots. We consider this to be desirable and important in these times of rapid social change and communicative and mediatic globalization.[190] As we have shown in the previous chapters and even in more detail in some of our other books[191], geopolitics has been shaped for more than a century according to a pattern that is one-sidedly Western, and tends to be Anglo-American. Within the framework of this kind of geopolitics, we observe a systemic feature that makes the world no longer able to escape these "eternal wars". We assume, furthermore, that Europe has to start at home, if it wants to find a way out of the crisis mode. It

---

areas and can now be considered popular.

[190] Independent observers, we will lead the Club of Rome, Buckminster Fuller and Gregory Bateson, have been citing the three most important challenges facing humanity for decades: wars, resource scarcity together with climate change, rapid demographic growth.

[191] The reader may refer to the following books:
Europe lost her Sovereignty. History-Background-Perspectives, published in 2024, by Georg von Goldbach.
The New System of Global Governance: The ongoing Paradigm Shift, published in 2024, by Georg von Goldbach.
Europe on the Way to Her Apocalypse. History-Background-Perspectives, published in 2024, by Georg von Goldbach.

leads nowhere to blame others. Therefore, in the quest to break free of the recurrent crises in Europe, a paradigm shift must be induced that allows the peoples and nations in Europe, to interact according to different, new rules. This will eventually change the patterns of interaction with the other peoples and nations dwelling on earth. New thinking and new ways of acting are therefore important for all of us to escape this negative spiral[192] of violence and war.[193]

CALL FOR A SOCIAL AND POLITICAL PARADIGM SHIFT

We therefore call for a paradigm shift in politics and in the way we are shaping through our institutions as well as our personal behavior in

---

[192] On the topic of the scope of action and the spirals of action, we also refer to the following source: Interview with Wolfgang Streeck from the Max Planck Institute for the Study of Societies about the scope of action of states. https://www.mpg.de/6360276/handlungsspielraum_des_s taates.

[193] In the tradition of modern psychoanalysis, Arno Gruen, for example, shows this need for action and shows ways out of this "psycho trap". Alienated from Life, 2019, Arno Grün. See also, Christoph Bördlein, Introduction to Behavioral Analysis. 1st edition, 2015.

the living environment of our societies[194]. Our primary aim is to show how attitudes, cultural prejudices and historically engraved ideologies hinder and prevent the redesign and consequent transformation of social processes. At the same time, we will bring some striking real-life examples, thus providing evidence for the possibility of choosing a way towards a paradigm shift in Europe. Such evidence will show us how rules have been changed in social interaction and in politics, and have finally led to new and better results. Our powerful and governing elites have brought us into difficult situations in several critical areas of life. We live in an age of permanent and general crises, [195]because these power elites pretend that their

---

[194] The term paradigm shift was coined by Thomas S. Kuhn in 1962 and refers to "the change of fundamental framework conditions", whereby Kuhn in his work primarily refers to the scientific-theoretical and scientific-historical context by tracing and analyzing the process of change in fundamental framework conditions for individual scientific theories. In his book, he showed how paradigm shifts take place in the scientific field, what laws such a paradigm shift of rethinking and other actions follows. Since that time, the term has been used in many areas and can now be considered popular.

[195] In a guest article for the Federal Association "Energy, Water, Life", Christian Schuldt writes in 2021 about the "Age of Crises". In an article in the FAZ of May 15, 2022,

thoughts and actions are the right ones, without alternatives. Notwithstanding the increasing and general situation of crises, they are not willing to change their minds or escape their ideological traps. They still want us to follow their rules. We no longer agree with this. This is why we are calling here to openly question and redefine the currently applied rules for the future shaping of our societies in Europe and for living together with our cohabitants on earth. The examples we bring will show that other ways, other solutions, and other paradigms of political action and the shaping of social and political coexistence are feasible.

We are aware that such a paradigm shift in political thought and social action, as we are calling for, would lead to profound social change. The subsequent social and political transformation will lead to far-reaching consequences, if implemented consistently. All areas of people's public and private lives in Europe would eventually be affected. We presume that this profound change is desirable and even urgently needed, if we wish to improve the quality of life in our societies.

Philipp Krohn asks "Permanent turning points and new crises - how do we endure it?"

Of course, we also know that change and transformation are not only associated with new challenges, but also with risks. This is a reason why people are usually hesitant and reluctant, and why they shy away from change. This fear of change is innate in us. [196] It is therefore only natural that significant social forces and individuals are afraid of a social and political paradigm shift[197] and will prevent it as far as possible. Out of fear of change and the inherent risks, opportunities for social and political transformation are faded out and usually not seen, suppressed, and not seized.[198] As with all

---

[196] In his studies, Konrad Lorenz has demonstrated in detail that "fear of change" is part of the basic equipment of the human psyche and human behavior. He was convinced that "for eons of time in natural history, those who were most afraid had the best chance of survival." On the subject of fear, see also Fritz Riemann: Basic Forms of Fear. A depth psychological study. 10th revised and extended edition (52nd–63rd thousand), Munich, Basel 1975.

[197] The Anglicism "paradigm shift" is also often used in German. We use paradigm shift and paradigm shift synonymously here.

[198] In Germany, Karl Steinbuch published good and stimulating books on the subject decades ago. To start with, I would like to mention "Wrongly Programmed – On the Failure of Our Society in the Present and Before the Future", 1968.

major changes, there are people and forces, who have a self-centered interest in maintaining the *status quo*. They will consequently resist change for reasons of self-centered interests.

The reason for rejecting a paradigm shift is therefore mainly twofold. Change is rejected either out of a natural fear of the inherent risks, or the fear of having to give up one's own interests and losing previous claims. This is completely normal and does not fundamentally call into question our intention, the validity of our approach, or the call for a paradigm shift in Europe. As we know from psychology, we should learn to cope with fears and anxieties and should not suppress them in the long term, because, in one way or another, they will erupt and break out, often in destructive ways and in the form of aggression. In the political context, such uncontrolled "eruption" of suppressed fears and anxieties often leads to violence against others and, in the extreme case, to war. It is a well-known fact that the psychological pressure on a nation's feelings and injured self-esteem will often be directed towards an enemy and, in many cases, lead to violent actions.[199] However,

---

[199] Refer to the classical and principal biographies "Hitler", 2007, by Joachim Fest and "Hitler", 1998, by Ian Kershaw, which provide convincing evidence for these phenomena.

we know that fears and anxieties can be consciously overcome. The energy that is released by such consciously managed processes to combat anxieties and fears, may then be used sensibly for processes of creative change and fruitful transformation.[200] If we apply this consideration to the political sphere, then we would say that the energy and costs that we have spent since many years on conflicts and wars would have been used much better and more sensibly to improve people's living conditions. However, this would have required rejuvenating the mental mindsets of the nations in Europe. Blinded by their fear, people have not seized upcoming opportunities for change in the past. This is the reason why we are bringing up now our proposal for a constructive paradigm shift. This will open great opportunities for huge benefits to all of us, except for those, who can

Further useful reading on this topic from the psychological side: Der Fremde in Uns, 2002, Arno Gruen.

[200] Refer to Heinz W. Krohne: Psychologie der Angst. Kohlhammer, Stuttgart, 2010.

In the therapy of Traumatic events the potential for "Post-traumatic Growth" is well documented: refer to "The Body Keeps the Score: Brain, Mind, and Body in the Healing of Trauma", 2014, Bessel van der Kolk.

This is what we mean, when we say that "every crisis opens the way to new Happiness".

see their salvation solely in the selfish pursuit of short-term profits and the strive for hegemonic power.

By paradigm shift, we mean the change to a fundamentally new pattern of thought, that will lead to a change in familiar reflexes and ways of acting in Europe. Such change will lead to a new path based on new rules, inducing a fundamental transformation of social processes and political action. A paradigm shift is often compared to a quantum leap.[201] This points to the magnitude of the actual challenge. A paradigm shift is not easy, but we will show that it is desirable and basically feasible.

We should also mention here that not every paradigm shift will automatically be meaningful and good in itself. One negative paradigm was certainly the globally widespread smoking of cigarettes that began to spread in the 19th and, in particular, the 20th centuries. This paradigm prevailed and spread through intensive advertising[202], especially after the First World

---

[201] The physicist Prof. Dr. Markolf Niemz speaks of the meaningfulness and social necessity of a "spiritual quantum leap". https://spirit-online.de/ein-spiritueller-quantensprung.html.

[202] Today, the "Marlboro Man" has almost completely disappeared from the public eye.

War. The American and European tobacco industries made huge fortunes out of this harmful habit. At the same time, however, many people suffered considerable damage to their health. So, what applies for cybernetics and system thinking is also valid for a paradigm shift: without the right rules, a lot, or everything will go wrong. As Gregory Bateson says: The rules have to change. And we would add: Rules have to be changed in free and open debates, in *a global competition for better ideas*, where power and short-term profits[203] are not the decisive factors.

Every paradigm shift begins with a first step, which is often taken by individual personalities [204]who, in the face of a challenge, recognize the

[203] The reader will have noticed that we apply throughout our book the distinction between "profit" and "benefit". These are two notions with seemingly similar connotation, but with clearly distinct meaning and value. While "profit" is a term applied in economic exchange, "benefit" usually is used in social interactions.

[204] The years-long struggle of European physicists over the understanding and interpretation of quantum mechanics and quantum theory, about the quantum leap in physics, is described very insightfully by Thomas Hürter in his book "The Age of Uncertainty", 2021. A paradigm shift is therefore not a matter of course. In the book by Thomas Kuhn mentioned above, the prerequisites for the success of such processes can be understood.

usefulness of and opportunity for an alternative approach to a challenge[205]. Following such a first step of increasing awareness of an opportunity, an additional ingredient is required. It takes courage to make conscious decisions and move towards consequent actions. Finally, we have to recognize that only charismatic leadership can induce processes. Only convincing and charismatic leadership is capable of leading people to consistently implement new knowledge and insight gained, which will finally lead to new patterns of action. As is well known, action is taken through a group structure. The charismatic individual is acting as a catalytic individual, but action will always grow out of a group. Such a decisive first step through coherent human action has been overdue for

---

In the political sphere, we dare to mention Mahatma Gandhi here, who, through his courage, his personal example, but also through his perseverance, finally forced the British Empire to end the occupation of India. The "naked fakir," as Churchill called him, had managed to encourage the Indian people to shake off British rule.

[205] For an introduction to the question of social and political paradigm shift, we recommend the conversation, published in issue 16, Sozialimpulse 4/10, with Roland Benedikter, Stanford University. The questions were asked by Thomas Stöckli MA, Director of the Institute for Practice-Oriented Research, Solothurn, Switzerland.

decades in politics in Europe and, from a global perspective, also for the USA[206].

---

[206] We will be told that European unification means a paradigm shift in German politics. We agree with this assertion insofar as we accept it for the policy of European integration with its so-called four 'freedoms', which concern the free movement of persons, goods, services and capital.

As we have been able to show in the previous chapters of this book, however, the paradigm shift that we demand for the fundamentally "better functioning" of our societies has not yet been seen and implemented by the EU. Freedom and sovereignty are indispensable prerequisites for the formulation of meaningful rules for shaping our societies. However, the EU, on the other hand, has become embroiled in wars and unprecedented dimensions of political and economic dependencies by subordinating it to the interests of the US and NATO.

PART TWO
THE ROOT CAUSES OF THE CRISIS IN EUROPE

Chapter 2
The Global Governance System Shaped by Europe[207]

"The vast majority of humanity is, of course, its non-Western part, and the paradox is that we people of the West are people whose view of history often resembles that of the time before Vasco da Gama. Personally, I do not believe that this antediluvian, traditional conception of the history of the West will last much longer. I have no doubt that a reorientation is imminent, and in our case it will, I think, be a reorientation in the literal sense of the word."

Unification of mankind and its world-political future
in: Outlook on the Future, Anthology, 1968
Arnold Toynbee

---

[207] For a quick introduction to the topic, we recommend Helmut Willke's "Global Governance, 2006.
An additional source to consult is "A Theory of Global Governance, Authority, Legitimacy, and Contestation", 2018, by Michael Zürn.

INTRODUCTION

In this first second of Part Two of the book, we will start with an analytical description of the Global Governance System as it has grown out of Europe's economic and political development since the Renaissance. We will show that the current system of global governance is intimately linked to the development of capitalism and deserves to be called a structured system since the time of the British Empire. It started to develop out of the organizational structures of the East India Company and reached its apex with the end of Victorian Great Britain, right before the First World War.[208] We wish to make a clear point at this stage: it is not our intention to undertake a formal criticism of capitalism. We consider such an endeavor far beyond the scope of the present book.

This line of development continues without interruption with the US, which inherited the Global Governance System from Great Britain after 1919 with the Treaty of Versailles, and has further developed it at its will and intention.

---

[208] Refer to "The Honorable Company: A History of the English East India Company", 1993, John Keay. A good source for further orientation is "Empire: How Britain Made the Modern World, 2018, by Niall Ferguson.

We will further show that there are clear indications that this Global Governance System, dominated by the West, will come to an end and will be transformed into a new system with new organizational structures and following new rules. The paradigm shift is already ongoing[209]. The emerging system of "global governance"[210] will change in the medium and long term due to China's economic rise and increasing political importance. There will be a paradigm shift in the functioning of international relations and structured interactions between countries and nations on earth. This process of developing the emerging new system of global governance is already underway and is at the origin of the current geopolitical turbulence. This transformative process of changing global governance structures confronts Europe with a huge challenge. Obviously, Europe does not

[209] Refer to "The New System of Global Governance: The ongoing Paradigm Shift", published in 2024, by Georg von Goldbach.
[210] We use the English term "Global Governance" throughout, which is also commonly used in the German-speaking world. In German, this would be called "global governance", or "rules-based global order beyond the nation state". The Berlin Social Science Center (WZB) offers a blog on this subject:
https://www.wzb.eu/de/forschung/internationale-politik-und-recht/global-governance.

have the capability and does not dispose of the required organizational structures to play the role of a creative actor in this process. We will show that the root causes are of a cultural and mental nature. They are underlying this refusal to change the current global governance system. The rejection and fear of change are among the most critical factors in the crisis in Europe.[211]

Obviously, the details of the organizational structures and the mechanisms of their functioning in the new system of global governance cannot yet be known. The outcome is linked to human, social and political processes. It's not like replacing an old, dysfunctional machine with a new one. We talk here about complex human, social and political processes. Nevertheless, we will endeavor in this chapter of our book to bring to light the dimensions of the challenge, while at the same time giving some indications relative to the forms and structures the New System of Global Governance may take.

---

[211] Rafael Poch-de-Feliu published in 2024 a series of articles entitled "Gaza, Ukraine and Eurasia in the Crisis of the Decline of the West". He sees the year 2024 as a watershed, "a turning point in the crisis of the decline of the West and its hitherto unchallenged dominance".

We are aware that this part of the book would deserve to be further expanded in scope and depth. We recommend that this work be undertaken in due course as part of a larger research program, perhaps led by the Berggruen Institute[212] as a neutral platform. Such an endeavor should be organized in cooperation with universities and research institutions from different countries, with interdisciplinary researchers coming from different cultures.

Our analytical description will serve its purpose if it sufficiently demonstrates the need for a paradigm shift leading from the European and Western dominated system to a new global governance system bringing other nations to the table and integrating other political and cultural features. The essential trains of thought developed in this context will clearly show the contours of the current challenges Europe and the US are facing. The contours that will appear in the course of our analytical description may serve the purpose of providing a distinct orientation for future research.

It should have become clear by this point that we make a consistent reference to cybernetics in this book. The critical feature of cybernetics is

---

[212] https://berggruen.org/

linked to its approach as a general systems theory that is based on humans learning from living, self-regulating systems. As a consequence, we intend to provide useful guidance for the formulation of new rules according to which the coming system of global governance might function.[213]

As a starting point and for the purpose of initial guidance, we would like to introduce this part of the book with a working hypothesis, pretending that *further global geopolitical development will not develop in a linear sequence*. We assume that the system of global governance is to work and meet with the approval of the majority of the countries and nations involved, then the rules for its functioning must be changed. The hegemonic system of global governance that we have witnessed for more than a century, with the principle of armed conflict as the main political tool, will no longer be able to function. We presume that *the main reasons for this are of cultural origin*.

---

[213] More details on the rules and functional mechanisms can be found in the book "The New System of Global Governance: The ongoing Paradigm Shift", published in 2024, by Georg von Goldbach.

In our ideas and line of thinking, we have partially been inspired by the discussion of imperialism that has been going on in Germany for decades, initiated by the publications of Hannah Arendt.[214] A number of other important sources were also consulted.[215]

However, we derive the essential rationale for our hypothesis from our own long-term observations, studies and reflections on the subject.

The direct reason for the specific approach chosen within this essay on the topic of the paradigm shift in global governance was taken from the work of Stefan Schmalz[216]. He repeatedly refers to the peculiarities of the

[214] Recommend reading: Hannah Arendt: The Origins of Imperialism in: The Hidden Tradition. Eight Essays, 1976. Further recommended reading: "The Origins of Totalitarianism". Furthermore, "The Human Condition".

[215] On the Political Relevance of Historical Theories. The Imperialism Discussion in the Shadow of the Cold War, Federal Agency for Civic Education, Issue ApuZ 20/1972, Author: Timothy W. Mason.

Recommended reading: The Age of Imperialism (in Oldenbourg, Grundriss der Geschichte, Volume 15). 4th edition. Munich, 2000, by Gregor Schöllgen. This is an excellent, comprehensive and research-oriented overall presentation with 1223 literature references on various individual topics.

"succession arrangement" within the evolution of the capitalist system. The process of formation of the capitalist order, as it has been described by Fernand Braudel and approved by most scholars since then[217], took place along a line of development with three clearly interlinked steps: a) origin in Italy, during and as a result of the Renaissance; b) then rapid and globalizing further development led by several European states, until the formation of the dominant role of the British Empire in the 17th and 18th century; and finally c) after the end of

[216] Schmalz, Stefan (2015): China's New Role in Global Capitalism. In: Prokla 40 (4):483-503.

Schmalz, Stefan/Ebenau, Mathias: Auf dem Sprung – Brasilien, Indien und China, 2011.

The Role of China in the Current Disputes about the Operational Mode of Globalization, in: Journal of International Relations, Vol. 25 (2018) Issue 2, pp. 144–163, Jenny Simon.

[217] Refer to Fernand Braudel, "Histoire et Sciences sociales : La longue durée", in : Annales, Année 1958, pp. 725-753.

German Edition: „Die lange Dauer". in: Schriften zur Geschichte, Bd. 1: Gesellschaft und Zeitstrukturen. 1992, pp. 49–87. Very important in our context is "The History of Civilization from the 15th to the 18th Century, 1982, Fernand Braudel. The original was published as "La dynamique du capitalisme". Paris, 1985. German edition: The Dynamics of Capitalism. 2nd edition. 1991.

the British Empire and the Victorian era in 1901, takeover of the system and its principal results by the United States, with a following systematic consolidation and development of its political and economic mechanisms and with a continuous increase in dynamism up to the present time.

While these three major steps are considered essential, we observe a multitude of intermediate stations and meanders in this history that were often very important in promoting this whole movement of capitalism over the past six centuries. We will however focus closely on our line of argumentation.

At this stage, we should not overlook a very important and critical point that is characteristic of this movement and the development of capitalism[218]: This kind of "capitalist civilization" was of European origin and driven by Europe.

With the re-entry of China as a player in world history[219] since the end of the 20th century, this

---

[218] We use the term "capitalism" here in a comprehensive sense that includes the different dimensions of social, political and economic action. So we are talking about the "global development process" of capitalism.

[219] There are now numerous studies and books on the topic of China's "new" entry into the active shaping of world history. We have acquired our knowledge mainly through

situation has changed dramatically, especially since China's dynamic economic rise, which was initiated under the reign of Deng Xiaoping towards the end of the 20th century.

At this point, it might be useful to further clarify our initial working hypothesis by putting it into the adequate global context: Since China belongs to a different cultural area[220] than the Western countries, the further development of global capitalism, and in particular of the new system of global governance, will not remain one-dimensionally European, and will thus not follow a linear path. There is necessarily a paradigm shift to occur. The previous "succession arrangements" between European powers will not apply anymore.

---

our studies at the Free University of Berlin in the 1970s and through the reading and study of the classical books of Jonathan D. Spence, and Craig G. Benjamin. We also refer the reader to "The New Silk Roads, Present and Future of Our World" by Peter Frankopan, 2018. This book introduces the period of development of trade relations and cultural exchange between the Orient and Occident.

[220] By using the word "culture", we do not want to limit the scope of related research to "cultural studies". Rather, we are concerned with opening up a field of scientific, historical, and philosophical reflection for research on the topic of global governance, which should encompass a wide range of relevant topics and areas.

Putting Part Two of this book into the context of our overall approach, we have to draw the attention of the reader to the fact that this paradigm shift towards the new system of global governance is one of the root causes of the deep crisis in Europe. We are, in fact, in the midst of a tremendous change of Europe's role in world history and of its place at the table of the global players. We are all part of a global birth process that will eventually bring to light new global governance structures.

We should also mention here that, in recent decades, India has become an increasingly important player on the world political stage. India will certainly play an increasingly important role in the future structure and mechanisms of the system of global governance. But while India is still searching for its specific role in this global power game, China has already established itself as a major player.

Oswald Spengler intuitively predicted this necessary paradigm shift of the global governance system in his highly informative introduction to his book "The Decline of the West".[221] There he elaborated on this issue in

[221] Spengler, Oswald; Der Untergang des Abendlandes, erster Band 1918, zweiter Band 1922. Published in English

some detail. Spengler refers to other cultural areas that he does not include in the Occident, i.e., the West. This comprises not only the Arab world, but also Russia and Latin America. We presume it is important to include Africa in this extension of the global scope, whose cultural power and importance are still not understood and whose potential impact on the shaping of future global governance systems is fundamentally underestimated.

In the further course of our analytical presentation, we will show why the further geopolitical development will not be driven by Europe and will not follow a linear sequence, and why the new system of global governance will follow new rules that will not be defined by Europe or the USA.

CULTURAL FOUNDATIONS OF CAPITALISM

In order to substantiate our hypothesis and help it to be well understood, we will present a brief overview of the cultural background of global political and economic developments as an essential part of our considerations. The background, on which this development of

as: "The Decline of the West".

modern capitalism has taken place is, on the one hand, of a political and social nature, and on the other hand, it arises to a decisive extent from the scientific and technical development in Europe.[222]

There are an infinite number of studies and books on the social, economic and political formation of the "modern world" and capitalism[223]. Most of them refer to a "secularization" as an essential prerequisite. This hints to an event in the spiritual realm that has to do with an increasing awareness of the "absence of god" or other external forces. In consequence, this implies man's individual responsibility for the shaping of humanity's living conditions. The eminent German sociologist Max Weber has called this process the "disenchantment of the world" and linked it directly to the "intellectualization" and "rationalization" of our world, which presumes that "all things can – in principle – be controlled

---

[222] We refer here to "The Renaissance, the Reformation and the Rise of Nations", an audiobook in the series "The Great Courses" produced by "The Teaching Company", in 2005, by Andrew C. Fix.

[223] For an introduction to the topic, we recommend "The Renaissance, the Reformation and the Rise of Nations (1348 – 1715)", published in 2005, by Andrew C. Fix.

through rational calculation". Max Weber explicitly considers these processes as the direct impact that scientific development has on our societies.

On the more practical side of daily life, the development of the modern monetary system has been one of the most critical aspects of the birth of modern capitalism, as the British historian Niall Ferguson, among others, has worked out clearly and in detail[224]. Let us tentatively call this aspect of the process of modernization of our societies the tendency toward the general "economization of the lifeworld". This modernization of European societies means an increasing control of all social institutions through a progressive penetration of structures, organizational models, concepts and patterns of social and political action. We called this process the progressive "auto-domestication" of human action, and linked it here to the progressive institutionalization of our societies. This tendency for "total control" has to be seen in contrast with individual human freedom.

---

[224] By Niall Ferguson, The Ascent of Money, 2008. Of course, there are also numerous other good studies on this topic of the money economy.

A third important prerequisite and concomitantly growing feature of modern capitalism has been the increasing "juridification" of private and public life, which goes hand in hand with the development of the contractual system and the determination of the individual person as the bearer of public rights and duties.

However, most scholars converge in their conviction that beyond these various social aspects, the decisive foundation for the emerging form of capitalism in Europe during the Renaissance has been provided by scientific and technical development. Science and technology have challenged the European societies in an unprecedented way. The answers to these challenges have led to completely new forms of human, increasingly anthropomorphic environments. The societies in Europe have taken up the challenges and have done their best to take advantage of the new opportunities and adapt to the new requirements that have arisen again and again through the science- and technology-induced development of capitalism. The rapid progress of science and technology since the Renaissance and the subsequent Age of Enlightenment has led to a fundamental change in the living environments in all areas.

This scientific and technological progress has developed faster and faster, with a momentum of its own that, it seems, cannot be tamed anymore.

Historically, this development of scientific and technological progress in Europe has been dynamized since the Middle Ages with the use of watermills and windmills, then continued after the Renaissance with the construction of mechanical looms and finally the development of the steam engine. This technology driven progress then continued with the production and use of electrical energy in industrial production and for the construction of increasingly complex, later also self-controlling machines. These scientific and technological developments have led to the science of cell biology and DNA research applied to medical treatment. Essential for the functioning of our mass societies have been the construction of automobiles, airplanes, nuclear power plants, satellites and spacecraft. Finally, all areas of life have been conquered by modern communication technology and social media. This vector of development has now become global and seems to be inexorably following a forward-looking dynamic in today's world with the use of robotics and AI. This is considered commonplace today, and no one will seriously deny the revolutionary significance and impact of these science- and technology-driven developments for humanity.

We would all agree that economic development has always made extensive use of the potential of modern science and technology and will continue to use it for its further development in the future. In view of current developments, this is also commonplace. The reason for this is the universality of scientific laws, what Buckminster Fuller calls "universal principles".

At this point and as a reminder, we would like to briefly point out the universal principle of feedback in communication, which is understood in cybernetics as the basic intellectual mechanism for learning from experience. This implies that the feedback mechanism is highly relevant for human-driven systems, i.e. the functioning of our societies. Communication and observation, as the principal faculties relevant for the feedback mechanism, are seen as the basic human competencies for social experience and learning. Hence, these social mechanisms are critical to the design of our societies. At the same time, the feedback mechanism is equally relevant for system-theoretical functions that are used in the control of machines.[225] What is important for us, is the dynamic interplay of these basic human competencies and system-theoretical functions, which is at the same time feeding the further dynamics of scientific and technological progress. The universal principles are responsible for the linearity and cumulative mode of this scientific and technology-driven development. While this is obvious for the technical side of development, it remains difficult to grasp its essence and impact on the development of human societies and the relationships and interdependencies between societies and nations.

It is exactly at this point, that we come in, asserting that science and culture do not obey the same laws and universal principles. We assume that natural science and technology follow a linear development driven by universal principles. On the other side, social development and politics are considered part of culture. Hence, the specific mechanisms of global

---

[225] In this regard, we recommend the article by Arthur Koestler "Beyond Atomism and Holism – The Concept of Holon", in Das Neue Menschenbild. Revolutionizing the Sciences of Man", 1970, ed. Arthur Koestler and J. R. Smythies.

capitalism that are related to Global Governance will follow a non-linear development. In the area of culture, social and political development, ever bigger, ever faster or ever more does not automatically mean ever better.

Cultures do not follow the universal principle of causality or the laws of thermodynamics in their development. Relations between states follow rules as we know them from game theory, i.e., movements within living systems characterized by correlations and dynamic, contingent and random relationships. Such systems not only depend on physical power and energy for the direction and course of their development, but their principal catalytic force lies to a great extent in human "willpower"[226], as we could have learned already in the early days of the 20th century from scientific research concerning self-regulating systems. Global governance is therefore about open relationships and the interaction of actors with different ideas and

---

[226] In the writings of Alwin Mittasch, former research director of BASF, Germany, we find enlightening reflections on the relationship between "Katalytische Kraft, Lebenskraft, Willenskraft" (our translation: *Catalytic energy, life energy, willpower*), p. 285 ff., Von der Chemie zur Philosophie, 1948. (our translation: *From Chemistry to Philosophie*).

interests. The laws of physical causality cannot be applied here, or only to a very limited extent, for example, in strategic models or simulations. Therefore, the new system of global governance will not evolve in line with a linear system driven by the accumulation of power, as is the case with energy in the field of science and technology. In the domain of global governance, which is critical for the geopolitical organization on our planet Earth, a paradigm shift will have to take place through the development and application of new, commonly shared rules.[227] Currently, such a paradigm shift is obstructed by the hegemonic forces of the US, which refuse change that is not following their self-determined rules. This leads to a situation where international relations are increasingly tense, full of violence and war.

In the creation of the new system of global governance, dominance and violence will have to cease their regulative functions. New rules

---

[227] We agree with authors such as Helmut Willke, Global Governance, published in 2006, that this transformation of the system of global governance has to do with the emergence of a "knowledge society". In our understanding, however, "knowledge" will not become an "instance" that could replace "law" as the authority in the decisions on how to function.

will come into play. Confrontation will be replaced by cooperation. Hierarchies will function differently during the communication processes that will have to be engaged to set new rules organizing the upcoming system of global governance. Hierarchies will not follow the rules of multi-level governance, as it is promoted within the EU, where this mode of governance is functioning without democratic accountability. The kind of multi-level governance preferred by our "modern" leaders and power elites is only a disguise for autocratic government. In cybernetics, rules play a different role, because they can never be set unilaterally. This is the principle of open societies. They cannot function like an army. Societies are considered peaceful organizations with *open participation and friendly competition for better ideas*. Hierarchies in cybernetics, i.e. in the general system view of organizational behavior, are understood as an interplay among multiple levels and layers, each with its own set of subsystems and related processes. These various levels and layers are interconnected and interdependent. No decision taken at any level or layer can be overruled by a higher level or layer. The principal purpose of interaction and working together among the different "forces", actors and elements is to maintain the functioning, stability and balance within a given social and political system. The purpose of communication and interaction is not about gain or profit.

This is what we learn from cybernetics and from our growing knowledge of self-regulating systems. This knowledge and insight that has grown out of scientific work with catalytic processes, living self-regulation systems and quantum physics has to be applied to global governance. Consequently, we will have to accept that one-sided dominance built on political, financial and economic power cannot hold anymore. This system, which we have inherited from European capitalism and the hegemonic imperialism of the US, is outdated and has become obsolete. Newton's mechanical thinking does not apply to open systems characterized by contingency and rules of open communication.

The new system of global governance will not emerge in a linear sequence from the previous, European-dominated pattern, nor will it follow the European model in the sense of a causal relationship. Other factors from other cultures will come into play, so that this new system of global governance will eventually take on a new structure and form. It will be regulated by a new set of rules agreed upon by the participating actors in this system, who come together from a great variety of different cultures.

The overall dynamics in the system of global governance, i.e. the regulation of mechanisms, institutions and organizations of international cooperation, will definitely have to change in the future. The current system of the UN requires a complete overhaul that will go far beyond cosmetic changes. We presume that this overhaul will comprise a review of the legal system as it is currently applied. We know that the legal system currently in use is built on "western values". Communication patterns that are currently valid may be adjusted and brought in line with the traditions of different cultures. Once the current UN system is broken up, the scope of potential changes will become increasingly visible. For the successful and peaceful cooperation of countries and nations within our "*global society*", new rules will have to be found and put into effect in order to enable a prosperous coexistence of people on our planet in the long term.

The maximization of economic utility as the primordial principle of liberal capitalism, with its emphasis on individualism and the formation of rigid hierarchical systems and structures linked to the exertion of power and obeying the principles of dominance and domination, will not remain valid in its current form in the field of global governance. The European model of global governance, which is based on power and money as the critical instances, as well as on the all-pervasive rule that *the winner takes it all*, will be supplemented by other forms. This is going to happen in the relatively near future. The paradigm shift has already been put into motion and is ongoing under our eyes. The current system of international relations will probably be replaced by a completely new concept of global governance in the not-too-distant future. This is the conclusion we can draw at this point in our analytical description.

The ongoing paradigm shift is an indication of the important role that has been played in the past by the "succession arrangement", i.e. the "handover" of the previous form of capitalism. The linear successions among European and Western nations enabled the continued functioning of the system based on domination through the means of power and money. This "handover" has so far followed a linear pattern as long as it has taken place within the European and Western world. This linear handover has assured the continuation of the capitalist system on an ever "higher" level of progress within the Western cultural area of Europe and the US. This handover was brought about by the addition of new and innovative elements and components, while the system and the rules did not fundamentally change. As long as this "handover" was carried out within the same cultural area, in which largely identical rules apply, progress could take place along a direct and consistent line, i.e. linearly.

In summary, these succession arrangements among European powers have taken the following steps, leading to ever higher stages with the aim of ever-increasing capitalist efficiency: starting with the commercial capitalism of Venice and the capital formation through robbery, theft and extraction of gold and silver from South America by Spain and Portugal, the Netherlands has added a sophisticated monetary system and an innovative financial system as driving forces. England has reshaped this system through "indirect rule", i.e. a more civilized form of colonialism (as opposed to a mainly brute

Spanish-Portuguese approach), and added Manchester capitalism on the production side, i.e. the value-adding processing of raw materials, often with the extensive use and brutal exploitation of human productive power. The British financial system represented essentially a continuation and improvement of the Dutch central and private banking systems. The British system had eventually grown out to become a general European colonialism. The British Empire collapsed in consequence of the First World War, due to the "imperialism of others", especially of Germany. The USA then took over the essential elements of the British system and supplemented them with Ford capitalism (consumptive production and "prosperity for all") and further forced geopolitical expansion through financial and military dominance.

This linear sequence of capitalist development has largely functioned unbroken, as long as it has concerned only the European cultural area, both in the area of social and political organization, as well as the development of science and technology. The effects of this cumulative development are evidenced today by the still-prevailing global dominance of Anglo-

American financial conglomerates and the Bretton Woods system.

China initially had no choice, but to fit into this linear development scheme in pursuit of its economic and technological development. Thus, within the scope of its own possibilities, China initiated the development of the socialist "Shenzhen capitalism"[228] to open up new perspectives for the country. We all agree that this initiative has been very successful overall. This development brought an end to the era of wars and internal power struggles in China and lifted hundreds of millions of people progressively up to ever higher living standards. For the time to come, capitalist development in China can be expected to follow the European, linear-cumulative model in the field of economic development, because it builds mainly on the potential of scientific and technological progress.

However, we encounter a different situation, when it comes to the regulation of social coexistence, or the regulation of interstate

[228] "Shenzhen: The Future Made in China: Between Creativity and Control", 2021, by Frank Sieren. Or "Future? China!: How the New Superpower is Changing Our Lives, our Politics, our Economy", 2020, Frank Sieren, Josef Vossenkuhl, et al.

relations, i.e. international relations. If we enter a new cultural sphere, then linearity applies only to technological and economic development. Linearity of development does not apply to the area of social development or to the system of global governance. Science and technology follow universal laws. Cultures, however, differ in the rules according to which they shape the coexistence of their members.

TRANSFORMING THE SYSTEM OF GLOBAL GOVERNANCE

According to our understanding, the economic development of capitalism will therefore, by and large and for the foreseeable future, follow the current pattern for the time being.[229]

The situation is different, however, with global governance, which, according to the still

---

[229] Refer to Immanuel Wallerstein, "The Capitalist World Economy", 1979. In "The Rise and Future Decline of the Capitalist World System", (zur Grundlegung vergleichender Analyse). In: Senghaas Dieter (ed.): Kapitalistische Weltökonomie. Controversies about their origin and their development dynamics, 1979 and 1982.

prevailing understanding, is about the "struggle for power and money".[230]

As we mentioned in the first part of the book, dominance in capitalism - let's call it economic power - was explicitly tied to the political and hegemonic power of European countries and, after the First World War, the US. This was already the case at the time of the British Empire, with its dominance over the seas and maritime trade. After 1919, the USA made it a fundamental principle of its own foreign policy. Since then, trade and international economic policy, as well as security policy, have always been closely interwoven.

It is also interesting to observe how a kind of "interregnum" occurs again and again. This is also pointed out by Stefan Schmalz in his work mentioned in the introduction. The consecutive stages of capitalist development were characterized by learning processes and important adjustments made. There was no existing blueprint that could have been followed exactly. When the US adopted the Monroe Doctrine at the beginning of the 19th century, it did not yet know that 150 years later it would

---

[230] Money as financial strength, as potential to finance development.

need the Bretton Woods system to secure and continuously expand its global rule.

Making a few comments on the "innovative pressures" that occur during the development and transformation of the global government system will help to further clarify our reflections and endow our considerations with more persuasive power. The link to the symptomatic pressures arising in the current and intensifying transformation of the system of global governance will become obvious. For this purpose, we will make here a brief, but important insertion, that refers to research and considerations coming from Western historical science, but which also comes from studies and sources related to the "Particularity of Chinese Science" and "Scientific Universalism".[231]

There is already a broad international academic discussion ongoing on this topic of the transformation of the system of global governance[232], on which we will not further

---

[231] We refer here to the diverse and profound work of Joseph Needham in these areas. Under his direction, the Needham Research Institute has published a book series, "Science and Civilization in China," on the history of science and technology in China since 1954.

[232] On this topic: https://de.wikipedia.org/wiki/Global_Governance. Then

elaborate here. The important point to retain from this discussion is that it is always limited to possible modifications of the current system. Hence, it is biased toward Western thinking and tradition. Its primary, mostly hidden interest is, to secure Western dominance and promote the continuation of the current system, with the application of some minor adaptations. With our approach and considerations, we intend to go beyond the limits of Westernized organizational systems. This brings us to refer at least briefly to two important historical pioneers from Europe. This will make it clear, on what intellectual basis our considerations and arguments have grown out.

To this end, we would first like to point out the structural relationship between transformation and history. We have to realize that when we look at social or political transformations, we are moving in the "historical space of time". Therefore, we consider it indispensable to make a few comments clarifying our understanding of "historical time", at least to some extent. This will bring us to a more comprehensive understanding of the ongoing transformation of

---

also in the German-speaking area:
https://www.wzb.eu/de/forschung/internationale-politik-und-recht/global-governance.

the current system toward a new system of global governance.

In this regard, we can glean from Reinhart Koselleck many good and useful thoughts on the concept of time, in particular of "historical time".[233] In Christopher Clark, we see intelligent and further historical explorations of Koselleck's considerations, e.g. in his book "Time and Power".[234] From these two historians, scholars, and authors, we can absorb important thoughts on the concept of "time" in the historical context. In their studies and books, they demonstrate the importance of the different perceptions of the "historical space of time" concerning the specific terrain for political and geopolitical development. This cultural relativity of the historical space of time has its impact on the specific conception of political constitutions, the control of decision-making processes in countries and nations, as well as on the shaping of their international relations. The highly instructive considerations of these two historians mainly reflect historical processes and

[233] Refer to "Vergangene Zukunft. Zur Semantik geschichtlicher Zeiten", 1989, Reinhard Koselleck. (our translation: "Past Future: On the Semantics of Historical Times").

[234] Refer to "Of Time and Power", 2018, Christopher Clark.

events in the German and European geographical areas.[235]

However, for our concerns, we still have to supplement the considerations of these historical scholars by lifting their fundamentally trend-setting understanding out of the European context. For, in the future, Europe and its intellectual world will no longer be the exclusive global benchmark, and the pattern, according to which people and their nations on earth will shape their mechanisms and rules of coexistence. Oswald Spengler already points to this issue[236], when he warns of the limits of the "Ptolemaic system of history", in which "the high cultures make their rounds" around the "Western European", as "the supposed center of all world events". Already before the First World War, he foresaw that following the "Copernican discovery in the field of history... a system takes its place, in which European antiquity and the West do not occupy a privileged position in any

---

[235] For France, the historian March Bloch has traced the historical birth of France in the space known as the hexagon with its social and economic structures in his masterpiece "The Feudal Society", new edition 2019, French original from 1939.

[236] In chapter 6 of the introduction to "The Decline of the West", originally published in 1918, the quoted edition is from 1922.

way, and in which India, Babylon, China, Egypt, and the Arab culture, as individual worlds, will weigh just as heavily in the overall picture of history".

It may prove to be useful, if we supplement our argumentation, with a very brief reference to an idea from organizational theory. Therefore, we will insert a few additional reflections that will further clarify our approach. In line with the general system theory related to organizational development[237], the concept of culture has been common for a long time. Different models concerning organizational development are frequently discussed in their relationship with the meaning of "culture" in organizations[238]. There is general agreement that "core values" and "beliefs" determine how the world is seen, and how life in it is considered best and most

---

[237] Donella H. Meadows writes in her classical book "Thinking in Systems": A system is a set of things — people, cells, molecules, or whatever — interconnected in such a way that they produce their own pattern of behavior over time.

[238] For an introduction, we suggest reading "Understanding Organizational Culture: A Systems Theory Perspective", 2023, by Markus Perry. A more comprehensive understanding can be gained by reading: Kreitner, R. & Kinicki, A.; Organizational Behavior, 2004, New York: McGraw-Hill.

meaningful. In German, this is often referred to as "Weltanschauung", i.e. the particular way in which things, people and the world are seen in their ever-specific context. These "basic values" and "beliefs" can be shaped very differently depending on the culture to which they belong and from which they emanate. Such a culturally shaped form of organization is often referred to as a paradigm, i.e. as a special social form with certain values and rules that have arisen historically. There is also agreement that these forms of organization must, in order to survive, adapt to constantly changing circumstances and pressures caused by external factors from the environment, or by internal factors, such as the behavior and interventions of internal actors in the system. There exists a general agreement in these discussions, that there are always changes to be taken into account and adaptations to new challenges to be made, without which no system can survive. This is a well-known principle from cybernetics and general systems theory.[239] We would like to add that this is also common sense.

In the current era, with exponentially accelerating technological innovations, the system of global governance is particularly exposed to such innovative pressure that requires organizational adaptations. We recall at this stage that the growing impact of economic growth, which is linked to exponential population growth, is creating intense pressure on our living environment. The growth rate of the economies on the globe, is exponentially growing through the exponential demographic growth we have been witnessing for more than a century now. We do not talk about the growth rate of individual economies. We have to take into account that ever more people are pushing economic growth and material consumption. As a result, the system of global governance has come under intense pressure. Rational

---

[239] In an essay by Niall Ferguson, which was published in the NZZ on December 31, 2021, under the title "A nation is not an individual, and an individual is not a nation", he dispels in a convincing way one of the oldest ideas in Western political thought, which assumes an analogy between the individual human being and the political body of society. In the same sense, we reject the analogy between scientific and technological progress and social development.

adaptation and a paradigm, short of the past *modus operandi* of global governance, are imminent and cannot be avoided. The constant glowing and flaring up of wars and conflicts is symptomatic of this increasing pressure. Violent confrontations and wars contradict the principle of rational human efficiency for the majority of countries and nations on earth. Only a few countries consider themselves to be winners and are able to draw ever-increasing profits from the wars and conflicts. On the other side, most countries and their people are paying a high price. Unipolar, interventionist and violent hegemonic strategies cannot be justified from the perspective of a global world. The majority of people and nations claim a peaceful settlement of conflicts to facilitate the coexistence of nations. At the same time, such unipolar and violent hegemonic strategies are counterproductive in the sense of a sensible approach to the living environment on earth, which is not divisible and will remain the basis of life on our planet.

It can further be learned from organizational theory, which has been shaped by systems theory, that a paradigm shift will necessarily occur, when an existential threat to an organizational system occurs, i.e. when the system is fundamentally endangered. In our understanding, such a threat to "Spaceship Earth", a term coined by Buckminster Fuller[240], can no longer be denied. Humanity is therefore faced with the challenge of developing a new paradigm, a new form and new rules for the system of global governance. In the sense of cybernetics, it can be assumed that for such a paradigm shift, neither the necessary processes can be fully planned, nor will the results be predictable. This is a typical case of an "open system", for which the contours and basic principles have been elaborated by Karl Popper in the years after the Second World War[241]. Hence, such a step towards a paradigm shift is not merely a technical undertaking; it requires a deliberate commitment for the future of humanity and life on earth.

---

[240] "Operating Manual for Spaceship Earth", 1969, by Buckminster Fuller. "Instruction manual for the spaceship Earth", German translation.

[241] "The Open Society and its Enemies", 1945. German Edition in 2 Volumes, "Die offene Gesellschaft und ihre Feinde", 1957 and 1958, by Karl Popper.

THE FUTURE SYSTEM OF GLOBAL GOVERNANCE: THE CULTURAL BACKGROUND

Our task here is not to discuss theories of global governance, i.e. to present possible models. However, we would like to point out here that all the discussions that are being held on this topic in the European and Western scientific fields are fundamentally short-sighted, if they do not take into account and include the knowledge and lessons to be learned from the living traditions of other cultures.

We understand that knowledge and its availability will be hugely important in the discussions about determining a future system of global governance. But we do not assume that the current logic of power, as the only instance dominating global political governance, will eventually be replaced by a logic of knowledge[242]. Both, power and knowledge, are not following logic. Their validity can only be examined and eventually confirmed through action or communicative acts that always offer the possibility of varied responses and interpretations from an external world. At the

[242] We refer here to "Global Governance", 2006, by Helmut Willke, who discusses the potential of knowledge for the system of global governance.

same time, we do not assume that a global legislature, functioning as a central legislative authority, can play the role of a coordinating and controlling instance. We do hope that nobody will come up with the idea to set laws prescribing that all people obey and function according to the same laws[243]. This would mean the end of free will and of human action. There may in the future exist collectively binding rules, perhaps rules of conduct or principles, but no globally and collectively binding system of law.[244] Globally binding laws will have to be limited to issues of a global scope. But even there, humanity will need global courts. International practice shows that adherence and obeisance to such courts function in a very selective way, and enforcement of court orders will always remain limited. Such international court orders are either dominated by the selective interests of power brokers, or they will become effective

---

[243] Even with a new assessment of "law" as a means of controlling action, we should recognize that the coming changes will pose a major challenge for the West.

[244] Stephen R. Covey presented such a principle-driven behavioral model in his bestseller "The 7 Ways to Effectiveness", originally from 1990. The German edition is from 1996. There, he also speaks of the need to initiate a paradigm shift in thinking and acting.

only at a moral level.[245] As we all know, the law has to be interpreted and does not function automatically. Hence, culture will again come into play to interpret laws in their specific context. We assume that at the level of global governance, everything will be decided according to the rules of discourse, i.e. rules that control human communication and decision-making processes. At the national level, the legislature may continue to determine policies, but at the global level, rules will have to be applied that are culturally sensitive and subtle. International organizations may not be enabled to take on executive functions. The international community may, in specific cases, delegate temporary mandates for the implementation of decisions to international organizations. However, they must not be given permanent executive functions. The experience of the WHO, IMF and World Bank shows extensively that international organizations are inclined to lead a life of their own and tend to serve exclusive rights and interests following pressure or incentives from their "hierarchical masters",

---

[245] The Nuremberg court trials did not have any effect on the quality of future political behavior and did in no way prevent political crimes and criminal acts. They were just effective for the show.

from private and public "pay masters", or from big business and lobby associations. These organizations act in the interest of their masters, not for the people or the public. Again, this is nothing new, but well known and due to recognized laws of organizational functioning. This is the main reason, why multi-level governance cannot be considered a democratic tool. International organizations will always tend to escape the control of the system of global governance. They are not inclined to respect the shared interests of a future-oriented community. It is mainly for this reason that no executive functions should be delegated to international organizations.

It will not be enough to expand the resources of the politics of power and power-based decisions beyond money to include the resource of knowledge. Values that are formulated on the basis of knowledge are culture-based and therefore cannot be used for formal, politically effective control through the system of global governance, even in the context of a knowledge-based world society. Obviously, subsidiarity and the authority for decision-making at the local and regional level will be required features for a functioning global governance system. Ironically, subsidiarity has been part of the political approach promoted by the EU under Jacques Delors. However, it did not fit into the expectations for "efficient leadership" of the US hegemon and was only applied, as long as it did not contradict US interests. The limitations of current proposals for the coming system of global governance lie in the fact that the Western social sciences and humanities are currently still under the influence of orthodox methodological and conceptual individualism, i.e. the one who has the power decides for the others.[246] They cannot imagine, or do not want to accept, that global networks and culturally differentiated conditions require new rules of governance. Only under this premise of culturally accepted rules will the new system of global governance bring to a bearing the effectiveness of human intelligence. The application of our knowledge concerning self-regulating systems will bring humanity in line with integrity and generalized patterns of human communication, as we know them from cybernetics.

---

[246] In his book "The West and the Rest: Discourse and Power", 1992, Stuart Hall analyzes this issue of cultural relativity. Interestingly, Niall Ferguson has referred to this fundamental polarity that is characteristic for the modern era in Europe. Refer to "Civilization. The West and the Rest", 2012, Niall Ferguson.

The challenge of creating a new system of global governance is already well understood in China. There is now a broad, open and lively discussion about this issue, but it is largely conducted by the Chinese and in China. The Berggruen Institute promotes this discussion in China by funding an open scientific platform. In Germany, Richard Wilhelm commented on this challenge that the West would have to face with China very early on[247]. British historians, such as Arnold J. Toynbee in his "Study of History", have also taken into consideration other cultures, but mostly with limited access to scientific literature from China. In the current Chinese discussion, Zhao Tingyang stands out with his impressive presentation of "Tianxia"[248] as a potential model for future global governance.

---

[247] Refer to his biographical account of his experience in China "The Soul of China", 1928, by Richard Wilhelm. The German original was published in 1925. Also interesting is his little booklet "Wisdom of the East", published in 1951.

[248] German edition "Everything under One Sky: Past and Future of the World Order,", 2019, Zhao Tingyang. ZHAO first tried to explain the concept of Tianxia in more detail in a monograph in 2005. In this book, there is a detailed bibliography on the subject. In January 2016, a new version of his Tianxia theory was published (Tianxia de dangdaixing: Shijie zhixu de shijian yu xiangxiang 天下的当代性:世界秩序的实践与想象, Zhongxin chubanshe).

From our perspective, the most convincing contribution from Western science comes so far from Joseph Needham. In his series of writings and books on "Scientific Universalism", he has published an essay entitled "Time and Eastern Man". Needham writes: "I believe that I can show that the 'man of the West' did not have a monopoly on the sense of linear, continuous time, and that the idea of the 'timeless Orient' is nonsense"[249]. In this essay on the "Concept of Time in the Orient", Joseph Needham has presented a comprehensive overview based on a detailed study of the relevant Chinese and Western sources. It is not our intention to reproduce this presentation here in detail. The essence of his statements, however, seems to us to be of the utmost importance and essential for the argumentation we wish to put forward.

Following Joseph Needham, it does indeed seem to be the case that Chinese thought and culture, which have been shaped in China for more than 3000 years, is strongly fed by a source of synthetic[250] perception and understanding of

---

[249] Quoted from "Scientific Universalism", 1979, by Joseph Needham, from the chapter "The Concept of Time in the Orient", pp. 176–250.

[250] An introductory discussion on understanding synthetic thinking vs. analytical thinking can be found in the book

things and processes. Opposites are not a problem in principle, but are seen as a challenge to find what they have in common, or even to see how such opposites can coexist in a complementary way and perhaps even complement each other fruitfully. In the sense of dialectic thinking[251], opposites are expected to create fruitful synthesis at a higher level.

Needham shows that China asks us to take a differentiated view of the concept of "time", in which not all processes are linear. In the

on legal theory by Prof. Mahlmann, University of Zurich, which clearly presents "Basic Philosophical Teachings". https://www.rwi.uzh.ch/elt-lst-mahlmann/rechtstheorie/kant/de/html/unit_u2.html.

A basic presentation of the questions on analytical and synthetic thinking can be found in "Grundlagen der Systemtheorie", 1989, by Heinz Neubauer. Further information on this topic: https://de.wikipedia.org/wiki/Systemtheorie.

[251] We wish to draw attention to the impressive reception of Hegel and Marx in China during the years of the revolution in China after 1900. From Chairman Mao to Zhou Enlai and Deng Xiaoping, up to Xi Jinping of modern-day China, Dialectic thinking has consistently been applied. This represents a link between East and West, between Eastern and Western thinking and world view, that is usually overlooked. In China, a dialectic view of the world is considered by most people to be a fundamental principle of its functioning.

aforementioned essay on the "Concept of Time in the Orient", Needham addresses the question, that is critical for our concerns, in a special chapter on "Time and History in China and the West". In the synopsis of Needham's studies on the "concept of time in the Orient", we learn that three dimensions of time can be distinguished in China, each of which is applied to specific areas:

- In the field of natural sciences, in China, as in the West, the "linear view of time" applies;

- In the area of society and state, time is essentially oriented towards social traditional rites. The great French sinologist Marcel Granet[252] calls this the "liturgical" time. We would prefer to call this societal and social time "publicly organized time", or in a more modern and holistic wording, the "time of rites, rhythms, and rituals";

- A third concept of time is "cyclical time", which results from the observation of nature and the understanding of the

---

[252] Marcel Granet, "The Chinese Civilization. Volume 2: Chinese Thought. Content, Form, Character", 2019. First published in German in 1985. Original: "La pensée chinoise", Paris, 1938.

processes and evolution of events in nature and in the cosmos.

It is not really difficult to understand, when looking at these three different concepts of time, that there is a big difference between the Chinese and the European cultural spheres in their understanding of the passage of time in the social and political spheres.

In Europe and the West, the concept and understanding of linear time is applied in a rather one-sided and generalized way, not only to the natural sciences, but also to the understanding of the organization of societies, as well as to economic and political life[253]. Even regarding cosmic evolution, Western scientists will raise questions about when it started, how it works and what the outcome will be at the end. A cyclical approach to time seems to have no place in the Western scientific mind set. In

---

[253] On April 11, 2022, the Mises Institute published an article by Eduard Braun entitled "Pseudoliberal State Interventions and Neoclassicism. Thoughts on Homo Oeconomicus and the True Value of Things". There, he shows how an "unrealistic image of man" must lead to irrational assumptions about human behavior.

From this alone, i.e. from a new assessment of "law" as a control of action, we should recognize that the coming changes will pose a great challenge for the West.

Europe and the West, societies are always expected to focus on quantifiable and measurable progress. The final purpose, that is imposed on "time", is to produce results that are quantifiable, if possible.

Obviously, our politicians and power elites have not yet learned the lessons of modern physics and natural science. If they had done this, they could have learned quite some time ago, that in catalytic processes, there is often no experimentally defined beginning and no end. Even the direction of processes may change over time. In quantum theory, we have to do with events, such as quantum leaps, about which no data can be found and for which only the situation before and the situation after a specific event can be measured. The absolute requirement for quantifiable results is a concept that can generally not be applied to social or political processes, such as decision-making in a global environment. Our power elites could also have learned that laws that are recognized in astrophysics are not the same as those used in atom physics. The same universal principles apply in both cases, but for practical reasons and to facilitate understanding, the explanations for observed processes are explained in different terms. Communication is key.

Understanding is a human communicative function and cannot be automated or entrusted to machines or computers. If we transfer these insights to the sphere of human life, then we must come to the conclusion that humans in China, Cameroon, Russia, or in Peru take different views on life on earth. The law of gravity is accepted everywhere. However, the laws that govern social and political life are not uniform among cultures. The acceptance of this fact is the fundamental challenge for the paradigm shift concerning global governance.

In his "Manuel d'Ethnographie" of 1926, Marcel Mauss, a French sociologist, introduced the term of the "ethnological turn" into sociology. Marcel Mauss made important contributions to the analysis of civilizations in terms of distinct material, institutional, and spiritual functions. He emphasized moral exchange and learning among the nations and their cultures. Mauss argued for the usefulness of ethnography and anthropology in developing "humane, smooth, and productive colonial relationships" and to promote long-term cultural exchange and partnerships in reimagining social possibilities within modern societies. He challenged humanity to engage seriously with the full diversity of human categories and self-understandings, rather than extending European concepts of humanity as a supposed universal standard, against which all others are measured. Unfortunately, the *ethnological turn* has remained within the domain of science. It did not produce a significant impact on the design and practice of Western politics. The egoistic and exclusive focus on the quest for more money and power prohibited the power elites from opening up their minds to serious and consequently culture-sensitive international debates.

We do not want to conclude these remarks on global governance without briefly referring to the example of India. The Berggruen Institute has been promoting research and studies on the topic of governance in India and China for decades. In an important and trend-setting publication, classical Chinese and Indian political philosophy and theories of the state are compared in their practice and implementation.[254] This anthology also presents models of political organization from the Indian

---

[254] Refer to "Bridging Two Worlds, Comparing Classical Political Thought and Statecraft in India and China". The book was published in 2003 by the University of California Press in the "Great Transformations" series. Edited by Daniel A. Bell, Amitav Acharya, Rajeev Bhargava, Yan Xuetong.

cultural sector that are very different from those, we in the West consider to be the "right" or the "best". In this book, the limits of the current political thinking based on the model of "Eurocentric International Relations" are criticized explicitly and in a well-substantiated manner.

With these indications, our preliminary anticipation of the need for the development of new, cross-cultural mechanisms and rules for the system of global governance takes a quite concrete form. From now on, it will be important to intensify practice-oriented research across cultures according to known system-theoretical-cybernetic methods with the interest of opening up new perspectives and viable paths. Humanity is required to create innovative mechanisms and define new rules, providing orientation for the design of the coming system of global governance.

In this respect, the suppression of this topic and the inability to take up the related challenges constructively and creatively are remarkable and symptomatic of the situation, especially in continental Europe. Jürgen Osterhammel, who is considered an important German historian on the topic of globalization and the "Far East", concluded his reflections and remarks in an article in the FAZ in 2022 with the title "All under one sky" by stating that there is not much to gain from this *Tianxia* system. Because, in the end, Osterhammel writes, hierarchical decision-making power is necessary. According to him, without a "boss", no system can function. This shows the helplessness, at least of German historians, but unfortunately also of European scientists in general and of the public in Europe, which remains trapped in their usual one-sided European thought patterns. [255]

It is therefore not surprising that the document published by the State Council of the Republic of China in September 2023, entitled "The Global Community of a Shared Future: China's Proposals and Actions", has largely been ignored in Europe. This document explicitly points out that the Chinese government sees *humanity at a crossroad*, i.e. the world at a *tipping point*. With an explicit reference to their deep roots *in history*

---

[255] The Tianxia model has, of course, been discussed in philosophical circles. In Band 7, Heft 1, 2020, S. 376–380; ref.: "www.praktische-philosophie.org", we find a short article reflection on "Tianxia und die Herausforderungen des Kosmopolitismus" (Tianxia and the challenges to cosmopolitism". However, these discussions, which remain shallow, have never reached a broader public.

and cultural traditions, the Chinese then dare to put forward a proposal for future paths, i.e. *a Blueprint for the Future* for discussion, in order to even consider the *Direction and Path*, that they think humanity should take. In conclusion, they also take the liberty of pointing out China's actions so far and their contribution to the formation of a "Global Community of a Shared Future".

To us, this sounds like an invitation and an offer for an open discourse about the future design of the common path for humanity with a shared future. Unfortunately, such offers are not being taken advantage of in the newly proclaimed Euro-American age of ideologies, confrontations and wars. Geopolitical hegemonic striving cannot be justified in such open discourses. So, the power elites from Europe and America prefer to stay away from the talks on these global platforms and keep widely quiet about them. Contributions are left to scientists, without concern for public life and without remarkable impact on the ongoing transformation of our societies.

Conclusions

In our book on "The New System of Global Governance: The Ongoing Paradigm Shift", we have presented various details related to the functioning of this new system. We refer the reader to this book, where we discuss further important considerations concerning the form this new global governance system may take, as well as the rules it may follow. We did not include these details here, because they are not directly relevant for understanding the root causes of the crisis in Europe, which is our principal topic here.

With our analytical description of the current system of global governance and the ongoing paradigm shift, a few important points have become clear concerning the root causes of the crisis in Europe.

It has become obvious that the current global governance system has its origins in Europe and is a result of European development since the Renaissance. This governance system is part of the development of capitalism as it has been forged over the past 600 years. With the globalization of capitalism, the European governance system has become the global reference.

With the re-entry of China on the stage of globalized capitalism since the end of the 20th century, the global governance system has come under pressure, and a paradigm shift has since then become inevitable. The ongoing paradigm shift will change the rules of geopolitics, and the new global governance system will present a new form regulated by newly defined rules. The European model is no longer the global benchmark.

China has presented, with its history and knowledge-based Tianxia system, a model for a future organizational scheme that could become the reference for the new global governance system. The Chinese government has taken up this stream of Chinese thinking and is operating its international relations and foreign policies according to the principle of a "Global Community of a Shared Future".

Our analytical description has also made it clear that Europe and the US are twin brothers and sisters. The US has dissociated from Europe through a process of colonization of the Americas that started in parallel, when the Renaissance began to spread its innovative impulses over Europe. The US is a cultural offshoot of Europe, but has dissociated economically and politically, to become a power of its own. Since 1919, with the Treaty of Versailles, the US has become the power progressively dominating Europe. After the Second World War and the establishment of the Bretton Woods system, the US has become the hegemon of the West. As the US, joined by Europe, has undisputedly been the largest economy and dominating global power during the second half of the 20th century, the US has progressively built and consolidated her position as the hegemon of the world until the beginning of the 21st century.

With the creation of the European Union, Europe has taken a major step that could have led to severing herself from the US to become an independent and sovereign actor on the world stage of politics. However, the US has succeeded in incorporating Europe into her economy and financial system. This has led to a situation, where Europe has become the most important pillar of US global hegemonic strategy.

The current situation is globally to a large extent shaped by the categorical refusal of the US to cede her hegemonic power and to share it with other partners, such as China, India or Russia. This situation cannot endure and will require creating a new system of global governance without the hegemonic dominance of the US. The US is deploying any means, economically and politically, to maintain its hegemonic position. It does not have the military power to achieve this strategic goal on its own. The US is operating increasingly through proxy wars, in which the financial and military burdens have to be borne by the strategic partners. Thus, Europe has been driven into the war against Russia, where Ukraine is the platform and implementing partner funded and militarily equipped by Europe and the US. For East Asia, we have a similar scenario looming, with Taiwan becoming the platform and implementing partner for the war against China. This war is expected, following the US strategy, to be funded, and the armies militarily equipped by Japan, Korea and Australia. This scenario of proxy wars is the latest Business Model of the US strategy for maintaining and consolidating its position as the global hegemon. With our essay we have provided evidence that the paradigm shift concerning global governance cannot be avoided.

In conclusion, this means that there exists a growing tension between, on the one side, the hegemonic strategy pursued by the US, NATO and their partners, and, on the other side, the other major nations on the globe, such as China, India and Russia. They are relentlessly pushing the ongoing paradigm shift of the current global governance system.

Hence, the choice of war or peace lies with the US, NATO and their partners.

In summary of our conclusion to this essay on Global Governance, we dare to predict that the change of the global governance system cannot be avoided. It is an incremental part of the current global developments. The refusal to accept the peaceful transformation of the existing system of global governance has been identified as one principal root cause for the crisis in Europe. This result of the analytical description we have presented in this chapter also corroborates the first part of this book, where we have identified war as the principal symptom of the crisis in Europe.

In the next chapter of this book, we will focus on the analysis of the paradigm that is represented by the impetus for progress and material growth that is characteristic of the science- and technology-driven development initiated in Europe since the Renaissance and copied by other nations and people around the globe. This science- and technology-driven development has increasingly become one-sided and exclusive, to the detriment of mental and spiritual development in Europe. We will provide evidence that this one-sided development is an additional root cause lying at the foundation of the crisis in Europe.

PART 2

THE ROOT CAUSES OF THE CRISIS IN EUROPE

Chapter 3

Europe's mind-set: origin of the crisis

INTRODUCTION

With the following chapter, we wish to point to the roots from which the striving for reckless economic and geopolitical expansion has emerged. We will show that this drive for expansion comes combined with the ideology of growth without limits, that characterizes Europe style global capitalism today. Finally, we will recognize that the US quest for geopolitical hegemony is a direct expression of these drives for reckless expansion and limitless growth.

In doing so, we will analyze the mechanisms to better understand the conscious motivations and unconscious drives that push within our societies for social, economic and geopolitical growth, and which are so characteristic of our Western societies. This will lead us to a clarification of the term that is usually referred to as "progress". Understanding the interdependent functioning of these motivations and drivers of growth and "progress", will lead to an increasing awareness of our self-image, which usually remains, to a good extent, unconscious. This growing consciousness will increase the capacity for making deliberate decisions and foster a proactive and creative attitude towards problem-solving and focusing on the critical issues. Together with increasing awareness of the underlying drives, the basic conditions required for Europe to find rational orientation for its future behavior and actions in this world will progressively be created. Consciousness refers to rational behavior -knowing where we are, what we are doing, and why we are doing it. Consciousness is closely linked to knowledge and action. Awareness has more to do with the meaning we attribute to these actions. Awareness refers to the conscious recognition that is combined with a secondary reflection on the actions, processes and outcomes that we are experiencing and living. Awareness leads to the inner dimension of our lives and follows attentively the inner processes that are linked to the creation of self-consciousness. In the positive sense, becoming aware of the inner life of oneself will lead to self-awareness.

These considerations may sound complicated and almost esoteric. However, we see Europe acting with a lack of awareness of its actions. Europe is lacking both, a strategy for its actions, and a principle-based orientation for its existence. Europe does not know the reasons, why it is doing what it is doing. At the same time, Europe cannot tell its people and populations what its undertakings are good for or what they are aiming for in the long term. As we have shown in Part One of this book, this necessarily leads to increasing autocratic political behavior, i.e. governance without people.

We refer to these individual, psychological learning processes for increasing consciousness and enhancing awareness, because they do also apply to nations and their power elites. It is the declared purpose of this book and its various analytical descriptions to progressively facilitate reflection on these processes in Europe. Consequent self-reflection will contribute to increasing consciousness and enhancing awareness in Europe. In the long run, Europe has to find back to herself and create a new self-image.

We presume that we all wish Europe to look more confident into the future and also be more peaceful than what we experienced in the past 600 years since the Renaissance. Reading and understanding this book will further people in creating a Europe on its way to a more peaceful and increasingly prosperous life.

NATURAL SCIENCES: THE PRINCIPAL DRIVERS OF MATERIAL GROWTH AND PROGRESS

The prevalent paradigm in Europe and the Western world, that has shaped the development of humanity since the dawn of the modern era, i.e. over the past 600 years, has its foundation in a vision and the belief in unlimited progress. This attitude takes its root in a concept of the natural sciences that has progressively been limited to the materialistic aspects of nature. Natural science has been expected to provide humanity with the possibility of unlimited material growth based on the use of the earth's natural resources.

This paradigm of science-driven economic growth is closely linked to the emergence and evolution of capitalism, which began in the 15th century in Europe and has, since its inception, directly gone hand in hand with geographic expansion. Since the Renaissance, this development of capitalism has been mainly determined by the application of intellectual intelligence in the sciences and by the utilization of the results of science for the development of technology in a progressively industrialized and increasingly knowledge-based world.

This "traditional", still existing paradigm of exclusively "positivist", abstract scientific reasoning and application of objectively verifiable methods[256], that are forced on all areas and aspects of life, has reached its limits in our time and has probably already exceeded them[257]. Nevertheless, there has for decades not been a thorough and open public discussion on "progress" going beyond its materialistic dimension. Privately, people may look for

---

[256] The methodological features of such "objective scientific knowledge" and the philosophical foundations of modern science were defined for a first time in 1620 by Francis Bacon in his «Novum Organum Scientiarum».
[257] This was already understood by Hegel, who wrote in his "Diary of the Journey to the Bernese Upper Alps", 1796, "to perceive a border means to cross the border". In: K. Rosenkranz, G.W.F. Hegels Leben [1844]. Darmstadt 1969: 470–89.

alternative ways, but public life continues unaffected by such expressions of spiritual longings. The question of what we expect from this materialistic progress and expansion for the future of humanity is not seriously pondered in public. Nowadays, statements that are concerning "progress" are usually funneled by the mainstream media and the power elites, or left to "activists". These activists are mainly idealistic people, who feel the need for change, but usually neither have the skills, nor the economic and political power, to implement or manage social and political processes of change. In most cases, they also do not have the knowledge to provide a well-reflected orientation on the direction future development might take.[258] In fact, these activist movements often provide politicians and our "world leaders" with an excuse for taking the lead. The adult or older generation in Europe seems to have already resigned in the face of the bleak prospects for "progress".

---

[258] Activists are usually people who want to force changes of any kind. This often also applies to meaningful changes, which is why activists can also play a positive role. In most cases, however, activists do not want to take responsibility for the results of the requested changes. They often lack the basic skills to do so.

Westerners generally do not expect alternative solutions to emerging problems to grow out of socially and politically induced processes. Their technocratic molded mindset expects solutions to all problems to come from engineering and technology. That's the side of life for which they have been trained, and they know best. That's their principal skill base. Social and mental skills and capacities are mostly underdeveloped or not used in the Western world. Social and public life is, to a large extent, managed by the government and informed by TV programs. Transhumanism is the logical consequence of these processes. Human beings are not good enough, so we better build machines with human faces and appearances.

Improving human life on earth and taking our chances for a better quality of life for humans do not come to mind anymore. This seems to be out of reach for most ordinary humans. Therefore, politicians, power elites or leaders of think tanks have to be called for. Otherwise, humanity may be lost, at least that is what people are told. Some hope to find escapes in outer space or on other planets. In the end, however, the aim is usually to continue what we are currently doing at a higher level, i.e. muddling along with our various problems as before. This leads to the crisis mode, which has become so characteristic of Europe and has spread over most parts of the globe.

We increasingly notice in Europe a general deficiency of creative imagination and the ability to think in pictures. Thinking or talking of utopia is considered incorrect by the mainstream. In 1969, R. Buckminster Fuller challenged humanity in his book "Utopia or Oblivion: The Prospects for Humanity", with the following words: "To make the world work for 100% of humanity in the shortest possible time through spontaneous cooperation without ecological offense or the disadvantage of anyone". We understand that this definition of utopia is different from the approach suggested by the UN with its Sustainable Development Goals (SDG). While the UN is mainly monitoring what humanity is doing and handing out gifts to her employees, humanity needs primarily to understand herself and the options it has for her actions. With an increasing awareness of her situation, humanity might be able to take the right course without the bureaucratic interventions managed by the UN or other technocratic institutions.

All these UN organizations promote these one-sided technocratic approaches, of which WHO is the best example, with "big pharma" and "general vaccination" in its back. This closes humanity off to the non-logical and intuitive parts of its inherent genius and prevents humanity from making use of its undeniable capacity to find solutions for the management of complex processes. This generalized technocratic attitude, which is an image of the European and US worldview, hinders the use of the eon-old genius of people that exists everywhere on earth. In the currently dominant environment, actions are not human-driven, but are exclusively directed towards technocratic solutions. The reason for this is all too obvious: technocratic and technological solutions are the most promising ways used by our power elites to cling to power and to make money. This prohibits the use of the greatest part of human mental capacity. Only the intellect and sciences oriented to technology are deployed. Access to the human mind is called irrational and is prohibited, because it is considered illogical and incorrect. The human mind is not considered directly useful for the creation of wealth, as understood by the power elites, and does not conform to the mainstream and its expectations.

The perception and understanding of the earth as a living body, as it was presented by Lynn Margulis and James Lovelock with their *Gaia principle* as early as 1974[259], is met with incomprehension and rejection. A purely technocratic mindset has become the rule and is spread globally through all the school and education curricula. Possible advantages of looking at the earth as a living body with a singular biosphere, are not publicly discussed and are rejected as "esoteric" or unscientific. This *Gaia principle* assumes that the earth is a dynamic, living system, in which "life" is characterized by an inherent ability to eternally regenerative self-organization. Only thinking, that is based on cybernetics - only a system-based approach to earth and the understanding of evolution of complex organisms and living beings on it – opens the mind to this kind of holistic understanding. This makes it clear to everybody with an open mind that this understanding of the earth and our life on it is not "esoteric", but scientific. However, this is modern, quantum-science and system-based thinking of cybernetics, not the Newtonian mechanical science, with her scope limited to

[259] The German edition "The Gaia Principle. The Biography of Our Planet", 1991, James Lovelock.

the application of mechanics in the visible and tangible world. We all could and should have learned that Newtonian thinking is very useful for mechanics, but it does not apply to living systems, or mental and spiritual processes in humans.

The revolutionary power of Newton's new science was so great that mechanics, as a scientific principle, was transferred to most areas of life, as well as science. The book "L'homme machine" ("Man as a Machine"), published in 1747 by the French writer La Mettrie, is a well-known expression of this attitude. In medicine, the application of this mechanical principle has enabled many scientific and technical findings, but at the same time, it has also led during centuries to a dehumanization of medicine and the repression of the mind in the consideration of man. Early psychiatry proves this very impressively. As we can learn from C. G. Jung, at the beginning of his professional career as a psychiatrist, at the beginning of the 20th century, "soul" or "spirit" were not considered in the treatment of patients. Mental problems have exclusively been considered problems of physical medicine. C. G. Jung relates this fact in his biography. Paraphrasing C. G. Jung, we might say that man has even in our days not completely recovered from the "loss of his soul".

Cybernetics is obviously a scientific countercurrent to this generalized Newtonianism. Cybernetics is both, the science, and the art of mindful insight into and control of self-regulating systems. Cybernetics in the management of human affairs requires human skills, such as social and intellectual competencies. Cybernetics in the management of human affairs calls for the use of mental capacities and a range of communicative capabilities, which only humans dispose of. Cybernetics requires that the context, the living environment and specific situational context be included as co-decisive parameters in the determination of rules to be applied for the design and control of social and political processes. This is further strengthened today by the scientific concept of second-order cybernetics[260]. This deepening understanding of cybernetics includes conscious reflection, i.e. conscious feedback, through awareness, on the

---

[260] This concept of "second-order cybernetics" was developed in the context of research into cognition. The term was coined by Heinz von Foerster.

For cognitive research, see
https://www.mpg.de/11857515/kognitionsforschung

understanding and knowledge gained through participatory observation of living, self-regulating systems. This awareness is precisely what is meant by learning through feedback from experiences made. In this sense, a new and constantly renewing self-image of individuals or groups emerges, who can thus take responsibility for the control of social and political processes with ever-increasing consciousness. In management, which controls processes and makes decisions on the basis of such cybernetic principles and understanding, there is no longer a need for a "boss", who ultimately tells everyone what to believe and what to do. This understanding of cybernetics should also make it clear that geopolitical hegemony, i.e. global dominance of a single nation, can have no place in an openly formed world community of sovereign states. Cybernetics can thus become an efficient tool to control power.

For the two great questions of self-aware and self-reflecting humanity, "Who are we?" and "How do we want to live?", this constantly renewing self-image of humans and of humanity through experience and learning is the prerequisite and provides the future basis for the formulation of shared rules for decision-making processes. In human life, there exist no eternal or absolute truths. Hence, everybody will agree that no final or definite answers can be given to these questions. We, as human beings, have to give ever-new answers to the upcoming challenges in an ever-changing world. Our answers, consciously reflected in processes of increasing awareness, will determine the quality of life on our planet.

Widely untouched by these considerations concerning a needed mind-shift, the entire public life and political discussions have switched into crisis mode. We remain stuck there since many decades now. Our power elites have refused to engage with these fundamental insights that would have provided the intellectual and mental means and tools to get out of the various crises. These fundamental insights made available by modern science would enable humanity to derive and formulate new rules bringing hope for peaceful orientation of human action and for the transformation of human life to increase the quality of life for all creatures on earth. Instead, we continue our lives in the crisis mode without any prospect for a sustainable and peaceful future.

Politics in Europe is no longer discursive and creative, as it has been the case during the Renaissance[261], but is limited to providing simple answers and linear solutions to complex challenges. The time of the EU technocrats has come. This process concerning the loss of the belief in the sovereignty of humans and their governments has, in an excellent manner, been reconstructed by the British historian Christopher Clark. In his book on "Time and Power", he shows convincingly that, since the Peace of Westphalia in 1648, i.e. at the onset of the Baroque era, German citizens and their governments have progressively lost their faith in the capacity of humans to manage their lives and living conditions with sovereignty[262]. This testimony of the decreasing self-confidence in Germany is just an example of what has been going on in Europe in general. The historical processes may have followed a different pattern for the nations in Europe. However, history has been shared in Europe, and the outcome is very

---

[261] For a thorough appreciation of the open mind and creative spirit of the Renaissance, we refer to "How to Listen and Understand Opera", 2013, by Robert Greenberg.

[262] The violent and self-destructive implosion during the Nazi-regime only corroborates this picture. It has been the apex of this process, leading to the decline of the West.

similar, with national and cultural specificities of no critical significance for the overall picture. A deep reflection on the subject makes it evident that the rise of Fascism and the catastrophe induced by the Nazi-regime in Germany are in their impact not limited to Germany. The catastrophe of the Second World War and its horrendous impact in all its dimensions is engraved in the collective memory[263] of Europe as a whole and has been a watershed for European culture. Europe as a whole has yet to draw its lessons from this era of the past century. Europe will have to recognize and acknowledge at the same time that it has been thrown out of the center of the world, which it occupied widely uncontested for more than 600 years. The US, as a direct offspring of Europe, will also have to accept the consequences of the new situation. Western hegemonic power has reached its limits and is approaching its inevitable end.

---

[263] We refer with the notion of "collective memory" to the work presented in 1925 by the French philosopher and sociologist Maurice Halbwachs in his book "Les cadres sociaux de la mémoire". Since then, this concept of the collective memory has been further analyzed and advanced by various researchers, such as Qi Wang, researcher in psychology at Cornell University.

The lack of comprehension and self-reflection of the power elites in Europe have been the source and direct root cause of most of the crises that have arisen over the past century. These crises have been caused by humans and their power elites in Europe, who have refused to slow down the detrimental processes to reflect on their own actions. This was still corroborated by the fear of becoming aware of Europe's own shadow that grows out of its violent past. Europe, until today, has refused to become conscious of the root causes of this unending sequence of crises. Europe has not acted as a continent of Enlightenment, but rather as a clinical patient that stubbornly refuses to undergo a transformative process based on deep self-reflection leading to a new integration of her cultural identity. The blockage of the increasing inner pressure for the transformation process in Europe has been externalized. Nowadays, it's the Russian and the Chinese people who are accused of being guilty of all the problems in Europe. As has become evident now, Europe refuses to acknowledge that all the problems of modern times have started under her influence and their root causes lie in Europe's own development.

This is the present challenge Europe is facing. It is primarily of a mental and psychological nature. The symptom of war as the ultimate crisis, as we have shown in the first part of this book, is a clear indication that time has run out. There is no escape. Either Europe takes up the challenge, or it will continue on the way to her apocalypse and the process of self-destruction. A continent that has been in the span of one century at the origin of three devastating world wars should eventually look into its soul to reach out to the inner energies that are driving its behavior and actions[264]. Only a profound understanding of these mental energies will enable Europe to manage life in a different way, in which the destructive energies will be directed toward peace and fruitful cooperation.

The crisis in Europe is human-made and self-inflicted. It is the expression of the dissociation of intellect and mind that has, until now, not been mastered consciously. The direct results are mental deficiencies taking their root in a lack of awareness. This is the root cause of the *vicious circle* and the downward spiral, in which Europe is caught. In Dante's *Inferno,* this is called *the*

---

[264] In Analytical Psychology, these energies are directly associated with the libido. In the Indian Vedantic thinking, libido is another form of Prajna, life force or life energy.

road to hell, which is created, on the one side, by a lack of trust in the capacities of the human mind and, on the other, by the one-sided reliance on the materialistic utilization of the intellect's capacities. While mind should be the master, currently only intellect is at the steering wheel in Europe. Dante's insight provides us with a useful orientation for understanding humanity's current situation on our planet Earth. Progress in a downward spiral! Do we not perceive the contradiction here? And if we perceive it, what are our consequent reflections, decisions and actions?

We are all aware of the potential advantages and benefits of science and technology-driven progress. If we think of the Internet, the development in the field of communication media, and the potential of artificial intelligence, then it is certainly not absurd to look at these accelerating developments of our time as "overwhelming", increasing human capacities in an unprecedented manner. So far, there exists certainly a broad agreement. However, we should also become aware that we need the will and determination to use these resources creatively for the transformation of social and political development to get out of the crisis mode. The wars we are leading globally, together with the general crisis mode, are proof that we do not make creative use of our existing knowledge and the creative potential of our mind. We do not improve the quality of life through the improvement of communicative, social and political processes. We do not seek to shape the future on our earth in jointly created organizational structures and with the support and within the framework of the possibilities offered by this technical progress.

The United Nations, its General Assembly and its Security Council have been created in a time without TV, without the Internet and without smartphones. However, until today, these delegates are sitting in the same chairs and in the same environment, using the same communication patterns and rituals, and are operating within the same hierarchical organizational structures, where a few decide for the rest of the world. We should understand that nothing will really change, if Germany, India or Nigeria will have a seat on the UN Security Council. With the same mindset operating, these old-fashioned organizations will not lead us to a new, sustainable world order and a new and inclusive system of global governance. Politics, with its mechanisms and power games of confrontation, is lagging behind the dire need for a general mood of cooperation and open communication. It is, as if the great powers are all sitting in these international meetings with a pump gun under their jackets, ready to shoot down each other at any moment. Their armies, nuclear weapons, and other highly effective weaponry are their pump guns. The emergence of the prerequisites for the smooth operation of humanity as a self-regulating system is nipped in the bud, before getting the chance to blossom. Let's not forget that when the UN and the UN Security Council were founded, humanity was still living in an era, when most of the nations were not even engaged in the process of industrialization. Globalization at that time has been organized by Europe, without responsibility of the major part of the world's population, their peoples and nations. The UN and her many sub-organizations still act today according to rules that date back to the time of the Treaty of Versailles in 1919. Obviously, there are reasons, why that can't work anymore and why we are living in a persistent crisis mode.

It is clear that over the past hundred years, the world has been organized according to policies based on the thinking of Napoleon and Clausewitz, in which "war" has always been the most important and decisive means[265] of helping the strongest to gain money and power. Until today, the "value of better ideas"[266], as a basis for progress in the geopolitical shaping of the world community, is still not recognized or acknowledged. The greatest part of the world is still expected to stay outside geopolitical decision-making.

---

[265] Carl Clausewitz wrote his unfinished book "On War" between 1816 and 1830. From this comes the quote that "war is the continuation of politics by other means". These theories about strategy, tactics and philosophy of war still form the basis for training at military academies today. It would be interesting to compare these Prussian-influenced remarks on war with the work of the Chinese Sun Tzu "The Art of War", which was written about 500 BC.
[266] This is the title of a book by Ludwig von Mises, written in 1958 on the basis of lectures given in Buenos Aires, Argentina.

THE NOTION OF "PROGRESS" AND ITS MEANING FOR THE COLLECTIVE MEMORY[267] OF EUROPE

It will gradually have become clear by now what we mean by the root causes of the crisis in Europe. We are not talking about unemployment, digital transformation, inflation or the exchange rates used by the FED or ECB. Albeit, we would agree that all these issues, and many more, are of great importance for the immediate well-being of people in Europe and the USA. However, they are all symptoms of root causes that are acting from below and are triggers for these symptoms to appear, with their specific impact on the quality of life in our societies. With our analysis, we are looking for the root causes that lie below the appearance of the symptoms. These root causes are orchestrating, to a large extent, the functioning of our societies and even the way our power elites function. If we wish to become masters of

---

[267] We refer with the notion of "collective memory" to the work presented in 1925 by the French philosopher and sociologist Maurice Halbwachs in his book "Les cadres sociaux de la mémoire". Since then, this concept of the collective memory has been further analyzed and advanced. As an example, refer to "On the Cultural Constitution of Collective Memory", 2008, Qi Wang, researcher in psychology at Cornell University.

our own lives again, we will need to understand these root causes. We will need to understand the reasons and causes why things happen in the real world in a specific way. This will provide us with the means and tools to counter the events and actions in our societies that are against our interests.

One root cause, that we find at the origin of the specific functioning of the societies in Europe, is the specific way the notion of "progress" is being translated into specific social, economic and political actions. Therefore, we will need to examine "progress" and what it means for us in Europe. We will not develop a philosophical ontology of the notion of progress. We will rather develop a historical reconstruction of the notion of progress, its utilization and its impact on human action and life in our societies.

Progress means, in the sense of the word, to move from one stadium of action or event to another one. Usually, progress has a positive connotation, which indicates a development from a certain level or stage of development to a higher or better one. Progress is not informing about a static situation. It is linked to things happening, linked to actions that are leading to situations that change.

Concerning the complex processes that are characteristic of our societies, we will therefore have to ask several important questions concerning our understanding of progress. We will have to ask whether progress, as we perceive it, means deliberate and targeted changes. As we will see already, with such a question, the answers are not always simple and straightforward. We would probably all agree that no one could have foreseen the progress and the "overwhelming" technological developments and innovations that humanity has realized over the past century. Individual inventions and innovations may be considered the deliberate results and products of individual or teams of scientists and technicians actions. However, technological progress in its entirety and in its result for humanity has not been deliberate and purposeful. This is an important point, because it means that we, as humanity, cannot determine, consciously plan and foresee our progress, i.e. the changes that will occur in our societies.

We may already perceive, albeit, in a subtle manner at this level of our examination the inborn "fear of change" that comes into play. If we cannot know the future, then how can we wish for such uncertain processes of change? On the psychological level, there is probably an additional factor playing a determining role in our persisting "fear of change": We talk here about the fear of the other, my neighbor or my partner in the various networks of interrelationships, in which we take part in this world. We are all aware, more or less, that the others and our relationships all constitute factors, that we do not fully know and which we cannot control. It seems that Buckminster Fuller was gifted with great intuition, when he proposed, already in the 1960s, a "great logistics game" and a "world peace game", later simply called the "World Game". This was intended to become "a tool that would facilitate a comprehensive, anticipatory, design science approach to the problems of the world", i.e. a communication platform to create a common understanding of the road to take for humanity in making good use of scientific and technological progress. Buckminster Fuller intuitively understood that people usually act together, assuming that they understand each other and that they share the aims and purposes of their actions. As experience shows us again and again, people usually have different ideas about the aims and purposes of their actions. This often leads to deception at the end. In the course of the actions taken this means that forces are not united for the attainment of common goals, because in reality, such common goals do in fact not exist.

We are therefore called to meet and talk together to come close to a common understanding of the aims and purposes of our actions. Buckminster Fuller has initiated this approach in his call on us to fight against "weaponry" to the benefit of "livingry". These are general terms that have a great chance to lead to a basic agreement as a starting point for common action. This approach has lost none of its relevance. The root cause of the deep crisis in Europe lies not in science and technology. The root cause lies in the restricted use we are making of our minds to reach a common understanding of our goals and purposes in the management of our human affairs.

Coming back to our analysis of the notion of "progress", we are facing an exciting situation. Taking our considerations seriously, we have to ask ourselves what we can and what we want to do as humanity in order not to abandon ourselves blindly and powerlessly to progress that is leading to ever more "weaponry", the dire consequences of which we all know too well. If we increasingly want to come to a conscious oversight and orientation of the processes leading to change and progress, then we must ask ourselves which rules will have to be applied to shape these processes for progress in a constructive direction. Obviously, we wish them to produce results that are fruitful and propitious for the coexistence of humanity as a whole. We then have to ask ourselves, according to which fundamental principles and laws our coexistence on earth will have to function. We must decide this again and again at every single place on earth, in every community and nation, as well as at the level of the world community, in open discourse and free communication.

These processes concerning the self-determination of humanity cannot work within an environment of dominance and coercion, as we have been living in over the past century. The application of such outdated rules will continuously lead to strong and destructive frictions and, as a consequence for geopolitics, to violent conflicts and wars. We are approaching a point now in our brief analytical examination, where we are starting to understand the root causes of the crisis in Europe. We start to understand that we need to change the rules. We also begin to understand where the lever is that will induce effective and constructive change in the way we manage our lives on "spaceship earth. The levers are not effective at the level of symptoms. As Gregory Bateson said: to further a profound change in the functioning of history, i.e. our world history, you have to ask, "Whether the rules have been changed".

The European crisis is, at the same time, a world crisis. To find a way out of its deep and long-lasting crisis, Europe will have to merge her potential with the "creative ideas" and potential of the cultural value systems of the other partners on our globe. Europe cannot solve the problems of the world. On the contrary, to solve its problems, it will need the help of others. Mentally, Europe has to open up and prepare itself for this communicative process that is the condition for a shared future. Europe is not the master anymore. Looking for friends and partners seems to be good advice in such a challenging situation.

At this point in our discussion of the notion of "progress", we also come across the provocative question of whether we humans must or should realize everything that is possible for us. Do mentally coercive mechanisms exist that are here at work, which are inherent in the human psyche? We are not sure. It is astonishing how spontaneously most people might say that nothing can be banned or prohibited forever. Most of us might also agree with the belief that most people will never deliberately accept being restricted in their actions. Most of us suppose that people always strive to be free. That is, at least, what we are told. As a trained social anthropologist[268], we are not really sure about this point. There are many examples of human communities that have never adopted certain things or tools, never applied their characteristic potentials, and never used their specific possibilities. These examples show that it is possible for people to reject things and not use their potential.[269] This does not only apply to individuals, but also to cultural communities. This puts into question the "innate compulsion" to make use of everything possible, or to give in to every mental compulsion.

Probably the most famous example of a tool that has not been adopted universally is the

---

[268] Studies accomplished in 1987 at the Free University of Berlin, honored with a PhD in Political Anthropology.
[269] This points directly to utilitarianism. These examples show that "benefit" can be understood in very different ways.

wheel. The wheel is, rightly, considered one of the most important tools in human efforts to promote technological development and facilitate human life. However, on the entire African continent below the Sahara, formerly known as Black Africa, the wheel was never used as a means for moving charges or other technological purposes. Archeological excavations show that the wheel was known in Africa. However, it was never integrated into the African societies as a technical instrument. No carriages and no bicycles were in use before the colonial era. The same applies to writing as a means of communication. Written languages as instruments of communication have never been developed and used in Africa.

The two examples certainly have nothing to do with any kind of suspected mental or intellectual inferiority of Africans. They are as intelligent as all other people on earth, and equipped with the same mental and intellectual abilities as all other people. Nor do these examples mean that Africa is hostile to technology or innovation. There are many examples, let's just mention the loom and also a great variety of complex musical instruments, which show that Africa has made good use of her technological and creative potential.

So what led to these culturally extremely important decisions to not use certain tools and instruments? And what were the positive and perhaps also negative consequences of these decisions? There are many more interesting and surprising examples of things, instruments and their characteristics that have been rejected or simply not made use of by certain societies. We believe that it would be worthwhile to take a closer look at the circumstances of these examples and how this behavior in societies came about. What we could learn from it would probably often be of great value, in the sense that it would often make very inspiring contributions to the "competition of humanity for the better ideas". The challenge would be learning to think what we have hitherto not thought.

We certainly don't want to deny that science-driven technological progress can bring good results. Nevertheless, we should have the courage to ask ourselves, in the light of our experiences, whether everything we call "progress" is really good, valuable and meaningful. In our understanding, it is time for Europe to rediscover and redefine the meaning of progress. This might provide some useful and mentally creative impulses for the transformation of our societies in Europe and the design of a new humanity. Modern psychology, a product of modern Europe, as well as the ancient Indian Vedic tradition, both maintain that the human being is in his evolution challenged to increasingly become master of his or her compulsions. It seems that there are lessons to be learned by Europe on its way into a shared future.

Sure, we all want the "steady progress... from the worse to the better", as Kant programmatically expressed it in his philosophy of history. As late as the 18th and 19th centuries, i.e. in the Age of Enlightenment, it was assumed that there was an inevitable process of perfection of man and the world, which was tied to the "domination of nature" by man. Contradictions and setbacks were only signs of a lack of knowledge and served as an incentive to further develop science and technology with the interest of further using them as the engines of progress. However, due to the ever-intensified scientific and rapid technological development, the human-caused changes in living conditions and the impact of industries on the societies of Europe, from the 17th and 18th centuries to the present day, became increasingly apparent.[270] Science and technology gave humans more and more means and power to shape their lives and their living environments. As a consequence, this also meant that human action on the planet in the course of the industrial revolution left increasingly visible and tangible traces. If, according to scientific understanding, we have until now lived in the Holocene, in the geological age after the last ice ages, we have begun to call our current, incipient age, the Anthropocene. This means that humans will, from now on, increasingly shape the earth and life on it. If that is true, then we humans bear a great responsibility. It seems that it is not yet clear to everyone what this newly recognized responsibility actually means.[271] One thing should, however, be clear to everybody: the answer to this challenge and the solutions will not come from Europe. The challenge has a global scope. It is shared by the global community. It cannot be met with an attitude of

---

[270] A detailed description of these events can be found in the book "The Pursuit of Power, Europe 1815–1914" by Richard Evans.

[271] Looking at the scope of this challenge from a global perspective, we should appreciate the sheer nonsense of politically driven attempts such as "Energiewende", i.e. energy transition.

dominance and a generalized war economy, i.e. the "weaponry", of which Buckminster Fuller is repeatedly warning us.

In their optimistic manner, Europe and the West have so far assumed that a better and fairer world would emerge on the basis of material progress. A truly human upswing and progress have been expected in particular since the time of the Enlightenment after the French Revolution. Increasing control of nature and the improvement of living standards were seen as a technical and mechanical cause-and-effect chain. Contradictions, setbacks and conflicts were seen as temporary side effects of progress, but they would not call into question the general trend.

In the 19th and 20th centuries, however, criticism of industrialization was increasingly voiced. The cause for such criticism came, probably and primarily, from the sometimes frighteningly poor working conditions in industrial production. This prompted attentive observers of the situation to have their first serious doubts about the general blessing of industrial development.[272] Not only the books of Charles

---

[272] An excellent overview, a kind of "history of the process of industrialization from the 19th to the early 20th century"

Dickens, Victor Hugo and Balzac, or the drama "The Weavers" by Gerhart Hauptmann, bear witness to this, but also the establishment and growing influence of trade unions and social movements can be traced back to the often miserable working conditions in this era of industrialization. It has become clear to many people that not all that glittered was gold. So there were increasingly more people raising their voices to fundamentally question the idea of progress[273]. Some people started to fear that the price of progress would eventually be higher than its benefit to the people.[274]

---

has been presented in "The Pursuit of Power: Europe 1815 to 1914", 2016, by Richard J. Evans.

[273] This was already the case with Nietzsche in his "Genealogy of Morality", 1887. Later, with authors such as Georg Lukács, in "The Destruction of Reason", 1955.

In exile in the USA, Max Horkheimer and Theodor W. Adorno wrote their "Dialectic of the Enlightenment", a book in which they subjected the Enlightenment's concept of reason to a radical critique. Like many others, they were shocked by the fact that society did not offer effective resistance to the forms of fascism and monopoly capitalism. These remarks on the criticism of "progress" could be continued indefinitely.

[274] Goethe is known to have been skeptical about technical and scientific development as it was pursued. His novel "Wilhelm Meister" expresses this skepticism about the importance of technical progress well.

Interesting considerations on this issue also come from the side of social anthropology and ethnology. The ethnologist Claude Lévi-Strauss, for example, distinguishes between two fundamentally different types of human societies. He calls them *cold* and *hot* cultures. The "cold" cultures, ethnic groups and population groups living close to nature[275], are now practically extinguished and have disappeared and dissolved in the modern civilizations of the "hot" cultures. According to Lévi-Strauss, these modern civilizations, i.e. our Western "hot" societies, are characterized by constant cultural changes due to people's growing ability to understand science, i.e. being inspired by the *scientific spirit*.[276] An important idealistic motivation that often characterizes these efforts by man for progress, in which he tries to adapt nature to his needs, is the striving

---

An important point to retain here: "Progress" is always thought of anthropomorphically, i.e. from the perspective of man, without placing him in a universal context of development.

[275] An approach to this topic can be found in Christian Sigrist's book "Regulated Anarchy". There is also a detailed bibliography for an in-depth study of the topic of "segmental" societies.

[276] An introduction to the topic can be found in Claude Lévi-Strauss in "The Wild Thinking", 1976.

for an "ideal society". These aspirations are then often linked to ideologies, leading to debates about who is the better one and who is right. Such ideological disputes tend to become emotionally intensified to such an extent that they frequently lead to violent conflicts and may then escalate to wars.

In fact, they often only disguise egoistic interests for power and money. Think of the ideological conflict between liberal capitalism and communism, which has been critical to human development for many decades during the era of the "Cold War". Such ideologies are basically nourished by the drive for the survival of the fittest, which is at the origin of the fear of one's own death and destruction - the fear of not being able to secure one's own survival or that of one's nation. It is the fear that the other person or nation will take something away that you yourself consider essential to survive. This has led to the paradigm of the "always limited resources" in the Western science of economics. From their observation and interpretation of these ideologies and the ensuing conflicts and wars, some ethnologists and social anthropologists then derive a general critique of progress. This critique often leads to a general critique of Western culture, which fundamentally questions the model of European-driven development and *progress*.[277]

We want to conclude this overview on the topic of progress by also pointing to the importance of colonialism, which must be seen as a necessary side effect of capitalism, as it has been initiated and shaped by Europe. This brief examination of the role of colonialism will highlight some aspects that are critical for a more comprehensive understanding of the new, future paradigm of the "infinite regeneration of our resources".[278] The future paradigm, according to our understanding, will not be a "Western" one, but will have to include humanity in its

---

[277] An overview of the topic can be found in Ralf Konersmann (ed.) "Kulturkritik: Reflexionen in der veränderten Welt", Reclam 2001.

For this general critique of Western "progress", the works of the "Critical Theory" of the Frankfurt School are an important source. The "Dialectic of Enlightenment" by Max Horkheimer and Theodor W. Adorno from 1944 can serve as a reference here.

[278] We have borrowed this concept of "infinite renewal" or "infinite regeneration of resources" from R. Buckminster Fuller, who repeatedly names it as a fundamental quantity in his writings. See h. Operating Manual for Spaceship Earth, first published in 1969. Then also his late work "Critical Path", from 1981.

entirety.[279] For the sake of illustrating our arguments about the newly emerging post-colonialist worldview, it will be helpful if we briefly refer to the "Geoscope" as it was developed by Buckminster Fuller in 1960 and reintroduced in his "Critical Path" in the fifth chapter[280]. This has now given rise to a global movement that is oriented towards a world "without borders". At the Technical University of Zurich (UZH), the Department of Geography publishes the journal *Geoscope*. According to the understanding of participants in this global *Geoscope* movement, borders are seen as challenges that must eventually be overcome. According to the Buckminster Fuller Institute, the *Geoscope* was one of Fuller's most profound ideas, a powerful tool for synoptic visualization and planetary stewardship. This brings us to a brief critical review of the role of colonialism in European-style capitalism.

European colonialism is usually seen as a necessary side effect, or accompanying

---

[279] It may be helpful for a better understanding of this new worldview if we take a look at the "Geoscope" as developed by Buckminster Fuller and presented in his "Critical Path" in the fifth chapter.

[280] For more details, please take a look at the website of the Buckminster Fuller Institute: https://www.bfi.org/.

measure, of European-style capitalism. A careful study of the emergence, historical development and expansion of the East India Company[281] and the British Empire replaces the study of many volumes of literature on this topic.[282] The expansive tendency, which became evident with the voyages of discovery and world circumnavigation of the 15th and 16th centuries, is directly linked to the growing belief in the progress of humanity. In general, Columbus' sailing voyage in 1492, is considered the signal for departure to new shores and the discovery of new continents and new worlds. Looking back, we understand today that this trip was the signal for the conquest of the world by the European-influenced capitalist economy and for the age of globalization, in which we have definitely arrived since the 17th and 18th century with the British Empire.[283]

---

[281] Refer to "The Honorable Company: A History of the English East India Company", 1993, by John Keay. A good source for further orientation is "Empire: How Britain Made the Modern World, 2018, by Niall Ferguson.
[282] In this regard, the book by Niall Ferguson, "Empire: How Britain Made the Modern World, 2003, is an excellent source.
[283] In his introduction to the "War of the Worlds", Niall Ferguson explains convincingly that globalization had reached its peak already before World War One.

The realization has grown in the sciences and among people in general that colonialism is not seen as an accidental historical concomitant, but as an important function and elementary component of Europe's and later the US imperialist policy. Thus, colonialism, i.e. the domination of other peoples and countries, has at the same time become an essential part of the still existing paradigm of modern Europe. This European model is characterized by the infinite progress of science and technology, together with the belief in infinite material growth and the infinite availability of natural resources, albeit for only a part of humanity.

When people talk about colonialism, they usually think primarily of the European colonial empires in Africa, Latin America and Asia. However, if we were to emphasize the importance of individual colonial empires, then this certainly includes India, but above all, the United States of America. These two states also make it clear that colonization often took very different forms.

The case of India shows that the colonial heritage is engraved in the collective memory of the country and cannot just be discarded or easily replaced. India still has to free itself of the mental bondage of the colonial era. India is an excellent example of the difficulty for a nation to find its own way to a sovereign development that is building on its own, very specific cultural identity.

The two distinct features of US colonialism were, on the one hand, the almost complete extinction of the Native American autochthonous population and destruction of their cultures, and on the other hand, the separation from the European "motherland" Great Britain. The special course and the concrete result of colonialism in North America, with the creation of large states and confederations of states, such as the USA, but also Canada and Mexico, is certainly a very special experience in the history of humanity. This colonialism in North America, which was then supplemented by the slave trade[284], produced economic, political and social consequences that still have a strong impact on

---

[284] For the sake of honesty, we will note here that the slave trade in the newly formed United States of America accounted for only about 10% of the total slave trade. Most of the slaves from Africa were destined for the predominantly British and French colonies in the Caribbean and for the Portuguese and Spanish colonies in Latin America.

humanity today and are to be considered part of its collective memory.[285]

There is one important feature that is characteristic of Europe's colonial mindset. This characteristic feature of the colonial mind divides the world into "we" and the "others", "we here" and the "others there". As Niall Ferguson puts it provocatively, "The West and the Rest" has until now been the world view of Europe and the US. [286] This puts the finger on the unspoken assumption of the existence of resources on the "other side", i.e. outside one's own premises. The European mind has strongly

---

[285] There is an extensive literature on the subject of colonialism. To start with, we recommend Wolfgang Reinhard's "The Subjugation of the World: Global History of European Expansion 1414 – 2015, published in 2017; or Reinhard Wendt, "From Colonialism to Globalization: Europe and the World since 1500", published in 2016.

Then on the importance of the British colonial empire, Niall Ferguson's book "Empire: How Britain Made the Modern World, 2003.

Also interesting is the book by Franz Ansprenger on the "Dissolution of the Colonial Empires", 1989.

[286] In his book "The West and the Rest: Discourse and Power", 1992, Stuart Hall analyzes this issue of cultural relativity. Interestingly, Niall Ferguson has referred to this fundamental polarity that is characteristic for the modern era in Europe. Refer to "Civilization. The West and the Rest", 2012, Niall Ferguson.

been shaped, and we may say it is still trapped, by this faulty and misleading experience. With the emergence of a global world view, this limited colonial mindset has lost its justification. Here again, we encounter a very specific reason, a root cause for the crisis in Europe, which is deeply engraved in the European mind. This is one reason why Europe, and with it the US, have great difficulties grasping or accepting the features of the new world order and the new system of global governance. Sharing power and resources on an equal foot with other nations requires a paradigm shift towards a new mindset for Europe and the US.

THE NOTION OF "GROWTH" AND ITS MEANING FOR THE COLLECTIVE MEMORY OF EUROPE[287]

GLOBALIZATION OF GROWTH

A symbolic event and a decisive step towards the paradigm of "growth" as we know it today, was undertaken more than 600 years ago by Christopher Columbus, when he set sail on a small sailing ship in 1492, to discover the "New World" in what is now the American hemisphere. It is not without significance that Columbus, a Genoese, received instructions for his journey from Toscanelli, a Florentine, who belonged to Leonardo da Vinci's sphere of influence. As a scientist and astronomer, Toscanelli was one of the pioneers of the early Renaissance, and he also designed maps, about which he exchanged information with Columbus in writing. From the

---

[287] We refer with the notion of "collective memory" to the work presented in 1925 by the French philosopher and sociologist Maurice Halbwachs in his book "Les cadres Sociaux de la Mémoire". Since then, this concept of the collective memory has been further analyzed and advanced. As an example, refer to "On the Cultural Constitution of Collective Memory", 2008, Qi Wang, researcher in psychology at Cornell University.

very beginning, the development of modern sciences, as well as the discovery of "new worlds", were closely linked to the generalized spirit of exploration, characteristic of the Renaissance. It was a time characterized by a new awakening of human consciousness, raising it to new heights. Even if the development of the foundations for modern natural sciences by Galileo Galilei had to wait for more than a century, the intellectual prerequisites were already created in Italy in this early period of the Renaissance. As we know, Nicolaus Copernicus formed his foundations for scientific thinking and acquired his most important scientific knowledge during his study visits to Italy. The Copernican turn to the modern era was finally initiated in 1543, with the publication of Nicolaus Copernicus' main work, "De revolutionibus orbium coelestium" (*On the Revolutions of the Heavenly Spheres*).

At that time, no one could have imagined the new dimensions, into which these scientific discoveries and developments would lead humanity. But the scientists and artists in Florence and the other cities of northern Italy during the Renaissance already suspected their explorations to open the doors to new worlds. Together with the groundbreaking developments in science and technology that followed the Renaissance, the dawn of uninhibited economic growth was heralded. The voyage of Columbus and the discovery of the "new world" were the symbolic preludes to this. Blinded by the gold and silver found in southern America that was increasingly mined by the colonial powers to fill the treasuries of the Spanish and Portuguese kings and emperors, there was no limit to the urge for European countries to conquer the world. Colonization soon reached the Asian and African continents. In 1770, James Cook reached the east coast of Australia. He took possession of the land in New South Wales for the British Crown. There was no hold. It had to be the whole world.

No person can bear better witness to this irrepressible urge to conquer the world through colonization than Cecil Rhodes, the lord of Rhodesia and the owner of large gold and diamond mines in South Africa and Botswana[288], which are still in Anglo-American possession today. From his biography, we take the following statement, which can also be seen as an "announcement" to conquer the world: "After reading the history of other countries, I realized

---

[288] We recommend Anthony Thomas' biography "Rhodes: the Race for Africa", 1997.

that expansion was everything, that the surface of the world is limited, and that the great goal of today's humanity should be to take as much of the world as possible". This statement leaves nothing to be desired in terms of clarity. In addition, it contains a reference that is important for our further argumentation. Cecil Rhodes speaks of the great goal of "today's humanity". For Rhodes, "today's humanity" was primarily formed by the inhabitants of Great Britain and the USA at his time. Rhodes was a well-known and avowed racist, who considered the British and the British Americans to be the "first race in the world." So it will come as no surprise that he dreamed of the reunification of the Anglo-American world, with the inherent purpose of forming a global Anglo-American empire. We must be deaf and blind to not hear and witness in this statement the announcement of the modern era, with the Anglo-Americans striving for hegemonic power, in which we still live today.[289]

Early colonialism, with its dramatic consequences, was the great prelude and

---

[289] It was Oswald Spengler, who has seen in Cecil Rhodes this exemplary character for the Faustian, modern times of the Western world. see the Introduction to "The Decline of the West".

complementary force for the formation of global capitalism in its present form, which had been in the making since the 16th century.[290] The center of this capitalism soon migrated, from the Catholic-church-dominated kingdoms of Spain and Portugal in southwestern Europe, to the northern countries of Europe, first to the Netherlands. It was there that the first modern, liberal financial and commercial center of capitalism emerged, and soon produced powerful offshoots in England, and subsequently also in Germany and France.[291]

In a parallel process of complementary evolution, modern science was definitely brought to light by Bacon[292] and Newton, with the development of the experimental scientific method to attain an "objective" understanding of nature. The definition of the calculus by Newton and Leibniz gave humanity the potential to think in systems and to create models of real or virtually existing things and

---

[290] For an overview of the historical processes, we recommend Fernand Braudel, "Civilization and Capitalism", 1967.

[291] These developments can be easily understood in Niall Ferguson's "The ascent of Money", 2003.

[292] Francis Bacon's "Novum organum", first published in England in 1620, is recommended for this purpose.

events. The rational-logical application of reason and intellectual thinking to science broke ground for the dazzling scientific and technological progress throughout Europe to finally usher in the comprehensive industrialization of the entire globe as we know it today.

This movement, initiated by Europe, fundamentally changed societies and the ways of life of people around the world. In the rural-agrarian societies of Europe, more and more centers of industrial growth were formed, ever larger cities grew, and more and more people and their living environments were driven away from nature and agricultural production to the industrial way of life. There seemed to be no escape. The suffering and sacrifices of many children, women and men who were mercilessly exploited in the mines and factories at that time cried out to heaven. Millions of black Africans were enslaved in the new colonies of the Americas[293], in order to create and increase the material wealth of the "masters of the world".[294]

---

[293] We are well aware of the old tradition of slave trade in the Arab world, i.e. along the coast of Eastern Africa down to the Comoros Islands and Madagascar. However, this is not the subject of our analysis here.

[294] In 1776, Adam Smith denounced the attitude of the "Masters of mankind", the new capitalist elite, in his

This industrial and economic growth seemed to provide humanity with unlimited opportunities to acquire wealth and power. The British Empire, the Netherlands and France founded more and more colonies and took mineral resources, agricultural products, precious woods and stones, as well as other sources of wealth, out of the colonies to increase their own wealth. America, the most important British colony, soon bought up its slaves coming from the African and Indian colonies. The colonies in Latin America, Africa and Asia flourished and increased, for hundreds of years, the wealth in the countries of Europe.[295] The new era of growth without limits seemingly had ushered.

LIMITS TO GROWTH

With the foresight of a great historian, Eric Hobsbawm brings together the end of

---

famous book "The Wealth of Nations": "All for ourselves and nothing for other people, seems, in every age of the world, to have been the vile maxim of the "*masters* of mankind".

[295] Obviously, we are writing here from the perspective of Europe. The Europe-driven colonization brought tremendous changes also in the countries and for the people colonized. We do not overlook these facts.

colonialism with the "end of empires".[296] The USA declared its independence from Great Britain in 1776. Brazil broke away from Portugal in 1822. India had regained its independence from Great Britain in 1948. The Netherlands gave up its colony in Indonesia in 1949, only after bitter fighting; the first Dutch trading posts had been established in Indonesia already in the 1600s. Most of the African colonies were granted independence in the years up to 1960. Algeria did not regain its independence from France until 1963. Portugal refused to give up its colonies in Africa until 1975. In South Africa, the racist apartheid system was not dissolved until 1994, and Rhodesia, named after Cecil Rhodes, was designated the independent state of Zimbabwe in the same year. So we see very well that these liberation movements reach far into the modern epoch after the Treaty of Versailles of 1919, which was the subject of our analysis in Part One of this book, concerning the most important geopolitical events in Europe over the past century. This recalls the fact that the rules applied to manage geopolitics have, until now, not substantially changed. This is the historical betrayal, to which Gregory Bateson refers in his

[296] This is what Eric Hobsbawm calls the seventh chapter in his book "The Age of Extremes" from 1994.

short essay on the two principal events in his lifetime. This also refers to the root cause of our current sufferings under the hegemonic strive of the West through forceful violent actions, sanctions and wars all over the globe. This brief review of the end of colonialism and the end of empires, which Hobsbawm links together, is at the same time a clear indication that the rules for the new system of global governance will have to change.

In Eric Hobsbawm's book, follow after the "Age of Empires" the "Golden Years". This brings us to the time that reached a temporary climax with the Cultural Revolution in the West at the end of the 1960s, and the mass opposition to the US war in Vietnam. It is therefore not surprising that the publication of the study entitled "Limits to Growth" was presented by the *Club of Rome* during the same time, in 1972, at a symposium in St. Gallen, Switzerland. Thus, the topic of growth had been brought to the attention of the new cultural movement in Europe and had consequently become an important part of the public discussion in modern societies for the first time. This rising awareness in the West also had a direct impact on the growing importance of global development policy in European and other Western countries, such as Canada and

Japan. As a result of this incipient public discussion on growth, which was originally mainly limited to Europe and the USA, the "North-South Commission" was founded in 1977 under the chair of Willy Brandt and in close cooperation with Olof Palme, as an "independent commission for international development issues".

At that time, something seeped into the consciousness of many people in Europe and the West. Unfortunately, however, the question of possible limits to growth has not really taken root and has been suppressed again and again by other, supposedly more urgent and upcoming events, challenges and processes. The call for action contained in the publication of the *Club of Rome* was soon rejected, ignored, or largely forgotten. Humanity seemed to have more important things to do, in particular to pursue the goal of increasing economic growth. The Rio de Janeiro Conference in 1992, to which the UN had invited 172 states, did not change this lacking commitment. The Rio Conference has been convened with the purpose of "finding solutions to problems such as poverty and the growing gap between industrialized and developing countries, as well as to the increasing environmental, economic and social problems, and to set the course for global sustainable development". Officially, environmental protection and social and economic development were from now on considered equally important for humanity. However, the subsequent global developments, with their increasing destruction of the natural environment and an ever-increasing exploitation of natural resources in combination with numerous destructive wars, show very clearly that the noble intentions and goals of the Rio Conference were followed by very little concrete action. The incessant struggle for money and power under the combined hegemonic powers of the US, NATO and Europe continued to obstruct a constructive global debate on a new system of global governance, i.e. what is today called a multipolar world order. This is unfortunately the situation we are still living today.

In any case, since then, human societies on earth have not adhered to an attitude that would have limited their destructive actions in pursuit of material growth. They did not set any limits on material growth for themselves. To the Western world "the limit was the sky", while limits, if at all, were only set for others. The uncontrolled and undistinguished, i.e. the unreasonable growth and expansion of our societies, has continued undeterred. Control and regulation of growth remained within the remit of the powers of the Western hegemonic powers, the US, Europe and the EU. Who else could better know the way to go than they? Moreover, the speed and extent of growth have increased rapidly over the past decades, driven by relentless technological progress. This increases, at least in theory, the chances of increasing the resources for the gain of power and money. The hunt for money and power was the driving force. This strive for material growth without limits created a psychological momentum that had the effect of a drug that is creating a narrow vision and reducing consciousness. Is it this effect that Christopher Clark refers to in his 2012 book, "The Sleepwalkers. How Europe went to War in 1914"? The hunt for money and power through limitless material growth leads to a situation, where reality is becoming increasingly blurred. Reality becomes the subject of a disturbed mindset that limits the capability to take responsibility beyond self-centered interests.[297]

---

[297] For a deeper understanding of these critical issues, we refer the reader to "The Insanity of Normality. Toward Understanding Human Destructiveness", 1987, by Arno Gruen, and The Betrayal of the Self: The Fear of

It is probably not out of place to say that, today, in Europe, we see ourselves overwhelmed by this growth. We are helplessly watching, as this one-dimensional strive for "progress", which is exclusively built on the mastery of power and money, as principal resources for the attainment of happiness, continues unhindered.

For now, the negative effects and disastrous impact of European and US-driven global developments are becoming increasingly apparent. This has become all the more true, the further this development of uninhibited growth has spread and intensified globally. To this day, many economists have the one-sided idea that this development has created wealth that was previously considered impossible. This may be true, as long as we talk about monetary income and financial resources. The wealth we create is usually limited to things we can buy with money. This approach does overlook the fact that before the total economization of the world's societies, many things, resources and services were received for free and shared among people and communities.[298] Think of water, forests, wild

Autonomy in Men and Women, 2007.

[298] Jörg Guido Hülsmann has just published a book analyzing the interdependence of between "Abundance, Generosity, and the State: an Inquiry into Economic

fruits and communal land. The scientific-industry-driven growth, stimulated by Europe, has definitely changed the world and has now spread over the entire globe. The total and comprehensive economization of human living conditions has finally become the ultimate goal, the utopia of this capitalism driven by Europe and the USA. The purpose is to make everything a commodity and make money out of everything. In this sense, and according to the ideas of the economists, politicians and power elites educated under this system, humanity seems to be on the right track.

However, these economists, politicians and powerful brokers overlook the negative side of the balance sheet of these developments. The back of the medal is not noticed and is often denied altogether.[299] This has also to do with the

Principles", 2024. There we can learn how the state has become the enemy of good neighborhood, of generous friendship and cheerful parenting.

[299] Very early on, at the end of the 18th century and in the course of his life until the second half of the 19th century, Alexander von Humboldt already pointed out these negative effects of economic activity in his travel reports and later lectures, sometimes in a language and clarity that could be applied to today's grievances in the same way. We recommend reading "Alexander von Humboldt and the Invention of Nature", in 2015, by Andrea Wulf.

fact that the negative impact is usually more important in the poorer countries of the developing world, euphemistically called "emerging markets", which have fewer capacities to manage their living environments. A striking symptom of this situation and the one-sided approach to development is, in our times, the export of garbage, such as plastic waste or used and broken electronics, to countries that do not dispose of the technical means for appropriate recycling. This is a striking symptom of the discharge of problems to others. In Analytical Psychology, this is called "externalization" of problems, i.e. repression of facts that are considered threatening.

Science- and technology-driven global growth had already reached its first peak at the end of the 19th century in the Victorian era of England. Since then, the negative effects and sometimes devastating impacts have become more and more evident, culminating in our time to a frightening extent. The "European model" of a scientifically and technologically driven infinite growth, has only worked for a limited time, as long as it was possible to live on an "island" and to get the resources, workforce and raw materials "from outside".[300] The "European model" has worked, more or less efficiently, for the "golden billion" of the world's population. While it has at the same time brought immense suffering to billions of people and produced devastating effects on the environment on an incredibly large scale.

We recognize today that we live in "one world". This world has not become culturally homogeneous, as many had naively hoped, assuming that all people in this one world would, in the end, function like Europeans or Americans. We have to recognize that this world has become a world, in which we have to communicate across geographical and cultural borders. It is a world, in which there is no longer a uniform canon of values, and in which all people and nations have principally the right to participate as sovereign participants in shaping coexistence.

This point, that the "outside" or "outer part of the world" no longer exists for humanity in a globalized world, has been considered by Lewis Mumford as a critical point[301]. It is deeply engraved in the mindset of the European

---

[300] And also to dump the garbage there, be it to sell it to the former colonies, or to dump it directly into the oceans.

"masters", a stubborn and devastating heritage of European-style capitalism. This is the "colonialist perspective", the perspective of "here we are, and there are the others". This perspective does not make sense anymore and no longer applies today. This was the perspective of the hegemon, that Cecil Rhodes dreamed of. However, nowadays, as the European capitalist model has finally globalized through the development of automobiles, airplanes, and the communication media, there is no longer any place that would be "outside", from which the resources could be obtained, or where the garbage and waste could be dumped. The limits of growth can no longer be overlooked. The world is a whole, and we as humans are all living in the middle of it. The pressure on people's well-being and on the natural environment is directly felt by each member of the world's population.

The distance to the results and consequences of one's own actions has been reduced or even completely annihilated. Every person has become part of the whole. Every individual action leads to global consequences. The consequences of the actions of the masses of individuals can no longer be overlooked. The

[301] Lewis Mumford, "Hope or Barbarism," Chapter VIII, "World Culture," pp. 159 ff.

consequences of growth are becoming more and more evident in their negative effects and their impact on the lives of the earth's populations. Unlimited growth, geographic expansion and demographic pressure combine to create a situation, where people and their living environment are suffering more and more. People are globally exposed to ever greater mental stress and economic pressure. In the Europe of today, we are living as the former masters of an era that is moving towards its end. It should have become clear to Europe that it cannot deny responsibility for the increasingly dire situation, in which the world finds itself today. The acknowledgement of this fact implies the duty to take responsibility for the future well-being of humanity. Europe is asked to take action - human action[302], not action driven by the strive for further increases in power and more money exclusively.

Due to the unbridled exploitation and extraction of natural resources, the large rainforests around the entire subtropical and tropical belt of the earth have been cleared by humans. There is nudged talk by politicians and in the media that

[302] "Human Action" is the title of the masterwork of Ludwig von Mises, an Austrian-born economist who immigrated to the USA.

these rainforests must be protected and saved. In reality, however, these rainforests and beautiful savannas no longer exist today. The natural resources of the oceans are increasingly being depleted. Their ability to regenerate decreases and is threatened. Most species of fish and creatures in the oceans are now threatened with extinction, and many have already disappeared. They are usually literally "eaten up" by humans. The wonderful coral reefs will soon only be admired on the screens. Fresh water is becoming a precarious resource in many countries. Even in highly developed Europe, there are hardly any fresh waters or sources left, from which the water can be enjoyed fresh and without cumbersome and expensive "treatment". Nature is also no longer a resource, in which people would find peace and relaxation. Population density in more and more countries is approaching that of Bangladesh, where there is no longer enough space to farm, where clean water is hard to come by, and where rural population density is approaching that of large cities.[303] In these countries, nature no longer has

[303] During his last working stay in Kenya, in 2016, the author of this book was shocked to see that at the height of the African Rift Valley in Kenya, one of the most fertile areas in the world, with an incredible biodiversity and impressive flora in the tropical forests a hundred years

time to recover. It is exploited as a vital resource until it is used up and depleted. The soils will need centuries or even millennia to recover, form anew and build up again to provide ground for the forests and prairies, as the basis for their regeneration. We could go on and on with examples of the dire consequences of human action under the current European and US-driven capitalist development system.

However, we want to take a break here to look more precisely at the dimension of the dilemma in which humanity finds herself. Once we have refined the diagnostic part of our analysis, we will be in a position to address the questions raised by this globally recognized dire situation more precisely in the following third part of the book.

THE DIMENSIONS OF THE DILEMMA

The path taken so far to solve the dilemma, in the midst of which we have placed ourselves through our one-sided behavior and exclusive belief in mechanical science and technology, consists almost exclusively of scientific and

---

ago, humans have spread to such an extent that even the water resources are hardly sufficient to survive.

technical measures. In Europe, this technological approach is generally called "energy transition". In this approach, citizens and humans in general are considered pawns and vicarious agents in the political arena managed by the Western power elites. Even worse, following the US model, Europe has now declared war to be supposedly the most efficient way to acquire the natural resources for the implementation of such technology-driven "transitions", i.e. ways out of the dilemma. The current war in Ukraine provides a living illustration.

When things are bad, they may still become worse. In this sense, Europe has now introduced a war economy, following the US model. It seems to be the most efficient way for our power elites in the EU and NATO to procure the resources for the implementation of such technology-driven "energy and political turning points".[304] Obviously, we are moving forward on Dante's *path to hell*, the path of a steep *downward spiral*. In paraphrasing Dante, we could say that the way out of the dilemma is not

---

[304] In its recent publication of the *Misesian*, Vol. 1, No. 4 | July–August 2024, the Mises Institute has published a series of articles, such as "American Imperialism and our Bipartisan Warfare State", by T. Hunt Tooley, that is confirming the general "warfare policy" of the US.

"paved with good intentions" but with "blood, sweat and tears", i.e. with ever more wars.

At this point, we may recall some of the major challenges and factors humanity is facing. These factors will have to be recognized, analyzed and understood in their context and with their potential and real impact. If we know these factors and principal challenges, we may be in a position to control them increasingly well in the future.

For this purpose, we will briefly show how this materialistic growth driven by science and technology has been accompanied by an equally exponential growth of the population on earth. All the important growth curves, that of economic growth, that of the growth of scientific and technical knowledge, as well as that of energy consumption are closely linked to the curve showing population growth on earth. They all run practically exponentially and in parallel. We therefore presume that there is a systemic relationship and interdependency among these different areas of human evolution.

GRAPHICAL GROWTH CURVES

GROWTH OF WORLD POPULATION
and the History of Technology

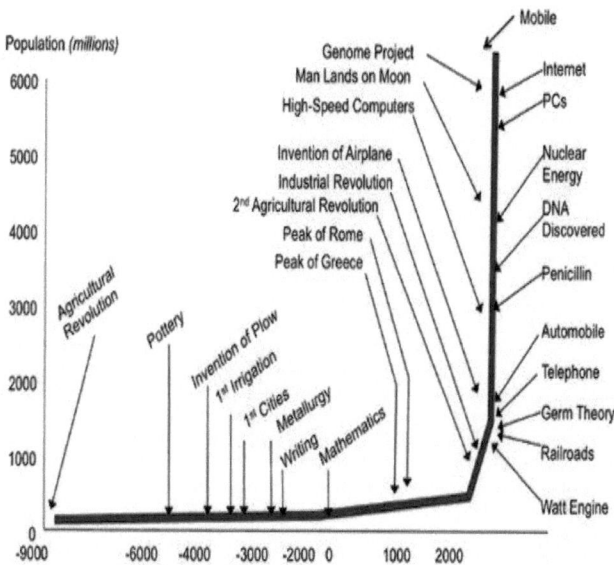

Source: Milken Institute, Robert Fogel/University of Chicago

GLOBAL PRIMARY ENERGY CONSUMPTION
BY SOURCE

Global primary energy consumption by source

Primary energy[1] consumption is measured in terawatt-hours[2], using the substitution method[3].

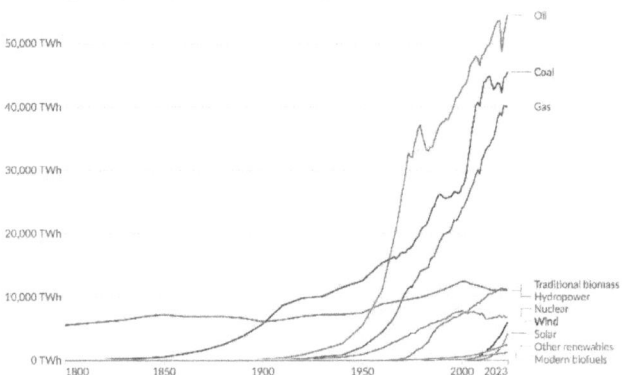

Data source: Energy Institute - Statistical Review of World Energy (2024); Smil (2017) OurWorldInData.org/energy | CC BY

Note: In the absence of more recent data, traditional biomass is assumed constant since 2015.

1. Primary energy: Primary energy is the energy available as resources - such as the fuels burnt in power plants - before it has been transformed. This relates to the coal before it has been burned, the uranium, or the barrels of oil. Primary energy includes energy that the end user needs, in the form of electricity, transport and heating, plus inefficiencies and energy that is lost when raw resources are transformed into a usable form. You can read more on the different ways of measuring energy in our article.

2. Watt-hour: A watt-hour is the energy delivered by one watt of power for one hour. Since one watt is equivalent to one joule per second, a watt-hour is equivalent to 3600 joules of energy. Metric prefixes are used for multiples of the unit, usually: - kilowatt-hours (kWh), or a thousand watt-hours. - Megawatt-hours (MWh), or a million watt-hours. - Gigawatt-hours (GWh), or a billion watt-hours. - Terawatt-hours (TWh), or a trillion watt-hours.

3. Substitution method: The 'substitution method' is used by researchers to correct primary energy consumption for efficiency losses experienced by fossil fuels. It tries to adjust non-fossil energy sources to the inputs that would be needed if it was generated from fossil fuels. It assumes that wind and solar electricity is as inefficient as coal or gas. To do this, energy generation from non-fossil sources are divided by a standard thermal efficiency factor - typically around 0.4. Nuclear power is also adjusted despite it also experiencing thermal losses in a power plant. Since it's reported in terms of electricity output, we need to do this adjustment to calculate its equivalent input value. You can read more about this adjustment in our article.

Global GDP over the long run

Total output of the world economy. These historical estimates of GDP are adjusted for inflation. We combine three sources to create this time series: the Maddison Database (before 1820), the Maddison Project Database (1820–1989), and the World Bank (1990 onward).

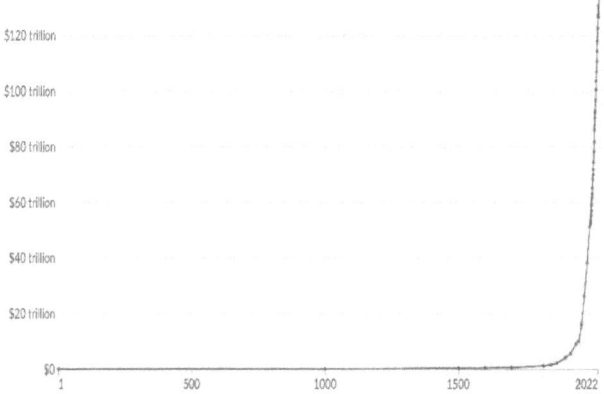

Data source: World Bank (2023); Bolt and van Zanden - Maddison Project Database 2023; Maddison Database 2010
Note: This data is expressed in international-$ at 2017 prices.
OurWorldInData.org/economic-growth | CC BY

1. International dollars: International dollars are a hypothetical currency that is used to make meaningful comparisons of monetary indicators of living standards. Figures expressed in international dollars are adjusted for inflation within countries over time, and for differences in the cost of living between countries. The goal of such adjustments is to provide a unit whose purchasing power is held fixed over time and across countries, such that one international dollar can buy the same quantity and quality of goods and services no matter where or when it is spent. Read more in our article: What are Purchasing Power Parity adjustments and why do we need them?

GROWTH IN SCIENTIFIC KNOWLEDGE
(1400 - 1900)

Evolution of the number of Researchers and Scientists (1400 - 1900)

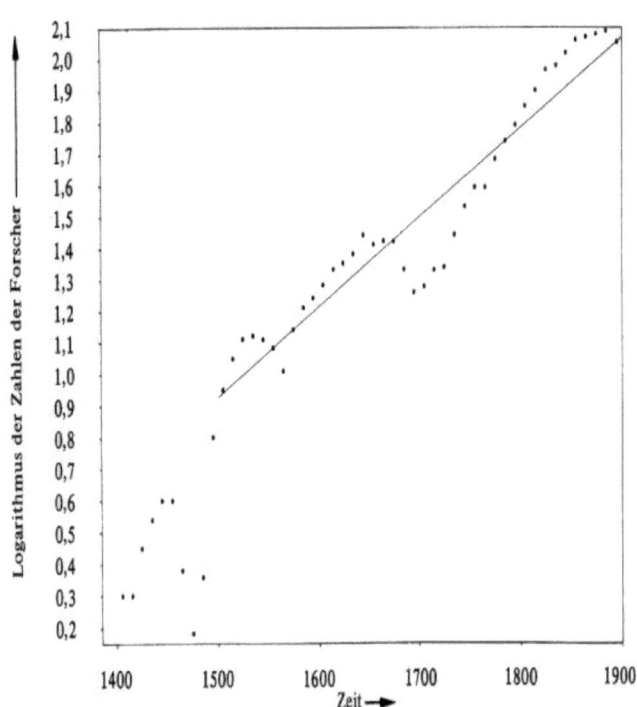

A whole series of more such growth curves could be shown, all of which would show this impressive parallel and exponentially steep development. We take this as a distinct indication that humanity is a living self-regulating system as part of the earth, which is itself a living and self-regulating system. This is a noticeable example of a hierarchy of systems, where the higher one comprises the lower one.

This presumption still receives stronger confirmation, if we take a look at a series of inverse growth curves. We all agree that it would not be difficult to show a series of growth curves with negative tendencies, i.e. that are exponential in a mirror image, but in a negative sense, indicating destructive results. These *inverse growth curves* could comprise one for biodiversity, one for available agricultural land, one for the areas of tropical forests, one for the depletion and decay of coral reefs in the oceans, one for the reproduction of fish stocks in the seas, one for the littering of large areas of land and seas, one for the degree of pollution of the world's oceans. The list could go on and on for a long time. So it is obvious that the negative trends are also moving steeply upwards, that they are also growing exponentially, but in a negative sense. These negative trends indicate the threat and harm that humanity is inflicting on herself, on her living environment. These negative trends are the result of this unchecked drive for global growth under the current paradigm for progress and of our Europe and US-driven way of life.

Looking at this synoptic picture of the parallel and exponential curves calmly, then the interdependence of the vital areas of development of our societies immediately makes sense to us. Currently, we are looking in the wrong direction, taking a false perspective. Humanity is looking for help through science and technology. This is what we are calling the functional and linear approach to solutions. This means searching for the solution in a way and with tools that rely on the principle factor that is at the origin of the current technology-driven paradigm. At the end, this will lead us ever deeper into our problems. We have to understand, however, that technology can only be a means, but does not provide the foundation and principal building block of the new paradigm. The foundation for the new paradigm has to be grounded in human beings and their behavior, as well as in nature as the living environment on earth. How could it be otherwise? We are human beings with a soul. We are not robots driven by electricity.

Taking these facts into account, it is obvious what these illustrations are showing us and to what consequences they point. Obviously, further unbridled growth, as depicted by these *exponentially growing curves,* can, with the consequences demonstrated by the *inverse growth curves*, not lead to a good end.[305] Obviously, a paradigm shift in what we consider to be "growth", will have to be induced in Europe and on a global scale. Growth in the broad sense will have to be consciously controlled by us as rational humans in a cooperative global approach. Furthermore, growth will have to be directly linked to a newly agreed definition of the meaning of "quality of life" for all humans. All our future challenges will have to be directly related to the progressive improvement of

[305] To further enhance the significance of these graphs, curves for species extinction or the decline of tropical forests could be cited, for example. If you are interested, you can look for the corresponding graphics on the Internet and look at them.

the quality of life for all humans, not just the golden billion. We will see in the following Part Three of the book in detail what we mean by that and what the role of Europe may be.

SUMMARY OF PART TWO: THE ROOT CAUSES OF THE CRISIS IN EUROPE

In Part Two of the book, we have focused our evidence-based approach on the descriptive analysis of the root causes of the *Crisis in Europe*. Our aim was, to attain a deep epistemological understanding of the root causes of this crisis.

We have analyzed the principal historical events and cultural factors that have shaped Europe and the social and economic life of its societies since the Renaissance. The origin of the historical memory and of modern Europe's self-image and consciousness in the 15th and 16th centuries has thus been brought to light. This has led us to a thorough understanding of the principal elements and their systemic interdependencies that are characteristic of the mind-set and mental framework of modern man in Europe.

Our examination has led us deeply into the historical and cultural context of modern-time Europe. The scientific tool we have applied is a concise historical reconstruction of the creation of modern Europe from the Renaissance until today. Through our evidence-based scientific approach, we could examine our hypothesis and the underlying assumption that a specific European mindset has grown out of its historic development since the Renaissance. Not only have the origins of the historical memory and of modern Europe's self-image and consciousness been brought to light, but we could also show that the modus operandi of Europe, the way it functions internally and operates internationally, has its origin in the collective historical memory and the subsequent self-image of modern Europe. We have examined this hypothesis in Part Two of the book and provided evidence for its reasonable justification.

We started Part Two of the book with a short chapter to present our research interest and the methodology applied to examine our hypothesis.

Thereafter, we have identified three critical areas and have put them in the focus of our descriptive analysis.

We started in chapter two with a detailed look at the current Global Governance system as a result of the growing Western economic and political dominance since the Renaissance. We came to the conclusion that a paradigm shift is ongoing. This puts pressure for change on Europe. However, lack of sovereignty, which we have brought to light in Part One of our book, makes it extremely difficult for Europe to embrace change and join the emerging new system of global governance. Here lies one root cause for the current crisis in Europe.

In the following third chapter, we have presented a deep analytical description of the critical and constituent elements that are characteristic of the mindset of Europe and its people. These constitutional elements are (a) the growing individual consciousness and the role played by the individual in society, (b) the specific view modern Europe and its people have developed with regard to "progress", and (c) the specific way "growth" is considered in Europe and by its people.

These three elements have been analyzed in their combined constitutional function for the specific mindset of Europe and its people.

The critical role of Europe in the development of modern science since the Renaissance has been included in the analyses throughout the chapters of this part of the book. We consider modern science a fundamental constitutional element for the mindset of Europe and the Western world. Life in modern Europe, in all its various aspects, cannot be thought without modern science, as it has been created since the Renaissance.

In their combination, these elements are constituting a complex, which is the driving force effective at the root of the Western model of capitalist development. This specific mindset is in its combination also representing the paradigm that is directing actions of Europe in its international relations. This specific complex of the critical elements is the constitutional force behind the mindset of Europe. It is in its combination considered the principal root cause of the economic, financial and environmental crises in Europe.

In summary, Part Two of the book has provided convincing evidence for the negative impact of the European social, economic and political model on global well-being and peace. In fact, the implementation of this specific European capitalist development model has brought life on earth to a threshold. This applies to the political level, where European-driven development has led to the creation of an ever-increasing arsenal of nuclear weapons that are not inspiring confidence in the sustainability of European and Western politics. In parallel, the world has obviously also reached a threshold through its exceeding pressure on the living environment on earth. Through our unique analytical approach, systemic interdependencies between the different root causes have become visible and are providing evidence for humanity functioning as a self-regulating system on earth.

Obviously, all these root causes for the crisis in Europe have, in their combining complexity, spread through the process of globalization and are exerting their impact globally. As a result, the crisis in Europe and the Western-dominated world has led to a crisis that has a global scope. At the same time, we are confronted with a lack of globally valid rules for governance that would enable the nations and international institutions to effectively cope with the crisis. Geopolitics in the age of the hegemonic strive of the US is mainly occupied with the building up of the war machines and armies to drive violent confrontations and wars. At the same time, it is undeniable that the "old" existing structures are breaking up. The forces, that are unconsciously effective in Europe's collective memory[306] and constitutional for its specific mindset, make it difficult for Europe to join in with the ongoing paradigm shift that is characteristic of the present era. This has put Europe in a general crisis mode. The geopolitical initiatives to manage humanity's actions concerning a globally overheating economy, an exponential demographic growth rate, and a generalized destructive

---

[306] We refer with the notion of "collective memory" to the work presented in 1925 by the French philosopher and sociologist Maurice Halbwachs in his book "Les cadres Sociaux de la Mémoire". Since then, this concept of the collective memory has been further analyzed and advanced. As an example, refer to "On the Cultural Constitution of Collective Memory", in 2005, by Qi Wang, researcher in psychology at Cornell University.

pressure on the living environment on earth are lacking efficiency and power. The suggestions and actions of the Western power elites are not convincing the Global South, and they find ever fewer followers. Sustainable solutions to the globally existing problems, which have taken their origin in Europe, are not found. Trust in the Western capabilities to successfully face the various challenges does not build up. Europe and its Western allies are losing steam and are getting out of breath. The Global South, representing the vast majority of the populations and nations on earth, does not consider Europe to be an honest broker anymore. We observe increasing evidence that Europe and the West are losing their last battle. Hence, it is high time for Europe and the Western nations to accept the new situation. They would be well advised to enter into negotiations with the Global South and the great nations of China, India, Russia and Brazil, to reach an honorable and peaceful outcome.

PART THREE

EUROPE'S WAY OUT OF THE CRISIS: PARADIGM SHIFT THROUGH HUMAN ACTION

"... how do I show the fly the way out of the fly-bottle?"

Wittgenstein, Philosophical Investigations,
§309

FOREWORD

In the introductory part of the book, we pointed out that it was not our intention to write a scientific work. Gaining scientific knowledge is not our goal. However, it should have become clear that we have definitely oriented ourselves towards science in our methodological approach. Evidence-based investigations only make sense if it is comprehensible how the respective insights and findings, i.e. the evidence, were obtained.

In the first part of the book, we have pursued a historical reconstruction of political economy as it is relevant for Europe and the EU today. In doing so, we have paid particular attention to the role and interests of the United States. The reasons for this should also have become plausible. In this historical reconstruction, comprising the critical events and facts, we have been able to show how Europe has lost its sovereignty. The role of NATO as the primary political instrument of the USA has been made clear. NATO is an instrument that was conceived to serve the USA by primarily enforcing its hegemonic aspirations, first within the European framework, then gradually expanding to a global scope.

In doing so, we made it clear that the proxy war in Ukraine, as it has been intensively prepared by Europe since 2014 and has been waged since 2022, is the most striking event to date, in which this loss of Europe's sovereignty has become clear. We have also shown that this war is the most emphatic symbol yet of Europe's subordination to US strategic goals. We have seen that Europe's integration into the US strategy, as expressed in NATO's policy, is ultimately the fatal consequence of this integration and subordination to US strategy. Europe has been "incorporated" by the US. Consequently, Europe has been forced by the US to wage wars and subordinate its economic and political interests to those of the US and NATO's war machine. For us, war and the inception of a war economy in Europe are the strongest evidence of the loss of Europe's sovereignty. We consider war the ultimate symbol of the crisis in Europe.

In Part II of our book, we then went one step further, moving progressively away from the analysis of events at the symptomatic level. We asked ourselves what the root causes of the crisis in Europe are, and out of which humus the roots of this crisis in Europe are growing. In doing so, we departed from the symptomatic level in order to go deeper and move towards an epistemological analysis. Our aim has been to conduct the historical and mental reconstruction of the mindset prevalent in the culture of Europe. This was done with the purpose of gaining a more thorough understanding of the roots of the crisis in Europe at the mental and spiritual level. Symptoms were only shown to the extent to which they created evidence for the underlying causes of the crisis in Europe. Here again, we have operated within the scientific framework of a historical reconstruction. In this second part of the study, we asked ourselves what the historical and intellectual roots are, from which the concepts of "progress" and "growth", which are so characteristic of Europe, have emerged. We were able to provide convincing evidence for the decisive role of the one-sided emphasis on scientific and technological progress, which is almost exclusively geared towards material prosperity.

In Part Three of the book, we will build on the results of our foregoing diagnosis of the crisis in Europe. We now want to take on the task of pointing out ways that can enable Europe to emerge from the crisis. We will show that there will be no liberation strike, or a great and singular blow of liberation. Rather, we will point out practical steps that are feasible and, if implemented consistently, will lead to concrete results on the way out of the crisis in the foreseeable future. This liberation from the crisis in Europe will correspond essentially to a transformation, through which the fundamental causes of the crisis will be progressively eliminated. It is not about combating and eliminating the problems at the symptomatic level. We believe that the causes must be tackled at their roots to be eliminated for good and in the long term.

Europe will have to rethink and learn how to recreate the concepts of "progress" and "growth". The one-sided scientific and technical understanding of these terms is the fundamental cause of the crisis in Europe. This transformation, through a new understanding of the two key basic intellectual concepts[307] that are the leading patterns of action for Europe, will eventually also affect the USA. The intellectual and mental framework apply in the same way to the USA, where it has attained its extreme expression. The point is, that Europe and the USA are of the same spirit, they are cut from the same cloth. This is important for understanding the crisis in Europe and for the transformation that must be initiated in order to find a peaceful way out of the crisis.

---

[307] We do not overlook the specific European concept of the "individual" and its "freedom" as a fundamental root of Europe. In our context, this will imply a change of the functioning of the nation state in the long term. The reader will accept that we cannot cover this topic in our book with its limited scope.

In the first chapter of this concluding Part Three of the book, we want to take a cue from Buckminster Fuller to see how his proposal for an "infinite renewal of energy and resources" can be implemented and what the results would be. We can only outline the design for engineering a cybernetic-induced overhaul of spaceship Earth in the context of our book. But the path should become clear. For the details about the procedures, processes and their meaningfulness, the reader should turn to the various writings of Buckminster Fuller, mainly to his book the "Critical Path".

In the second chapter of this concluding part of the book, we will refer to an example that we have identified and developed ourselves. We will show how a social transformation, or paradigm shift, can be initiated with relatively simple means. Here again, we will show that such a transformation cannot be tackled at the symptomatic level. Such transformations and paradigm shifts are ultimately initiated by gradually changing consciousness, followed by awareness of the need for rationally directed change. These are processes that interlink public discussions and communication processes with individual processes for increasing consciousness. Such transformations will consequently lead to conscious actions that make the paradigm shift concrete and ultimately lead to a social and political transformation. As an example for the possibility of initiating a paradigm shift in concrete terms, we have chosen the example of demographic change. We have good reasons to assume that demography has the greatest leverage effect for social and political transformation. All areas of private and public life change with the number of people living in a society. This is even more true at the global level, because there is no way to relieve one's own society at the expense of a neighbor. Demographic changes in each individual society always have an impact on coexistence with other societies. This is the principle of "One world".[308]

---

[308] The principle of "one world" for us is not that all people become equal, do the same thing, or live in the same way. So far, this has been the naivety of Europeans and Americans, who assume that all people will behave culturally like Europeans and Americans. The existing cultural diversity on Earth was overlooked.

Introduction

The wider public has been talking about New Thinking for years. The media talk and write that we need "new minds". Even the "New Man" is called upon again and again. Others speak of the new "image of man.[309] To us, these wishes and demands seem to be fundamentally right and good, because we need new skills in the rapidly changing world and have to adapt our behavior to rapidly changing circumstances. But we also know that the New Man or Woman, or "right" and "different" thinking, cannot be prescribed. The physical man is constantly renewing himself, but a new spiritual man is formed either through spiritual revolutions, as in the Renaissance, or through experiences in lengthy learning and transformation processes. For the individual, this usually requires lifelong learning processes, spiritual renewals or personal transformations.

So we want to ask ourselves how humans, we as humanity, can find our way to "new

[309] In 1968, Arthur Koestler and J. R. Smythies published the volume on the "Revolutionization of the Sciences of Life, The New Image of Man", as a result of the Alpbach Symposium at that time.

thinking" and to correspondingly new actions. - In today's specialist literature on this topic, it is often assumed that there is a difference, or contrast, between linear (convergent) and lateral (divergent) thinking[310]. Mostly, however, these remain philosophical or epistemological considerations. The question of the conditions and prerequisites of how to get from a certain way of thinking, an intellectual or spiritual attitude, to a certain specific is usually ignored. So the crucial question usually remains unmentioned, or is not dealt with in these discussions: how do I get from "right" thinking to "good" action? In the context of our topic, which is about geopolitics, this step, from theory to practice, is of course critical. Because this is where the question of power comes into play. In politics, it is the question of power that must be asked in order to really implement changes and innovations, including "new rules". And then it gets very exciting again, and we are back in the middle of our topic. Because the question of power is about how I deal with my own interests in relation to the interests of others.

[310] Psychologist J. P. Guilford introduced the terms "convergent thinking" and "divergent thinking" in 1956.

Do I want to see the interests of others as equals? Or is it about setting the rules of the game in such a way that my own interests always have absolute priority or even exclusivity in a one-sided way, as in a zero-sum game.

In the following chapter, however, we will not enter into a discussion about theories and philosophies, but we will bring examples and hints that, in our understanding, show how "new thinking" can lead to "different actions" and to new behavior, even in politics. We want to be careful here and therefore do not speak of "right action". For, a human being alone cannot judge about issues in an absolute way, as Immanuel Kant already showed in his treatises on the Categorical Imperative and Practical Reason. But we also do not want to shy away from intellectual honesty, and thus want to live up to what we consider our social and political responsibility. Therefore, we will represent our opinion clearly and openly, also give examples and give indications of what we consider to be "better ways and more sensible actions".

We assume that a change in the way people think and act in our societies would lead to a social paradigm shift[311] . We consider this to be desirable and important in these times of rapid social change and communicative globalization.[312] As we have shown in the previous chapters, geopolitics has been shaped for more than a hundred years according to a pattern that is one-sidedly Western, and tends to be Anglo-American. Within the framework of this kind of geopolitics, the world no longer seems to be able to escape these "eternal wars". Therefore, a paradigm shift must be induced that allows the nations and peoples on earth

---

[311] The term paradigm shift was coined by Thomas S. Kuhn in 1962 and refers to "the change of fundamental framework conditions", whereby Kuhn in his work primarily refers to the scientific-theoretical and scientific-historical context by tracing and analyzing the process of change in fundamental framework conditions for individual scientific theories. In his book, he showed how paradigm shifts take place in the scientific field, what laws such a paradigm shift of rethinking and other actions follows. Since that time, the term has been used in many areas and can now be considered popular.

[312] Independent observers, we will lead the Club of Rome, Buckminster Fuller and Gregory Bateson, have been citing the three most important challenges facing humanity for decades: wars, resource scarcity together with climate change, rapid demographic growth.

to interact according to different, new rules. New thinking and acting are therefore important for all of us to escape this negative spiral[313] of violence and war.[314]

ACTIONS LEADING TO A PARADIGM SHIFT

In the following chapters, we do not only intend to call for a paradigm shift in politics and the shaping of our societies[315]. In fact, our

[313] On the topic of the scope of action and the spirals of action, we also refer to the following source: an interview with Wolfgang Streeck, from the Max Planck Institute for the Study of Societies, about the scope of action of states.
https://www.mpg.de/6360276/handlungsspielraum_de s_staates.

[314] In the tradition of modern psychoanalysis, Arno Gruen, for example, shows this need for action and shows ways out of this "psycho trap". Alienated from Life, 2019, Arno Grün. see also, Christoph Bördlein, Introduction to Behavioral Analysis. 1st edition, 2015.

[315] The term paradigm shift was coined by Thomas S. Kuhn in 1962 and refers to "the change of fundamental framework conditions", whereby Kuhn in his work primarily refers to the scientific-theoretical and scientific-historical context by tracing and analyzing the process of change in fundamental framework conditions for individual scientific theories. In his book, he showed how paradigm shifts take place in the

primary aim is to show how a paradigm shift can be put into action. This will require overcoming obstacles such as attitudes, prejudices and ideologies, which hinder and prevent the redesign of social processes. At the same time, we want to use examples to show how rules have been changed in social interaction and in politics, and have finally led to new and better results. Our powerful and governing elites have brought us into difficult situations in several areas of life. We live in an age of permanent and general crises, [316]because these elites pretend that their thoughts and actions are the only right ones. Notwithstanding the deepening crisis situation, they do not change their minds to escape their ideological trap and still want us to follow their rules. We no longer agree with this, which is why we would like to call here to openly question and redefine the currently

scientific field and what laws such a paradigm shift of rethinking and other actions follows. Since that time, the term has been used in many areas and can now be considered popular.

[316] In a guest article for the Federal Association "Energy, Water, Life", Christian Schuldt, 2021, writes about the "age of crises". In an article in the FAZ of 15.05.2022, Philipp Krohn asks "Permanent turning points and new crises - how do we endure it?"

applicable rules for the future shaping of our societies and for living together on our earth. We want to use examples to show that other ways, alternative solutions and other paradigms of political action and the shaping of social coexistence are possible.

We are aware that such a paradigm shift in political thought and action, as we are calling for, would lead to social change, i.e. to a social transformation with far-reaching social consequences, if implemented consistently, which would affect practically all areas of people's public and private lives.

Of course, we also know that change and transformation are always associated with new challenges and risks. This is also the reason why people usually shy away from change. This fear of change is innate in us. [317] It is therefore only natural that significant

---

[317] In his studies, Konrad Lorenz has demonstrated in detail that "fear of change" is part of the basic equipment of the human psyche and human behavior. He was convinced that "for eons of time in natural history, those who were most afraid had the best chance of survival." On the subject of fear, see also Fritz Riemann: Basic Forms of Fear. A depth psychological study. 10th revised and extended edition (52nd–63rd thousand), Munich, Basel 1975.

social forces and individuals are afraid of a social paradigm shift[318] and want to prevent it as much as possible. Out of fear of change and the inherent risks, opportunities for social transformation are faded out and usually not seen, or suppressed and not seized.[319] As with all major changes, there are people and forces who have an interest in maintaining the *status quo*, i.e. who resist change. The reason for rejecting a paradigm shift is therefore a natural fear of change, or the fear of having to give up one's own interests and losing previous claims. This is completely normal and does not fundamentally call into question our intention or the importance of our examples. As we have learned from psychology, fears and anxieties should not be suppressed, because, in one way or another, they will come to light in often destructive ways and in the form of aggression. Fears and anxieties can be consciously overcome, and

[318] The Anglicism "paradigm shift" is also often used in German. We use paradigm shift and paradigm shift synonymously here.

[319] In Germany, Karl Steinbuch published good and stimulating books on the subject decades ago. To start with, I would like to mention "Wrongly Programmed: On the Failure of Our Society in the Present and Before the Future, 1968.

the energy that has been released by such consciously managed processes to combat anxieties and fears, may then be used sensibly for processes of change and creativity.[320] If we apply this consideration to the political sphere, then we would say that the energy and costs that we spent for many years on conflicts and wars, could be used much better and more sensibly to improve people's living conditions. Hence, our proposal for a constructive paradigm shift, which would bring huge benefits to all of us, except for those who can see their salvation solely in the selfish pursuit of profit and the pursuit of hegemonic power.

By paradigm shift, we mean the change to a fundamentally new pattern of thought that will lead to a change in familiar reflexes and ways of acting and to taking a new path based on new rules related to social processes and political action. A paradigm shift is often compared to a quantum leap.[321] This points to

[320] see h. Heinz W. Krohne: "Psychologie der Angst", in 2010.

[321] The physicist Prof. Dr. Markolf Niemz speaks of the meaningfulness and social necessity of a "spiritual quantum leap". https://spirit-online.de/ein-spiritueller-quantensprung.html.

the magnitude of the actual challenge. A paradigm shift is not easy, but we will show that it is basically feasible.

We should also mention here that not every paradigm shift will automatically be meaningful and good in itself. One negative paradigm was certainly the globally widespread smoking of cigarettes that began to spread in the 19th and, in particular, the 20th century. This paradigm prevailed, spread through intensive advertising[322], especially after the First World War. The American tobacco industry earned huge sums of money from this. At the same time, however, many people suffered considerable damage to their health. So, what applies for cybernetics and system thinking is also valid for a paradigm shift: without the right rules, a lot or everything will go wrong. As says Gregory Bateson: the rules have to change. And we would add: rules have to be changed in free and open debates, in *a competition for better ideas*, where not power and profit are the decisive factors.

---

[322] Today, the "Marlboro Man" has almost completely disappeared from the public eye.

Every paradigm shift begins with first steps, which are often taken by individual personalities [323]who, in the face of a challenge, recognize the usefulness of alternative approaches[324]. Following such a first step of increasing awareness, additional ingredients are required. It takes courage to make conscious decisions. Finally, we have to

---

[323] The years-long struggle of European physicists over the understanding and interpretation of quantum mechanics and quantum theory, about the quantum leap in physics, is described very insightfully by Thomas Hürter in his book "The Age of Uncertainty", 2021. A paradigm shift is therefore not a matter of course. In the book by Thomas Kuhn mentioned above, the prerequisites for the success of such processes can be understood.

In the political sphere, we dare to mention Mahatma Gandhi here, who, through his courage, his personal example, but also through his perseverance, finally forced the British Empire to end the occupation of India. The "naked fakir," as Churchill called him, had managed to encourage the Indian people to shake off British rule.

[324] For an introduction to the question of social and political paradigm shift, we recommend the conversation, published in issue 16, Sozialimpulse 4/10, with Roland Benedikter, Stanford University. The questions were asked by Thomas Stöckli, MA, Director of the Institute for Practice-Oriented Research, Solothurn, Switzerland.

recognize that only charismatic leadership can induce processes, i.e. lead people to consistently implement the knowledge gained to finally create new patterns of action. Such a decisive first step has been overdue for decades in politics in Europe and, from a global perspective, also for the USA[325].

[325] We will be told that European unification means a paradigm shift in German politics. We agree with this assertion insofar as we accept it for the policy of European integration with its so-called four 'freedoms', which concern the free movement of persons, goods, services and capital.

As we have been able to show in the previous chapters of this book, however, the paradigm shift that we demand for the fundamentally "better functioning" of our societies has not yet been seen and implemented by the EU. Freedom and sovereignty are indispensable prerequisites for the formulation of meaningful rules for shaping our societies. However, the EU, on the other hand, has become embroiled in wars and unprecedented dimensions of political and economic dependencies by subordinating itself to the interests of the US and NATO.

Part Three
Europe's Way Out of the Crisis: the Overdue Paradigm Shift

Chapter 1

The new paradigm: Infinite Regeneration of Energy and Resources

"... humanity now – for the first time in history, has the realistic opportunity to help evolution to do what it is inexorably intent on doing: converting all humanity into one harmonious world family and making that family sustainingly, economically successful."[326]

Buckminster Fuller in the foreword to "Critical Path", from 1981, on page XIX

"Therefore, our "main engine", the life-regenerating process, must operate exclusively on our vast daily energy income from the powers of wind, tide, water, and the direct Sun radiation energy".

Buckminster Fuller, in his "Operating Manual for Spaceship Earth, 1969

---

[326] R. Buckminster Fuller in the preface to his late work "Critical Path", from 1981, on page XIX.

Introduction

In the Vedic literature, which is considered to be the oldest written source of human knowledge, the pupil that is coming to his master to learn the scriptures and sacred books has to bring "fuel" with him to entertain the fire in his master's house. Energy and food are considered essential elements for entertaining the human being. In acknowledging this age-old knowledge, we will start Part Three of our book concerning the overdue paradigm shift with a short chapter on the "Infinite Regeneration of Energy and Resources". This is also to say that we do not intend to reinvent the wheel. Rather, we will use knowledge and wisdom available for orientation of our actions.

The "new paradigm" that is emerging will have to be shaped by our understanding of our world as a holistic and living being. The new paradigm will start with human beings that are liberating themselves from the bonds of old creeds and outdated paradigms. These liberated humans will become ready to take responsibility for life on planet Earth, even if he or she is aware that there will be no definite and final goal for the journey of humanity. In his book "Hope or Barbarism", Lewis Mumford made a courageous attempt to "create a new myth"[327] and describe the contours of an upcoming "world culture". In doing so, he places himself in the tradition of the Renaissance of Leonardo da Vinci, who at the beginning of this new epoch of humanity indicated the contours of a utopia, an image of the future human being, who has the ability and the will to set out in search of liberation from earthly shackles, while fitting in with the spirit of nature and cosmic laws.[328] According to the image of the human being of the Renaissance and of Leonardo da Vinci, humanity must further its scientific and technical skills in a complementary approach with the arts and directed by humanistic social action. During the Renaissance, the attitude prevailed that this development of

[327] "Hope or Barbarism," 1981, p. 11, Lewis Mumford. The original American edition of "The Transformation of Man" is from 1956.
[328] An easily readable, yet profound insight into this development since Galileo and through the Renaissance to the present day can be found in the small booklet "What does the world of tomorrow look like?", which was written by the quantum physicist Pascual Jordan in 1958 from a Christian-Protestant point of view.

humanity must go together with the spiritual development of the human being, out of which the new, modern human being would then arise. It was assumed, that through the ever-developing cooperation of intellectual (science) and spiritual (consciousness) all its talents, the human being would be prepared to place himself as a freely human actor and creator in the center, taking consciously responsibility for life on earth.[329] This was the idea of modern man, that was at the origin of a new, upcoming humanity in the Renaissance. In the perspective of our book, we would express this with the formula that the liberated human beings will have to write a new myth about humanity as a unit. Such a myth will go far beyond the image of the "One World". Such a myth will prepare the ground for a new era in which peoples and nations will work together for a shared future. People and nations will each create their own individual interpretations of the myth of a new humanity. Humanity will continue to use

[329] To understand Leonardo da Vinci's image of man, we recommend reading the historical novel "Leonardo da Vinci" by Dmitri Mereschkowski. Jacob Burckhardt, with his "Culture of the Renaissance in Italy", can also give us important insights again and again.

different languages but will learn to speak with one voice, when it comes to matters of global interest.

As we have already shown and will explore even deeper, this image of the humanistic human being, i.e. the holistic, intellectually educated, spiritually oriented and artistically inspired human being, was displaced over time. It was replaced by the ideal image of the exclusive scientific and technically educated human being. This self-education of modern man led over time to the one-sided materialistic world view through the development of the natural sciences in the 19th century. This educative process led to the "Man without Qualities" of Robert Musil, a mathematician, trapped in a hopeless search for orientation in a changing world. This one-dimensional scientific-technically educated man of intellectual knowledge was then increasingly completed by the one-sidedly profit-oriented merchant and entrepreneur.[330] This double-rooted man of

---

[330] This new figure in the European menagerie was brought on stage by Shakespeare with the "Merchant of Venice" with striking historical and cultural insights on developments, such as the establishment of the East India Company in 1606.

the Renaissance has over time become the modern European, whom we may see as a man caught in a *double-bind*[331], or we may else call him the "modern man in search of his soul"[332]. It seems that the *double-bind* pathology of modern man arises out of his fear that he will not be able to correspond to the image of the ideal modern man. This leads to the horrible fear of becoming either mad, poor, or both at the same time. The fight for dominance has brought Europe and the US a temporary relief from that fear. It is an engagement that seemingly preserves the old self-image for a while, as it provides satisfaction through the gain of power and money. As we know, this flight of responsibility is a futile undertaking in the long term.

[331] This term was coined by Gregory Bateson and his colleagues, when they understood that schizophrenia was not necessarily inborn, but was often a mental disorder grown out of the helplessness of a person being victim of a cognitive trap, a double-bind, of which he could not escape, whatever way he chose.

[332] This is the title C.G. Jung gave to one of his books that had initially not been published in his German native language.

INFINITE REGENERATION AND THE MIRACLE OF GROWTH IN NATURE

In the following chapters, we will show step by step that there exist ways for modern man to leave this fear behind, of not being good enough to fulfil the challenges of modern life.

In springtime, in the temperate zones of the earth, we can all experience this miracle of growth again and again. The power of nature makes itself felt everywhere, breaks through, shows itself in its irrepressible work, and casts a spell over us all. In the tropics, this infinite flow of energy can be experienced all year round. This experience gives the impression of powers, of life forces, that have the potential of growth without end. This growth of nature seems limitless. It will be worth taking a closer look at this phenomenon.

Buckminster Fuller calls this natural force "infinitely regenerative".[333] For him, this force of nature is of cosmic origin. It is therefore infinitely available to earth and infinitely

[333] For Buckminster Fuller, we recommend his late work "Critical Path" from 1981. In German, he also borrowed the "Instruction Manual for Spaceship Earth", published in English in 1969 as the "Operating Manual for Spaceship Earth".

regenerative.[334] The cosmos lives of this infinitely regenerative force and unfolds in it completely. Einstein made the paradoxical statement for the universe that it is finite, but unbounded. It seems important that humans grasp the essence of Einstein's insight to transfer it to their understanding of nature. Doing this, we will learn to live with paradoxes and to appreciate the functioning of open systems. This will help us to understand that, on the one hand, "energy" is "infinitely renewable", i.e. it is available to us without end and in unlimited, cosmic quantities. At the same time, however, we must also learn to understand that this infinitely renewable energy does not necessarily lead to unlimited growth of all natural elements. Nature takes an infinitely nuanced approach to life and creates an infinite variety of forms and species. Nature keeps herself all the opportunities open. This challenges people and humanity to make a

[334] This also refers to the statement from Einstein's general theory of relativity, where we learn that *space-time* has an inner *curved* structure and therefore the universe is finite but unlimited. Such a conclusion could also be drawn for "energy", which is "infinitely renewable" but does not necessarily lead to unlimited growth of all elements.

choice again and again. Nothing remains static or fixed in life. Humanity has to take decisions in line with nature's universal principles.

Let us deepen the understanding of these thoughts a little more and take a brief look at what we call "growth" in nature. It seems to be without limits. But does this always apply to all growth processes?

A grass or herb grows. It reaches a certain length and size, then it stops growing. It may form seeds, or roots and bulbs for propagation, i.e. to regenerate after a certain time. But its growth is not unlimited. The same applies to a tree. An oak or acorn tree may reach a very stately size, but when it has exhausted its natural potential, it stops growing. Yes, after some time it even begins to degenerate and decays to finally die to return to earth.

The same can be said in a slightly modified form for the human body. It grows, forms its organs, reaches its fully formed size and shape around the age of 28. It has thus reached a limit. From then on, it renews itself for a certain number of years. But the degradation of the human or animal body is inevitable, it ages, and after its physical death, when the life-spirit has departed from it, it dissolves completely and becomes earth again.

As we can see from these few examples, growth in nature always has limits. This even applies to the human disease "cancer", which strives to continually grow and proliferate. However, cancer will finally not succeed, because it finally "dies" together with its victim.

These considerations lead us further to a distinction to be made between the human mind and intellect, compared to the natural growth of physical objects. The laws for growth seem to be different for the intellect and mind compared to physical objects. Not only are the regenerative powers of human intellect and mind potentially unlimited, but the same is true of their growth[335]. We learn

[335] Rudolf Steiner, in his lecture "Light and Love" (GA 143, p. 209), makes the interesting, theological remark that, in his view, God can be neither omniscient nor omnipotent. This contradicts the principle of human freedom. If God were omniscient and omnipotent, then man would not be able to develop freely, which, according to Steiner, corresponds to his divine mission. According to Buckminster Fuller, this is the cosmic

relatively early in life that there is always more to learn, more to know and to understand. As we grow older, or more mature, sometimes both go together. In old age we appreciate, still more than in young age, that there seem to be no limits to mental growth, not only that which is built on intelligence, but especially on the growth of mental and spiritual powers.[336]

In this sense, then, in terms of intelligence and intellectually accessible knowledge, human growth seems to be unlimited. At any rate, this is how we perceive it. It is this fact that is misleading and bringing confusion. We erroneously want to generalize the power and potential for growth, be it material or mental. Growth is thus regarded as unlimited at all times and in any case. However, this is a logical error, a kind of "logical fallacy" that we fall for.

We will have to learn that not everything has to or will grow infinitely, and we will have to adjust our human actions accordingly. Human

mission of humanity.

[336] Already in Chuang Dzi "The True Book of the Southern Blossom Land", 2007, translated by Richard Wilhelm, we read on p. 64, Book III, 1: "Our life is finite; knowledge is infinite".

beings can decide on growth, or on limits of growth, depending on specific situations and the objects. Humanity will have to decide on the use and application of cosmic energy. This is part of the role that humans are playing on earth, with earth being part of the cosmos and its universal principles. We will have to learn to take decisions as one humanity, in common and consciously. This corresponds to our cosmic mission, in the view of Buckminster Fuller.

At this point, we would like to expressly note that with these statements, we do not contradict in any way the epistemology of Gregory Bateson, as he described it in his book "Spirit and Nature: A Necessary Unity".[337] On the contrary, we agree with him that the energy available for evolutionary development on earth is infinite, since it comes from the sun and from the cosmos. Likewise, there are no limits to intellectual and intellectual growth, in principle. We also agree that no object in nature can grow indefinitely[338]. Limits to growth are also set by

[337] "Spirit and Nature. A Necessary Unity", 1987, Gregory Bateson.
[338] The Veda teaches that all things composed will decay and will have to die one day.

the fact that there are numerous objects in nature that can only retain their existence, if they are not eliminated and extinguished by other objects. There is always exchange and interdependency among different elements and processes. Hence, the end of life of one living being will lead to the death of other living beings. There exists no single "thing" without interdependent relations to other things or energies. In the 1920s, Niels Bohrand Heisenberg, together with their colleagues, discovered and formulated the fundamental principle of complementarity, which has an essential function for "the success of the eternally regenerative universe".[339] The "thing-in-itself" exists only in the imagination of philosophers. In the life of man and his societies, as well as in nature, all things and forces are always in a necessarily complementary relationship.[340]

---

[339] We quote here from the introductory passages of the foreword to "Critical Path", 1981, by Buckminster Fuller. The translation is by us / WP.
[340] S. h. Fortes, Meyer; The Political Systems of the Tallensi of the Northern Territories of the Gold Coast, in African Political Systems, M. Fortes and E. E. Evans-Pritchard (eds.), First Edition 1940.

This principle also applies to other African societies, as has in detail been shown in the ethnographic monography „Ronga – Ein Beispiel politischer Komplementarität", 1987, Walter Pfluger.

PART THREE

EUROPE'S WAY OUT OF THE CRISIS:
THE OVERDUE PARADIGM SHIFT

Chapter 2

The End of Linear Solutions in Politics

Problems can never be solved with the same mindset that created them.

Albert Einstein

CRISIS, THE CHANCE FOR NEW HAPPINESS

For many decades, the great fear of "demographic change" has been spread by our power elites among the public in Europe and many other countries. This issue was highlighted as "particularly urgent" even by the WEF (World Economic Forum) in its infamous study on the "Re-set" of the world order[341]. We take the following warning from the WEF's Global Risk Report 2024: "Just as natural ecosystems can be pushed to the limit and become something fundamentally new; such systemic shifts are also taking place across other spheres: geostrategic, demographic and technological".[342] The risks listed are then referred to as structural forces. This report therefore assumes that these structural forces pose global risks to "structural conditions". You don't really get smart when reading these circular statements. However, the decisive factor for us here is that, from the WEF's point of view, "demographic factors" probably pose major risks to humanity.

In the document "Demographic Change and Sustainability" that has been published by the United Nations Population Fund (UNPF) in 2024, you will find a relatively well pondered

---

[341] It says: "Powerful economic, demographic and technological forces are creating a new balance of power".

[342] Our translation: "Just as natural ecosystems are pushed to their limits and can become something fundamentally new; Such systemic shifts are also taking place in other areas: geostrategic, demographic and technological."

reflection on concerns about both "overpopulation" and "underpopulation". We have to bear in mind that policies in Europe, until to date, are talking of "overpopulation", when it comes to Africa and the "developing world", while they are warning of the decreasing population in Europe as a threat of "extinction" and decline. This one-sided point of view, generalized at present in Europe, is our point of departure in this book. The fact that this point of view is almost universally accepted, is a further proof of the need for humanity to liberate herself from the one-sided Western world view. Humanity is challenged today to accept different thinking and learn from different worldviews coming from different cultures.

In Europe and the West, we take it for granted that this issue of "demographic change" is considered universally critical. Its impact seems well known in the wide circles of the global power elites. Due to its difficult ideological and emotional connotations, however, the topic is usually rarely covered openly in public in terms of content.[343]

[343] It is noteworthy that the topic of demography emerged with a negative connotation during the so-called Corona pandemic. There were "experts" who

Demographic change in Europe is usually presented as a threatening fact for our societies. When the topic is dealt with or discussed, it usually has a negative connotation. Demographic development seems to pose major challenges and even bring risks for the world. Demography is in these public debates in Europe, if they take place, usually directly related to "aging", with a low birth rate and the threat of "downfall". We will, in contrast, show in this chapter that "demographic change" can be a great blessing for all of us, if we meet the challenge with a meaningful paradigm shift[344] that positively affects our social and political thinking and actions. To show the advantages as well as the feasibility of this paradigm shift concerning demographic change in Europe is

were of the opinion that such pandemics would ultimately lead to the "natural" regulation of population growth. When the AIDS virus emerged, similar discussions began. We do not join these discussions because they are often racially motivated.

[344] As already mentioned, not every paradigm shift is "automatically" meaningful and good. The paradigm shift is like cybernetics: it's about changing the rules, setting them in such a way that they result in advantages for the vast majority.

the major purpose of this chapter in this book.

One thing seems obvious to us. If we[345] want to turn demographic change into a blessing, then we must not flee from this challenge into a one-sided policy of unchecked population growth and give in to the demand for more and more "skilled" workers, as has been the case up to now. As we will see later, this kind of industrial and social policy, which was characteristic of the industrialized countries in the last century, is built on fundamental fallacies that have consequently led to major mistakes and problems, not only for us in Europe, but also for most other countries on earth.

We will show that it would be much better to meet this challenge of "demographic change" with courage and intelligence in order to initiate a fundamental paradigm shift[346]. As

[345] The WEF Risk Report speaks of "demographic bifurcation". A definition for this term is attached. But what the term really means for demographic development is not clear. It seems to be a kind of "Orwellian" language formation, i.e. "Newspeak", to pretend to have great expertise.

[346] It is known, for example, that birth growth decreases at the moment when societies allow for

the saying goes: *Every crisis offers the chance for new happiness*.

The following proposal is not revolutionary, and it does not call for an uprising or a general strike. Rather, it is intended to raise questions that, if answered, could lead to a better understanding of the circumstances, as well as to a process of social transformation[347], as a meaningful contribution to shaping a better future for all of us. In this sense, we are showing more courage than the WEF, which makes general statements in its risk report[348],

higher prosperity, better education and greater self-determination for women. – But as long as the intellectual and material resources of humanity are used primarily for the production of weapons and for waging wars, these goals will not be achievable

[347] To clarify the term, we would like to briefly note here that by "paradigm shift", we mean a fundamental change in a certain area of social life, whereby, in connection with such a change, new forms of thought, new views on things, and the world emerge. Transformation is a rather general concept that is specifically formulated depending on the field, from mathematics to chemistry.

[348] The WEF report refers solely to problems in the "labor market". Of course, this is banal and, in our understanding, does not go far enough in view of the global challenges. We call this the thinking of "bean counters."

without offering practical indications for creative solutions to global challenges.[349]

We have chosen this topic of "demographic change" deliberately, because a paradigm shift in this area would have the greatest leverage effect[350] for a sustainable improvement in social conditions and for the quality of life for all people, in Europe. What applies to Europe also holds for people in other countries and societies on our planet.

With our call for a paradigm shift, we will often refer to Germany and Europe as the frame of reference, because that is where our home and origins were at the time we wrote this essay. However, we should be clear that what we say about Germany and Europe applies to many other countries in one way or another. After all, our call for a paradigm shift is not about "empirical" details. These serve as illustrations. We call for a paradigm shift, i.e. for a fundamental change and adaption of

[349] The recommendations in the WEF study are limited to the labor market. Hence, the focus is on profits, nothing more. How creative, this WEF!

[350] In American business jargon, this is called "the highest leverage". Today, one would say, "How can I best use my resources", or "How can I achieve more, with less".

new rules, to induce and guide future social and political processes in such a way that they lead to improving the well-being of all people. The interest of such a paradigm shift is not to increase power and profits for the self-proclaimed power and financial elites. It is also important to note that, according to our understanding, our statements about new rules only make sense, if they can be applied by other people and in other countries, in principle. We deliberately wish to avoid a Eurocentric view.

In the spirit of our argumentation, we want to tie in with the demand for a policy for a better quality of life, which was proposed for Germany in 1972 by the then Chancellor Willy Brandt[351]. In doing so, he called for a necessary paradigm shift in order to replace old, outdated ideas of politics that are solely oriented towards the growth of the gross national product (GDP). The aim of this new approach was to put policy on a new, sustainable and humane footing. In doing so, we refer at the same time to an international discussion that has since been set in motion

---

[351] Developed together with Olof Palme and other members of European governments and parties.

about how "quality of life" should be determined.[352]

We all know that Germany, together with the Netherlands, is still one of the countries with the highest population density in the world. Therefore, in our view, it is an error to promote population growth in these countries even further, while at the same time warning that other countries have high population growth, which is considered unsustainable, and which they should therefore correct. We believe that it would be better to take the current situation as an opportunity to rethink our options and to launch ourselves in a paradigm shift to see how we can live well, and may live even better, with a decreasing population density. This is, as we see it, the way of the future on our planet.

Just as the age of industrialization has ended for most countries in the world, and we are going down the path of knowledge societies, we will also have to regard exponential population growth as a temporary historical development.

---

[352] An overview of this discussion can be found here: https://de.wikipedia.org/wiki/Lebensqualit%C3%A4t

The fallacy we have fallen with Bentham's "the greatest happiness principle" is that happiness for humanity would increase with the number of people. This is the capitalist's reading of this principle. Today, we understand that this interpretation is no longer valid in our time. It has turned into its opposite and has proven wrong and misleading. Intuitively grasped, this interpretation of Bentham's "the greatest happiness principle" was still valid until the time of the first assembly lines in Ford car production. In 1913, Henry Ford developed the first flexible assembly line and revolutionized the industrial production process with his T-Model. This assembly line was located in Michigan, USA, and laid the foundation for industrial series production around the world. By this time at the latest, it had become clear that the old principle no longer applied, according to which more people are needed for the increase of industrial production. It could have become clear by that time to everyone that intellectual, scientific and technical progress in creating better and more efficient assembly lines and production facilities was the critical factor for greater industrial production. This is what we call the application of technological potential to constantly increase productivity.

Why, then, was it that the potential paradigm shift did not happen? – We will just refer here to one important point that will demonstrate capitalist thinking that is one-sidedly interested in increasing profits at the expense of social long term costs. The point is that more workers at the assembly line represent more consumers. Hence, the more workers operate at the assembly line, the more of his cars Ford could sell. We may recall that with the assembly lines for industrial production, the era of "consumer capitalism" was inaugurated. The potential growth for capitalist investment made a great leap forward during the following decades.

From that time on, this erroneous belief in the necessity of demographic growth has turned increasingly negative in its effects. With the assembly line production in more and more industrial sectors, energy and resource consumption also grew exponentially. Demographic growth grew in parallel at an exponential rate. This was the time, when the pressure on the living environment strongly increased in all industrialized countries. One may think of the "Dust Bowl" in the Great Plains of the USA, which happened right after the Great Depression. This was in the US during the time of President Roosevelt and the New Deal, a huge social program supposedly to "alleviate the plight of poor and displaced farmers". In fact, a huge migration to cities took place, and former landowners became wage dependent workers. In the Great Deal, the environmental degradation has been addressed for the first time in US history.

In consideration of these various facts, we understand that at this point in time, at the beginning of the 20th century, a historical *tipping point*, has been slept through by the "sleepwalkers in the modern states". There was a lack of intellectual understanding, and probably also a lack of courage, that prohibited a paradigm shift. The absolute priority attributed to the individualistic capitalist quest for ever more profits through ever greater investments was leading to ever-increasing social and environmental pressure. At the same time, the era of the interventionist, social democratic style of state, was increasingly taking pace.

With his ingenious intuition and based on his training as an engineer, R. Buckminster Fuller perceived the deeper sense of these events and their impact on human life. In his "Critical Path" and in other books, such as the "Crunch of Giants", he sheds light on the interests that have led the US on the wrong path with ever-increasing resource and land consumption, combined with high demographic growth. Buckminster Fuller shares our point of view and agrees with us, that the Ford assembly line was the historical *bifurcation* or *tipping point* that has been overlooked deliberately in favor of further inhibited capitalist growth through increasing consumer consumption.

Buckminster Fuller went even further in this understanding of the necessary paradigm shift in industrial production. As early as 1938, he coined the term *ephemerialization*.[353] It refers to the potential of technological progress to "achieve more and more with less and less, until you can finally do everything with nothing", i.e. an accelerated increase in efficiency in order to achieve the same or more output (products, services, information,

[353] Buckminster Fuller in "Nine Chains to the Moon", 1938. He further refines this concept in his Critical Path and also uses it in his "Spaceship Earth".

etc.) and at the same time spend less input (effort, time, material, resources, etc.).

The application of materials and technologies in modern mobile phones compared to older computers and phones is an example of the concept and application of *ephemerialization*. Ephemerialization leads to an increase in efficiency through technological progress. With the use of fewer materials, higher efficiency is achieved, while at the same time, greater benefits for the users are obtained. For the customer, this means more functionality at lower costs. For the production process, this means that resource and energy consumption are reduced. These are the basics of "Bucky" Fuller's vision of design science, as he saw it. He expected that judicious use of technological progress could lead to an ever-increasing standard of living for an ever-growing population[354]. In doing so, he argued fundamentally against Malthus' theory, according to which humanity, which

[354] We should note here that R. Buckminster Fuller saw strong demographic growth as a fundamental problem for the current situation of humanity, but he assumed that it would level off through enlightenment, education and a generally better self-awareness of humanity, leading progressively towards self-control.

has the inborn tendency to grow continuously, has only limited resources at its disposal. In the social sphere, the further development of Buckminster Fuller's ideas, in combination with cybernetic thinking, has led to the concept of societies that develop according to the principle of "self-organizing systems".[355]

At this point, at the latest, you can see, why we are calling for the "end of linear solutions". Our reference to Buckminster Fuller and the other examples mentioned make it clear that progress in industry is primarily achieved through intellectual revolutions and the consistent, courageous and intelligent implementation of new ideas leading to new paradigms. On the other hand, our politicians are looking for the continuation of familiar approaches and linear solutions due to their outdated understanding of progress and growth. We characterize this narrow-minded

[355] Refer to Francis Heylighen, "Accelerating Evolution", 2007, in Modelski, Tessaleno and Thompson William (eds.) of "Globalization as evolutionary process: Modelling global change. Rethinking Globalizations, London 2007. Other ideas in this direction have been developed in particular by Alvin Tofler, e.g. in "Revolutionary Wealth", 2006.

attitude by saying: *they just continue to muddle along, as always*. This attitude towards upcoming challenges is merely looking for outdated functionalist solutions, in which there is always "a little more of the same". If we want to come to further reaching and sustainable solutions to our social and political challenges, then the rules according to which the "games" are played, must urgently be changed in social as well as in political life and work. Sincere integrity is required in the sense of cybernetics and the consequent application of systems thinking. Only through the formulation and subsequent application of new rules can social and political systems function in new ways to effectively meet the challenges of the modern world. As C. G. Jung has explained, one major characteristic of the functioning of the Western world is its continuous drive for change. The Western mindset, with its strong egocentric and science- and technology-driven formation, is oriented towards rapid technological, but also to continuous social and political change. A rather fast rhythm of life, and even unrest, are characteristic expressions of the specificities of the Western mind.[356] However, politics with our power elites is always running behind this continuous change. As the poet Rimbaud remarked in 1873 in his "Une Saison en Enfer" (A season in Hell): Science is never fast enough. It always comes too late and understands processes only with hindsight. This is characteristic of politics, operating at the symptomatic level, but never going to the roots of the challenges.

Following the experience of the First World War and the mass killings of people, Europe should have turned to a new paradigm in the field of demography. Today, wars are waged using unmanned drones and supersonic missiles that are controlled and fired from great distances. The technocratic answers, which repeatedly tell us that the earth can "bear" 15, 20, or more billion people and that technically "everything is feasible", fall short here. The challenge for our future on earth is not about what we can do, it's about what we want and how we wish to live. These words directly indicate that we are talking here

[356] A summary of details on the specificities of the Western mind is presented in "The Origins and History of Consciousness", published in 1949, by Erich Neumann. It was first published in English in 1954.

about a change of the mindset in Europe, that is narrow-minded and focusing on results and quantitative outcome. We talk about attaining a higher level of consciousness. This is where, according to C. G. Jung, the real challenge for Europe and her people lies. We agree with C. G. Jung that such a transformation will, like any birth of a new being, require time and patience, and will probably not be achieved without pain and sacrifice.

However, help for Europe will not come from heaven. The transformation depends on our growing will and consciousness. The help and support from friends and partners will certainly further the process. Open dialogue with friends and partners will prevent us from making too many mistakes or going astray.

The big question Europe has to ask herself is: How do we want to live? We understand now that the answer must align with new rules in order to create and shape new social and political systems that are coherent with the well-being of all people on this planet.

We can only get meaningful, far-reaching and sustainable answers to this question, if we change our thought patterns and gradually build a new mindset in order to establish new rules that will guide our future social and political actions.

DEMOGRAPHIC CHANGE: THE GREAT OPPORTUNITY FOR A PARADIGM SHIFT

We will now return concretely to the challenge of taking demographic change as an opportunity for to seize on our way to new happiness. As indicated, "demographic change" is considered the optimum entry point for our impulse to bring the politics of linear solutions in Europe to an end. Population policy has the highest potential for a successful transformation of societies in Europe.[357] A fundamental change in demographic policies has the potential to demonstrate the validity of a paradigm shift in politics in Europe. It will pave the way and prepare for the end of linear solutions in politics[358]. If implemented consistently, such a paradigm shift would certainly have far-

[357] Presumably, this topic is relevant for all highly developed societies. It also offers an approach for countries such as China and India, where the challenges posed by population growth are well known and are part of the political agenda.

418

reaching social and political consequences that would affect practically all areas of the public and private lives of people in Europe. As we will show, demography is the social factor that exerts the greatest leverage effect on public and private life.[359] At the same time,

[358] The term paradigm shift was coined by Thomas S. Kuhn in 1962 and refers to "the change of fundamental framework conditions", whereby Kuhn in his work primarily refers to the scientific-theoretical and scientific-historical context by tracing and analyzing the process of change in fundamental framework conditions for individual scientific theories. In his book, he showed how paradigm shifts take place in the scientific field, what laws such a paradigm shift of rethinking and other actions follows. Since that time, the term has been used in many calculations and can now be considered popular.

[359] Demography, i.e. the composition and dynamics of population development, has an impact on practically all areas of life in modern societies. This can be gleaned from the following books, which shed light on the different aspects of demography: The Power of Demography: and How It Explains the Modern World, Paul Morland, 2019. The population discourse. Demographic Knowledge and Political Power, Diana Hummel, October 2000. Environment, Population Pressure and Economic Growth in Developing Countries, Burkhard Heer, October 2013. Empty Planet: The Shock of Global Population Decline, Darrell Bricker and John Ibbitson, 2019

a fundamental change in our attitude towards demographics would produce results in a short time span. Considerable effects would be felt by almost everybody already within one generation.

It is only natural that, out of fear of change, leading forces and people have not seen the enormous potential of demographic change and have not wanted to seize the opportunity for social transformation for more than a century. As with all major changes, there are people and forces, who have an interest in maintaining the *status quo*, i.e. who resist change. This is completely normal and does not fundamentally call into question our proposal and appeal[360], which we will explain and elaborate in more detail on the following pages.

---

[360] We will be told that European unification means a paradigm shift in German politics. We agree with this assertion insofar as we accept it for the policy of European integration with its so-called four 'freedoms', which concern the free movement of persons, goods, services and capital.
As we will show, however, the paradigm shift that we are calling for the fundamental functioning of our societies has not yet been seen by the EU and consequently has not been implemented.

So we take on the task of demonstrating the meaningfulness and feasibility of a paradigm shift, using the example of so-called "demographic change",[361] which refers to the so-called problem of the "aging" of our highly developed societies in Europe[362]. In fact, the real scope of this problem is very limited. We consider it much more a normal social process that has been inflated by interested parties to make profits out of it.

It is the usual process. Something is happening, and of course some people perceive it as an opportunity. Hence, they make an issue out of it to pursue their own egoistic interests. In a follow-up, government and our power elites use it as a pretext for

[361] In principle, this example can of course also be applied to the other states of the EU and Europe, as well as to the other highly developed societies and states. The fundamental meaningfulness of our demand for a paradigm shift is underlined by the fact that the People's Republic of China is already massively and directly affected by this challenge of "demographic change". for Japan, this has been an important political issue for decades.

[362] Richard J. Evans in his book "The Pursuit of Power", 2017, puts these social, economic and political powers in relation and illustrates their effects in Europe during the age of industrialization, i.e. 1815-1914.

interference and for strengthening their own interests. The so-called public is then "guided" to a reply on the issue that has been inflated by an often small interest group. The impact of the subsequent public actions on the welfare of the population may be relatively high, while the benefits may not exist or even be negative. Such misleading public policies are increasingly being used by the scientific community, which is considered to be at the service of society and public interests. The public policies during the so-called Corona pandemic have provided ample evidence for the abuse of science in the interest of the power elites. We have found out that the challenge of demographic change is now also being perceived and scientifically analyzed in China. Researchers at the University of Beijing pretend to have identified a problem, for which they are suggesting a solution at the same time. This is Western-style science made in China. A decline in population growth has been identified as a "problem". This so-called problem, the researchers suggest in their ignorance, can, unfortunately, only be met with the same stereotypical "Malthusian" thinking as in Western societies.[363]

This so-called problem of the "aging" of society is caused by the fact that the population in most countries in Europe is declining, which means that the birth rate, or "natural fertility", is lower than the death rate. The birth rate is no longer sufficient to allow the population to continue to grow at a fast pace, as has been the case over the past centuries. This is generally seen as a problem, or at least presented to the public as such. However, we presume that this effect should rather be considered a cause for reflection

---

[363] Wang Mingyuan, "Why Have Repeated Efforts to Revitalize the Northeast Failed? – Rethinking the Twentieth Anniversary of the Strategy of Revitalizing the Old Industrial base". Source https://www.readingthechinadream.com/wang-mingyuan-on-chinas-northeast.html.

The summary of the cited study then warns of "declining birth rates in China": "Wang, a law professor at Tsinghua University in Beijing, seeks to explain the Northeast region's persistent economic underperformance during reform and opening, and interestingly warns that all of China may be headed in the same direction, given declining birth rates in China and trends toward economic sovereignty throughout the world."

about the usefulness, or even necessity, of continuing population growth. Where does this widespread "belief" of the need for a steadily growing population come from? Of course, we know from the Old Testament that God gave us humans the task of "growing and multiplying", when we were expelled from paradise. But we also know that much of the Old Testament is meant metaphorically[364], and is not necessarily meant to directly guide action in modern societies. The media, politicians and other leading elites explain to us constantly that this aging of society creates the big problem that with a decreasing population, more and more costs arise for an increasingly older, unproductive population, which takes up an ever larger part of the total population. These growing costs have to be borne by an increasingly small, active and young part of the population. In concrete terms, this issue is considered the economic problem of covering the costs of an "aging population".

For decades, politicians and the public media have been telling us the story that this

[364] See the extensive work of Joseph Campbell on the understanding and interpretation of myths. The Joseph Campbell Foundation website: https://www.jcf.org/

problem can only be solved, if we take in more and more people through immigration, i.e. by taking in foreign populations, in order to have the working population grow[365]. Of course, this is a very selfish way of thinking, because it shows that we want to use other people to solve our own problems.[366] In addition, this path is very short-sighted and makes no sense in the long term. This negative policy, which calls for immigration, is demanded in particular by companies and industries with a generally low degree of

[365] We are aware that the UN with its International Organization for Migration (https://www.iom.int/global-compact-migration) is also playing an effective role in not only managing, but also in promoting global migration. Again, these are activist organizations that are raising problems for which they will not be accountable and will not have to pay for.

[366] This is the public narrative that has its origins in the economy, as an example the so-called "shortage of skilled workers", which has been adopted by politicians and the media by consensus and successfully propagated since the founding of the Federal Republic. The social costs that arise from this policy are never asked. This issue then always emerges as a consequence, as a result, and then forms a problem for politics that has to be overcome and for which the tax-paying population has to bear the financial and social burdens.

productivity in order to meet their need for cheap labor. The business associations of these less productive industries are therefore lobbying everywhere and incessantly talking about a shortage of skilled workers in order to promote their interests in cheap labor. This immigration policy also has very negative consequences for many countries of origin, for example for Croatia, Bulgaria, Hungary, Serbia and Romania, due to the emigration of trained, young workers. It is completely ignored that in these countries the villages are emptying, many houses are for sale and young families are separated, because part of the family works in other European countries.[367]

We have to be clear on this sensitive issue. We consider migration to be natural for human societies. Migration happened throughout the existence of humans. However, we refuse for migration to be used in the sense of social engineering. We reject this functional approach to human society. Looking at the systems of kinship that have existed since the dawn of humanity, we will learn to appreciate

[367] Refer to "Migration und Entwicklung im sozialistischen Jugoslawien", by Sara Žerić, Ulf Brunnbauer, 16. April 2024.

the genius of the human being, which is far more sophisticated than the pretended scientific tools our social engineers and power elites are applying today. The Western, science- and technology-driven approach to human life is always falling into the same trap. These people think that ordinary people, or people from other cultures, are stupid and that science is a tool to regulate every edge of human life. These scientists, trained in Western thinking only, overlook that their approach to life is useful in some ways, but is one-dimensional and often narrow-minded. Other cultures have developed their own sciences as well and acquired extensive knowledge about the functioning of nature and human societies. Such knowledge and insight are not below the level of knowledge created and insight achieved by Western science. It always depends on the solution you consider the best. Since the rise of Western science in the centuries following the Renaissance, only Western solutions are considered valid. In today's world, herbs are considered second best, far below the quality of synthetic pharmaceutical products and prescription drugs. The pharma industry constantly wants to increase production and profits. That has become its declared priority, not service to people.

It is true, however, that only Western science has been capable of producing electricity, constructing airplanes, and building the atomic bomb. On the other side, the organization of human societies has never and nowhere been better organized than in the traditional societies of Africa or Oceania.[368] Nowhere existed better or more sophisticated systems of the utilization of plants and minerals for medical treatment of ailments than in India or China. Western science as well as Western capitalism and colonialism have come over the world with a narrow-minded quest for general dominance. It came with the tendency to push everything and everybody aside that did not fit its own expectations. We agree that this narrow-minded approach with an exclusive focus on the intellect and "objectivity" might have

[368] We refer here mainly to "The Elementary Structures of Kinship" published in 1949 by Claude Lévi-Strauss in its original version as "Les Systèmes elementaries de la Parenté".
Robin Fox's study on "Kinship and Marriage", published in 1967, is an additional source providing further insights into the functioning of systems of kinship and alliances, not only in traditional societies.

been the price to pay for the development of modern science. Opening up this narrow mind is our task today in the interest to find a global balance, where mutual respect between cultures comes into play.

Concerning our topic of demographic change, we fundamentally question the arguments and assertions of our power elites and business lobbyists about the necessity of immigration. We counter these policies with our call for a paradigm shift with regard to demographic growth. These claims and the call for ever more demographic growth are directed by the short-sighted interests of individual lobby groups from industries and businesses. They are not in the interest of social development aimed at a better quality of life for all. The entrepreneurs of these, usually low-productive, industries are mainly interested in higher profits through the use of cheap labor. These entrepreneurs may win in the short term with this policy. However, the financial costs of this immigration must then be borne by the taxpayers' community. This migration policy is also creating social costs that are to the detriment of social groups that are suffering from the negative side effects of these immigration policies: kindergartens, schools and universities, are overcrowded, the quality of education is decreasing constantly, health insurance and hospitals have increasing deficits due to increasing costs caused by people, who do not pay themselves for the medical treatment and services, social and economic infrastructure is degrading, because funding is not secured, and so on. All this can be read every day in the newspapers. This is a good example of what happens when wrong rules, or specific rules, are applied unilaterally, without the general welfare and interest in mind.

So far, no one has come up with the idea that a declining population might not be a problem at all, but could be converted into a blessing.[369] In any case, no one wanted to tell us this story.[370] With our proposal for a

[369] In the politically important American journal "Foreign Affairs", readers are constantly brainwashed with terms such as "depopulation". How stupid and how malicious! As if the earth might be "depopulated".
[370] Of course, it is not quite right when we say here that it was nobody. There are also people in the Federal Republic of Germany and in other countries who have thought in our direction. We only want to refer here to Thomas Straubhaar, a Swiss economist and migration researcher. He is Professor of International Economic Relations at the University of Hamburg and was

paradigm shift, we want to call for a fundamental rethink in politics and society concerning demographic development. We suggest looking at these phenomena in a new way in the future, from a new perspective. It is for this purpose that we ask for the application of new rules. In doing so, we can show how entrepreneurs and the economy in general can achieve greater growth and higher profits without causing harm to the public or generating social and financial costs. Short-sighted and egoistic interests have to be avoided through the application of new rules that consider general interests. The power elites will have to give up their power for the benefit of people and their quality of life.

In line with our personal conviction, however, we do not consider it advisable to apply techniques of "social engineering", in which sometimes questionable proposals are made, which ultimately make people objects of science-driven and technologically-oriented

appointed Professor of Economics at the University of the Federal Armed Forces Hamburg in 1992. At the same time, he was President and Director of the Hamburg Institute of International Economics (HWWA, later called HWWI).

strategies and policies.[371] Notwithstanding the experience of daily atrocities committed by humans, we remain convinced that humans are capable of creating conditions for an improving quality of life and a propitious living environment. We rely on the potential and competence for human action through free people. We believe that humans are able to recognize what is good for them and know how to make the best of their situation. However, we know that people have difficulties deploying their potential and creativity in societies, where the state rules over all aspects of public life.[372] In our societies in Europe, people are not encouraged to take responsibility in order to search together for long-term and sustainable solutions that fit their expectations and needs. People cannot prosper in societies

---

[371] As an example of an approach to "social engineering" that we do not want to subscribe to in this form, even if we largely share the analytical findings on the negative effects of strong demographic growth, is Paul R. Ehrlich, The Population Bomb, New York: Ballantine Books 1968.

[372] In his book "The Road to Serfdom", first published in 1944, Friedrich August von Hayek has presented his work on political philosophy, cultural history and economics with a view to preserve individual freedom.

where the government pretends to know the cure for all the problems of life. We, on our side, are counting on the healthy self-interest of people, who want a better quality of life in the long term. We suppose that these same people can very well recognize that perpetual and higher demographic growth will be harmful in the long term. Let them look at the current situation and discuss the issue openly. We trust in the common sense of people more than in the interests of lobby groups or power elites.

The first step that is needed to progressively induce a paradigm shift is to open public discussions and take the psychological and economic pressure off people. Then, demographics will have to be introduced as an important topic in the public debate concerning quality of life. People will be asked to examine the validity of the existing rule that says that a better quality of life for the majority of people depends on higher demographic growth. This rule of "more people create more happiness" must be publicly examined. There is a great chance that it might be considered wrong. Consequently, this rule might be dropped. At the same time, people will be asked to openly discuss the establishment of new rules related to demographics and the quality of life. In these public debates, people will concomitantly learn to assess the existing social processes. People will increasingly learn to take charge of their lives and the living environment. Currently, what is good in life is determined by the government and promoted by their media, or through think tanks and the power elites. People have to accept what they get. On our side, we ask for a new environment of public debate to be created. These discussions will induce a learning process and encourage people to take responsibility for public life. We are convinced that such open discussions would bring to the fore striking arguments confirming that humanity has all the abilities to achieve a better quality of life. The means to create the economic conditions for a higher quality of life will be provided through higher productivity and increased efficiency in the use of existing resources. People are intelligent, and many of them are well-trained. They will understand these points and their systemic interdependencies without any doubt. However, in the current situation, the power elites are keeping them out of the decision-making processes.

In our context, we understand "existing resources" as the potential of intellect and the social competence of human beings to take decisions concerning the intelligent use of natural, "infinitely regenerative resources". People will have to learn that they do not have to fight for these resources. This is the old story that is told to us by the power elites to serve their narrow-minded and egoistic interests for power and money. We do not believe in that anymore. People can understand that these "infinitely regenerative resources" are offered to us on earth and made available to us by the sun on a daily basis. This comprises natural, regenerating resources and raw materials, as well as solar radiation, wind- and water-power.

To put it more simply, we have to rely on our own intellectual and mental abilities to make good use of the infinitely regenerative energy and resources. We have to get out of the crisis mode of constant short-term problem solutions, or the short-sighted pursuit of quick profits. We must find new self-confidence in the ability of the human being to master our fate on earth, without systematic mutual exploitation, and without systematically resorting to the means of violence. On the following pages, we will bring forward some convincing examples to show that paradigm shifts in this dimension are possible.

LINEAR THINKING LEADS TO A DEAD END[373]

The causal reason why there has not yet been a paradigm shift in relation to demographic change is that most of us have, so far, only ever thought and acted in a linear way.[374]

[373] That we do not get anywhere with such thinking, and how we can do it better, is very plausibly testified by Rene Egli in his book "The Lola Principle, The Perfection of the World", Editions d'Olt, 1994.

[374] In the book "The Discovery of Chaos", by John Briggs and F. David Peat, 1997; the original was published in New York in 1989 under the title "Turbulent Mirror", the authors convincingly and consistently show that the world of people cannot be grasped and understood with linear concepts. Nevertheless, these linear concepts still control the common narratives in politics today. Probably the best example of this is the publication of studies such as those periodically published by the Bertelsmann Foundation for the Control of Public Opinion.

Europe did not dare to look beyond the edge of its limited mindset. Europe is not really ready to share lives with other people. It's still locked in its paradigm of dominance and unique superiority. The geopolitics of the US are the extreme proof of this narrow-minded view of the world. For those, who do not yet agree with us, we suggest they read daily the publications of *Foreign Affairs*. All the mainstream media want us to believe that everything is expected to go on as before, only better, faster and further; always more and more of the same. We are all told, drummed into our brains in schools and universities and reinforced by the media, that everything has to go on as before, only a bit better; that is, faster and farther, but always only more of the same.

Let's be inspired by Buckminster Fuller and see which way he shows us to escape from this dilemma of linear thinking that we all know too well. In the chapter "Self-Disciplines of Buckminster Fuller" in his 1981 book *The Critical Path*, he summarized the decision he took at the age of 32 as follows: "*I tried to think in my own way and limited myself to information gained from experience... instead of trying to take into account the opinions, creeds, educational theories, romance and customs of everyone else...";* and further down, he says, reaffirming his social position: *"I tried to achieve everything in such a way that the benefit obtained for one person would never be achieved at the expense of other people".*[375] That sounds almost like a personal guide to the paradigm shift we are suggesting. As early as 1784, Immanuel Kant chose the motto of the Enlightenment as "sapere aude!", i.e. "Have the courage to use your own mind!" We would fully agree that this is certainly one of the most important prerequisites for paradigm shifts. The will to consciously take responsibility for the well-being of oneself and, within the scope of one's capabilities, also for others, is the foundation for a shared future on this planet.

Back to the actual challenge of demographic change, we could say that nobody really feels

---

[375] It says: I sought to do my own thinking, confining it to only experientially gained information... instead of trying to accommodate everyone else's opinions, credos, educational theories, romance and mores...; and further down: "I sought to accomplish whatever was to be accomplished for anyone in such a manner that the advantage attained for anyone would never be secured at the cost of another or others".

responsible. Governments are operating at the symptomatic level, and the UN publishes papers to be discussed in their talk shops and global meetings without any courage for relevant action or consequent follow-up. UN action has always had to side with the power elites and the paymasters. This is the sad reality today.

From our side, we criticize the fact that so far no one has come up with the idea of a fundamental paradigm shift. This seems to be a symptom of fear. Or is it a kind of prohibition imposed on people, to make good use of their own minds? We do not believe that it has to do with an intellectual or mental lack of human competence. We ask ourselves, why nobody has had the courage to say: Let's try it in a completely different way, not linearly, not on the path we have always taken so far. Rather, let us meet the challenge with a new attitude and a new way of thinking, looking for a fundamental and sustainable solution to the problem. People might have become aware that such a change would make a fruitful contribution to the transformation of our societies in Europe, leading to a higher quality of life in the long term. The precondition for this to happen is that people take back their right to think freely, to discuss all issues openly, and to take action, shaping their societies at their will.

With the following considerations, we want to explain in some more detail what exactly we mean by this, how such a paradigm shift can be justified[376], and what the necessary prerequisites are to set it in motion.[377]

An important premise, which Buckminster Fuller in particular points out, has been known since classical philosophy. He clearly distinguishes between the function of the "brain" and the potential of the "mind". While it is the task of the intellect to serve us in the description of "facts", it is given to the mind to discover the *universal principles and laws* in order to understand them and progressively move towards synergistic alignment. These synergies are not only effective at the level of

[376] We refer to Richard J. Bernstein: Beyond Objectivism and Relativism: Science, Hermeneutics, and Praxis, University of Pennsylvania Press, 1983.
[377] R. Buckminster Fuller in his "Critical Path", Foreword, page XI, but also on page 159, where he writes: "brain deals with… thingness" and on page 160 "only minds have the capability to discover principles". It is these "principles" that we call the "general rules" here in the sense of cybernetics.

physical energy. At the social and political level, synergies are combining the forces driving the processes that govern our lives and worlds. With this kind of systemic and cybernetic thinking, we approach the understanding of the function of catalytic processes and of societies as self-regulating systems.

Engaging in such thoughts and applying this kind of thinking during public debates, we might become aware that we are advancing into new dimensions, which can open paths for new thinking and new attitudes towards paradigm shifts. We talk here about the *universal principles and laws*, of which Buckminster Fuller speaks, and suggest applying them to social and political processes. In the context of social processes and political actions, we call them "general rules" in the sense of cybernetics.

Through the application of such "general rules", which are considered valid for humanity, the transformation of societies will lead to new dimensions for a shared future. We must question, discuss, and ultimately change the existing rules that currently shape our societies in such a way that they will meet our demand for a better quality of life for all in the future.[378] These debates and open discussions will have to examine the drivers and enablers of synergistic alignment, as well as the barriers and challenges to face. The key factors influencing synergistic alignment in societies are communication and culture. Charismatic leadership may function as an additional, catalytic factor driving and directing synergistic processes.

It is now time for us to bring at least a few examples of successful paradigm shifts to show that social paradigm shifts are feasible on a large scale and that they can make absolute sense.

[378] We do not wish to call this the "dawn of a new form of democracy", because we do not wish to recur to concepts that of earlier periods of the social and political evolution of humanity.

SUCCESSFUL EXAMPLES OF PARADIGM SHIFTS IN POLITICAL AND SOCIAL LIFE

Even in the Federal Republic of Germany, which certainly cannot be regarded as a state with great revolutionary energy, paradigm shifts have taken place in certain areas. We would like to briefly mention just two examples here in order to show that, even in Germany, it is principally possible to fundamentally change the rules for political and public action. With such new rules, political leaders did not react to problems by acting at the level of symptoms. Such short-sighted political action - we know it all too well - is always creating new problems downstream. This has finally led us into the present crisis mode. We are referring, with our practical examples, to political leaders of a different caliber and style. They took action, leading the country on new paths and initiating long-term, positive changes. This is what we understand by setting new rules to induce paradigm shifts in the long term with direction provided by charismatic leadership.

The introduction of the social market economy in Germany[379]

First, we would like to refer to a politician from the early days of the Federal Republic of Germany, after 1949. It is Ludwig Erhard who, with his stubborn advocacy, coupled with political skill, was largely responsible for the introduction of a liberal, but "regulatory economic policy", for the introduction of the Deutsche Mark as an independent currency, and for the shaping of the social market economy in Germany.[380] Any economist will

[379] We know, of course, that there are economists who will immediately contradict us by saying that other economic systems are better. However, we counter that the system of the social market economy in the first decades offered the Federal Republic and its people a good economic framework for reconstruction.

[380] As an easily readable summary of this topic, we would like to cite the book "The Order of Freedom and its Enemies: On the Uprising of the Forsaken against the Rule of the Elites", Finanzbuch Verlag, 2018, by Thomas Mayer.

Thomas Mayer is the founding director of the Cologne-based Flossbach von Storch Research Institute. Previously, he was Chief Economist of the Deutsche Bank Group and Head of Deutsche Bank Research. Before moving to the private sector, he held various positions at the International Monetary Fund in Washington and the Kiel Institute for the World

be able to confirm that this policy represented a fundamental departure from the paradigm of the managed state economy, which had been a valid paradigm for most economies in Europe until then, and was favored at that time, especially by the socialist and communist governments in many countries, not only in Europe.

This regulatory approach to economic policy is based on the assumption that the state defines the framework and determines the basic rules, in close coordination with the social partners concerned, through which the "order", i.e. functioning, is to be regulated politically and economically. In addition, this Ordo-Liberal system relies heavily on the creativity of free people and on their entrepreneurial spirit. At the same time, this approach implies that the economy also fulfills its social mission and undertakes to do its utmost to train its staff, i.e. mainly young people, so that no one is excluded or left behind. This approach is in line with the German Basic Law, which states that "property obliges", and that the private

Economy.

economic actors have responsibility for society.

In contrast, for 20, 30 and more years, we in Germany have taken a path, in which the "state quota" is reaching ever-new highs and the state is intervening more and more in all areas of public life and the economy. This is done in a manner that is supposed to show that nothing works without the state. Governments and the state institutions, together with their politicians and other power elites, pretend to always know everything better. The responsible citizen of yesteryear has degenerated into a subject of the power elites again. The never-ending government-driven reforms have so far not brought sustainable positive results, but have continuously increased the state's budget for social expenses and led to an overall reduction of quality standards in services, accompanied by a steadily decreasing quality of life. At the same time, the tax burden for income-generating activities increased, while the costs for social and public services continued to increase in parallel. Ever more money is in the hands of the government.

Striking examples of the negative impact of increasing government interventions in Germany are health policy, energy policy, education policy, and now most recently climate policy, to which we could add digitization and, most recently, "information policy". This list could be continued for a long time; unfortunately, and it includes practically all aspects of public and private life today. This is the process to which Hayek referred in his book "The Road to Serfdom". A social and political process, where the citizen is constantly losing power, while the power elites are taking over the lead in every aspect of life.[381]

The policy of reconciliation and peace under Willy Brandt

Another example of a successful paradigm shift in the politics of the Federal Republic of Germany can be found in the reconciliation

---

[381] The novel "The Silence of the Lambs", published in 1988, by Thomas Harris, provides us with a frightening background on the metamorphosis of post-modern life. Building on this novel, Rainer Mausfeld published in 2018 his book, asking "Why do Lambs remain Silent?".

and peace policy of the government under Willy Brandt (in office from 1969 to 1974). Today, we can no longer imagine how a large part of the population, instigated by political parties and political pressure groups, resisted this policy of reconciliation with Germany's eastern European neighbors.

With his charisma and the support of courageous and clever politicians, such as Egon Bahr and Hans-Dietrich Genscher, Chancellor Willy Brandt succeeded in implementing this new paradigmatic policy of reconciliation and good neighborhood. As a result, this policy has led to, among other things, Germany becoming a respected partner not only among its eastern European neighbors, but also in global politics as a whole. The trauma of the Nazi-era political past has since become a manageable part of Germany's foreign policy agenda. Germany has moved into a position, in which it could deal with its most important historical legacy in a self-confident and responsible way. This policy of reconciliation and good neighborhood has since become a widely recognized part of Germany's political profile.

Through this paradigm shift and this courageous step on the path to reconciliation and international cooperation, Germany has freed itself from the corset of the past. This opened the door to the possibility of a sovereign management of German foreign policy with regard to its Eastern European neighbors, but also in Europe as a whole, as a policy of good neighborhood.

SUCCESSFUL EXAMPLES OF PARADIGM SHIFTS IN INTERNATIONAL POLITICS

There are also good examples of successful paradigm shifts at the level of international politics, of which we will briefly mention at least three, to illustrate what we want to put forward here in our book.

Singapore: from Third to First World

In the modern history of the development of the Asian states, the state of Singapore certainly stands[382] out as a very special

---

[382] There is an extensive literature on Singapore, covering all areas of history and modern life. As an introduction to the topic, we still consider the biography of the founder, Lee Kuam Yew, to be very helpful, "From Third World to First".

phenomenon. Singapore is the result of a unique experiment that was not given much of a future, when it was founded, and it also had an ethnic challenge to overcome. Today, Singapore has become a model state in many respects, which unfortunately has not yet found successful imitators due to its uniqueness.[383] It is certainly not out of place to call Singapore a pearl, not only among the Asian states, but among the states of the international community. In Singapore, an exceptionally high quality of life has been achieved for all citizens on an unprecedented scale. This goes, at the same time, hand in hand with the realization of universal human rights, a low crime rate, and peace with all its neighbors.

[383] We know that there are vehement critics of Singapore as an "authoritarian regime", especially in Europe. If we consider how many "failed states" there are now on our globe, how many states are responsible for wars, and how many states do not succeed in offering their populations good health and education systems, or even in feeding them well, then we think it is better to be a little "authoritarian" than "failed" or "problematic" in development.

Perestroika and German reunification

Another example of a successful paradigm shift comes from European policy. We would like to refer here to the policies of *Glasnost* and *Perestroika* from 1989 to 1991 under the leadership of Mikhail Gorbachev. The policy promoted by the former Soviet leader has brought a non-violent end to the Soviet Union and to the Cold War. It also facilitated the process of peaceful and non-violent German reunification.

The Soviet Union's policy had reached an impasse. Internally, all attempts at reform failed. The system had too many flaws, preventing its successful transformation. In the era of the Cold War, this represented a complete defeat concerning international relations. What would have been possible geopolitical options? To detonate atomic bombs against enemies? To start a new world war? – Gorbachev chose a different path, he made a paradigm shift and, through his policy, banned violence and war from European politics, at least for a few years.[384]

---

[384] In an interview concerning this issue, Richard Sakwa explains the basics: "We are at the funeral of the old school of diplomacy", published in GlobalBridge on

Gorbachev relied, against serious resistance in his own country, on his political genius and took a different, non-linear path. Following a clear vision, he had the courage to take a step in a direction that no one had foreseen. He has extended his hand to the West in a friendly manner to usher in a new era by acknowledging the economic and political defeat of the Soviet Union. At the same time, however, he was concerned with proposing, on the basis of the given situation, a solution that would serve the long-term interests of the peoples of the Soviet Union, of which he was president, as well as those of the other peoples and nations in Europe.

This example provides evidence that there was not only the shift away from linear "business as usual" in Gorbachev's thinking, but that he also saw the possibility of changing the global political configuration in the world[385]. Mind you, to change the world,

May 21, 2024. To deepen the insights, we recommend reading his book "The Lost Peace: How the West Failed to Prevent a Second Cold War", from 2023.

[385] A good primary source for understanding the motivations of Gorbachev and appreciating his policies is "Gorbachev: His Life and Times", 2017, Taubmann, William.

and to do so without taking up arms[386]. What a noble policy!

China's economic and social transformation

The third example from international politics, that we would like to refer to briefly, is the change in the economic policy paradigm in modern China under Deng Xiaoping, the leader of the Communist Party and leader of China from 1979 to 1997. As an old comrade of and successor to Mao Zedong, he had taken on the role of "outstanding leader". At the same time, he initiated a fundamental change in Chinese politics, especially economic policy.

In his position, he could not say, we are now abolishing the Communist Party, or, we are turning China upside down as a whole. He was aware that, after many decades of uprisings and terrible wars, the country had to find itself and learn to function stably and reliably after 1949, according to its new rules. But

[386] It is worth mentioning here that Gorbachev also ordered, under his government, the withdrawal of Soviet troops from Afghanistan.

Deng Xiaoping learned and understood during his visits to the newly industrializing center in Southern China and to Singapore[387] that there might be an alternative, another way to lead China out of poverty and backwardness. With his policies, he paved the way to this new path and implemented it with a lot of political skill. This basically ended the previous paradigm of the communist mode of production and its rigid centralist administration in China, the legacy from the time of Mao.

Since then, China has taken this new path very successfully.[388] Deng Xiaoping, in his intelligent and pragmatic way, asked: Where do we stand? Where can we go? What do we have to do to achieve our strategic goals? What are our resources and opportunities?

[387] The relevant information can be found in the book "From Third World to First", by Lee Kuam Yew, the founder and long-time president of Singapore.

[388] We should remember at this point that China had successfully initiated its political transformation at the time of Mao Zedong, after unspeakable sacrifices, especially under the "Cultural Revolution". Economically, however, neither "the great leap" of industrialization had been achieved, nor had the rampant poverty of a large part of the population been overcome.

And, it seems, as if he has asked himself yet another question: Which path can fit in with our millennia-old culture and tradition?[389] – Together with the people, who worked with him, he found the answer to this challenge in the fruitful combination of the ethical rules and virtues from the tradition of Confucianism, with the drive for personal success and the renowned fervor for achievements, well known of the Chinese people. This complementary approach still governs life in Singapore today, as well as in modern-day China.

Based on the given situation, Deng Xiaoping understood that China had to fundamentally change the rules of the game for its economy. Free enterprise, within certain limits and in compliance with certain rules, was made possible and encouraged. At the same time, of course, this also brought great progress in the sense of individual development and the unfolding of personality for the individual people in China. Mao's strict and rigid, monolithic system had been broken up. There

[389] Deng Xiaoping, without speaking it out, had certainly recognized that Mao's policies of the "Grand Leap forward" and the "Cultural Revolution" have been a failure.

is a very telling saying by Deng Xiaoping in which he asked rhetorically: "Which is better, a black cat or a white cat?" He gave the following answer: "The main thing is that the cat catches mice". Please bear in mind that this paradigm shift led to the creation of modern China, as it unfolds today with seemingly unlimited vitality. This paradigm shift had an impact that was not limited to economic growth. Should we call it a successful step towards the "pursuit of happiness" for the Chinese people?

This example of China is a good illustration of some principles useful for a successful paradigm shift. It's not about choosing between black and white. Above all, it's not about doing more of what hasn't worked well before. So it's not about mixing black and white to give birth to a cat of a blurred gray color. No, it's about walking down a new path that no one has seen before. This was achieved through the synergistic unity of forces that have hitherto been separated. A new way of life was born leading China to an unprecedented leap forward to a better quality, as well as peaceful life for millions. Using China as an example, this path, starting from the Confucian tradition, meant trusting in the genius and creativity of the Chinese people within the framework of the order set by an always modernizing Communist Party.

From what we can observe, this paradigm shift in China is showing excellent results, unique in the history of mankind, in that a people, trusting in its own forces, develops in a way that provokes our amazement and admiration.

CRITICISM: LINEAR POLITICS OF BUSINESS AS USUAL

If we relate these examples and our previous remarks on the situation in Europe, then we have to ask ourselves what a new path, i.e. a paradigm shift in relation to policy with regard to "demographic change", could have looked like. How and by whom could such a paradigm shift have been initiated.

For several decades, we have been told by politicians, the public as well also privately financed media, supported by all associations, trade unions and churches, that we have a "demographic problem" in Europe. This so-called "demographic problem" consists, according to general agreement, in the so-called "aging of the population". This opinion is shared by almost all major think tanks, professional thinkers, politicians and associations, including the UN.

With so much "intelligence" behind the claim that the "aging population" is a major problem, it is difficult to argue against it. And yet that is exactly what we want to do here. In response to this supposed problem, all the groups and institutions mentioned are calling for continued growth, leading to migration, i.e. immigration of people to Europe, with the presumed goal of preventing population decline and the "aging" of European societies. The aim seems to be to reverse the negative trend in the "societies of decline". However, as we will show, these internationally driven policies are in fact at the origin of a decline in the quality of life in Europe. All these policies are looking for linear solutions, tend to tackle the issue at the symptomatic level, and consequently lead to ever-new problems downstream. We have become aware now that this will not work.

In our understanding, such policies for migration[390] and immigration are only policies in a linear direction, a policy of "always going on to do what we know", of "always doing more of the same". So these are policies that take us further, but always in the same direction, descending or ascending, as you like, but not out of the problems.

The experience of the past decades shows us emphatically that these politics are attempts to simply cure the symptoms. However, they have led us nowhere, and did not bring us any closer to solving the problems. As they are not changing the root causes, they will not lead us any further in the future either. Obviously, this kind of bureaucratic politics manages and administers the problems instead of overcoming them, in eliminating their root causes in the long term. On the contrary, through these politics, we are in the process of getting ever deeper into an imbalance and creating increasingly more and new problems for ourselves. In the meantime, the social and financial consequences of these misguided politics have become so great that they will soon no longer be manageable. The

[390] Please note the title of the UN organization. It reads "Organization FOR Migration".

crisis mode has been engaged in high gear already. To justify our position, we would like to briefly point out just a few important developments that are serious threats to the quality of life in our societies.

Urbanization: Relationship between Population Density and Aggression

Our politicians and power elites are coming with cunning and think that the best they can do is keep citizens happy and bring them on track with methods of "nudging" and "framing"[391], i.e. through sophisticated methods of manipulation through the media. We take the opposite position and assume that our societies would have benefited more, if the politicians and power elites had tackled the root causes of the arising problems and

[391] "Merkel wants to educate the Germans through nudging", the daily newspaper "Welt", on March 12, 2015.
"The ARD framing paper testifies to a crude understanding of democracy", The broadcaster has commissioned a manipulation manual to deal with criticism - the wrong way for more social acceptance, writes Hans-Peter Siebenhaar, on February 19, 2019, in the Handelsblatt.

existing challenges. We refer here briefly to the unrest of 2005 in the French "banlieues", but also to more recent unrest in the suburbs of London, or even in Sweden, in 2024. Obviously, these are symptoms of persisting and increasing problems related to immigration and population growth. How do our governments in Europe handle these issues? They ask for more money to cover the problems with social assistance programs. Certainly, these are not long-term solutions.

It would have been much more beneficial for social peace and well-being in our societies, and more would have been achieved if, for example, the evolutionary relationship between population density and aggression had been made transparent. These interdependencies are well known, and their consequences for the quality of life have been well analyzed and could have been publicly discussed[392]. This might have been useful in the sense of inducing a meaningful paradigm shift related to these issues of migration and

---

[392] As one of the many sources on this topic, we refer to the book "The Master Animal", written jointly by an economist (Lionel Tiger) and an anthropologist (Robin Fox). We recommend, in particular, reading Chapter 8 "The Noble Savage".

demographic growth. This is what we would expect of politics that are tackling issues at the root causes.

Historically, the phenomenon was perceived by artists and sociologists in Europe and the USA in the first half of the 20th century. The Spanish philosopher and essayist José Ortega y Gasset published in 1929 an intriguing essay on "La Rebelíon de las Masas", translated in English in 1930 as "The Revolt of the Masses". The American sociologist David Riesman presented in 1950 the critical study "The Lonely Crowd", showing the impact of "the mass phenomenon" in America's society on the American character. C. G. Jung applied aspects of his "collective unconscious" to politics and society. Jung examined mass movements in relation to mass psychoses. He came to the conclusion that "mass-mindedness" is a danger for the survival of human societies, and considered the psychology of the masses as a "dangerous germ".[393] In 1946, Jung wrote for a BBC broadcast, entitled "Civilization in Transition": "...industrialization, ...this new

[393] The term "collective unconscious" first appeared in Jung's 1916 essay, "The Structure of the Unconscious".

form of existence—with its mass psychology and social dependence on the fluctuation of markets and wages—produced an individual who was unstable, insecure, and suggestible." In the context of this chapter, the following quote by C. G. Jung is particularly informative: "Resistance to the organized mass can be effected only by the man, who is as well organized in his individuality, as the mass itself".[394] This remark is essential for our argumentation, because it hints towards a principal prerequisite, at the level of the individual personally, that is necessary for paradigm shifts in public and social life, as well as in politics.

This topic of the "masses" and the inherent social and political challenges is now increasingly observed by specialized sociologists worldwide, especially in relation to urbanization. There are warnings of an

[394] Jung has, in many of his works, elaborated on the phenomenon of the masses. In particular, he compared the function and impact on the individual psychology and consequently on social life of "groups" vs. "masses". Refer to "The Meaning of Psychology for Modern Man, Collected Works, C. G. Jung. More details can be found in his biography "Memories, Dreams, Reflections", 1961.

increasing number of "slums",[395] for which the symptoms in Europe, not only in the suburbs of Paris, London and Rome, but also in cities such as Duisburg, Berlin, Stockholm and Rotterdam, have become obvious to every attentive observer.[396]

[395] Using the example of "slum as a consequence of metropolization", Leonard Couvée vividly shows all the negative consequences that arise in his 2016 book.

[396] There is already considerable scientific literature on this topic and lively public discussion. A reference to the book "Planet of the Slums" by the urbanist at the *Department of History at the University of California* in Irvine, Mike Davis, should suffice for us here.
The book *Planet of the Slums* was published in German in 2019.
Perhaps even more inspiring is the speech by Mike Davis, entitled "Who will build the ark?", The Commandment to Utopia in the Age of Catastrophes, held at the first award ceremony of the "Culture Prize", which is awarded by the Munich University Society. The laudator was the former German Minister of the Environment and later Director of the United Nations Environment Program, Klaus Töpfer. In this speech, Mike Davis outlines strategies for dealing with coming disasters that are already current and can no longer be averted. In our book here, on the other hand, we argue that it is always better to look for an alternative solution via a paradigm shift than to settle into the catastrophe. We trust in our reason not to let humanity jump headlessly over the cliff like lemmings.

It is clear, and it should be obvious to every sensitive and intelligent citizen in Europe by now, that the solution to the problem of 'demographic change' is not to promote the population to grow ever more. Since 1972, when the study entitled "Limits to Growth" was presented at a symposium in St. Gallen, the topic of demography should have become a decisive element in the discussion about global development policy.[397] Scientific research provides ample evidence of the fatal consequences of unlimited population growth in various areas. For political reasons, the issue of demographic growth has been taken off the international agenda. Useless discussions are limited to means such as birth

[397] Even the original Keynesian and Nobel Prize winner Josef Stieglitz now points out that "the world's population cannot continue to grow forever, that's a law of physics," in the NZZ, January 18, 2020. Stieglitz does not have the courage to indicate any solution to the challenge. Why? Because population growth is a politically sensitive issue. The most striking example is Israel. The Palestinian population in Gaza and the occupied lands argues that they will demographically outgrow the Jewish population in the long run. Thus, demographic growth is instrumentalized as a "weapon". Talking about it is politically not correct for Westerners. This applies to other Arab countries as well.

control through contraceptives. The international community, in its present structure, is not able to engage in an open discussion on this issue. This might have led to questions about the existing power structures in these UN organs and institutions. On our side, we assume that there exists a constructive and creative answer to the "demographic problem" or the so-called "aging" of our societies. This is the position we take in our book.

CHANGING THE PERSPECTIVE LEADS TO FINDING A NEW PATH

As we have seen with the practical examples we have provided in the previous section, a paradigm shift in politics is not "witchcraft" and nothing that would be beyond our reach. It seems, as if we have been told for decades to always look in one specific direction only, because that is where the solution was supposedly to be found. We understand today that we have been led in the wrong direction. This misleading orientation given by our power elites has brought us into ever-increasing problems. It has led Europe into a crisis mode and finally a general impasse, of which we do not easily find a way out. Certainly, a paradigm shift in European politics does not fail because of a lack of knowledge, but rather because we fear change, and lack experience in taking new paths. We know well that it is often difficult for people to take paths that they do not yet know "from experience". The main obstacle, however, is probably fear, and the subsequent lack of will and courage to initiate and allow for major social changes to which a paradigm shift will inevitably lead. [398]

So we consider it high time now for us in Europe to change the perspective and direction of our thinking, to accept the challenge, and to see the solution that is openly in front of us within our immediate reach. We need to steer the development of our societies in a direction that takes us away from the current problems,[399] rather than just

[398] Horst-Eberhard Richter, the "grand old man" of the German peace movement, has dealt with this topic a lot. One of his books on this subject is "Morality in Times of Crisis", Suhrkamp Verlag, original edition, 2010.
[399] We borrow this concept from cybernetics, as it was initiated in 1948 by Norbert Wiener together with other colleagues as a science. at the same time,

managing them and replacing them with newly created problems.

however, we also refer to his socially critical, popular scientific work "The Human Use of Human Beings – Cybernetics and Society", in which he refers to the necessity of human control of systems and machines. It is this approach that we want to take into account here by appealing to the responsibility of humans for shaping the context of their lives.

The challenge: Securing and Increasing Prosperity

So our call is now to take up the challenge and finally take a first important step to enter the path that will lead to sustainable politics and a better quality of life for all people in Europe and beyond[400].

As we understand the situation from our side, there is no such thing as a "demographic problem", but rather a "prosperity problem". The challenge consists of the need to close the financing gap, caused by demographic developments, through innovation and a steady increase in productivity in the areas of production and services. For this purpose, we are of course ready to make good and intelligent use of science and technology, as well as of the constantly growing means of artificial intelligence (AI) at our disposal.

---

[400] In our presentation and analysis, we refer largely to Germany. But it should be clear that we do not want to take a nationalist or chauvinistic stance here. Other countries should also initiate their respective paradigm shifts, on their way and to their advantage. If others are better off, then that's good for everyone.

The lever has probably been the first important tool. The wheel has had an incredible impact on the technical evolution of mankind. For us, however, it is essential to use the technical tools at our disposal for the improvement of the quality of life of the people, not to constantly monger new wars.[401] The key is to undertake all our actions with consciousness and in a globally joint effort, without striving for individual dominance. We don't have to be afraid of artificial intelligence and science; on the contrary. On the other hand, we have to take a close look at how, for what purpose and with what goal we humans want to apply the means and tools offered by science and technology, including artificial intelligence. It is therefore a matter of a conscious attitude

---

[401] Because for us, artificial intelligence is not "artificial" but human. As R. Buckminster Fuller aptly describes it, sometime perhaps millions of years ago, a man, or even a primate-like precursor of man, understood and learned that he can increase his own physical strength many times over with leverage. The lever is therefore one of the early and most important instruments of "artificial" intelligence that humans have found and have been using consistently ever since. The wheel is another "artificial" instrument. Should we be afraid of that?

and an intelligent approach to tackle real challenges. Under these conditions, people will become ready to consciously take responsibility for their actions and their consequences for the environment and the well-being of Mother Earth. This means, in our eyes, also consciously taking responsibility for demographic developments and their social and political consequences.

We all know that the European countries have the highest population densities in the world so far. Therefore, we consider it a blatant mistake to promote population growth even more. It would be better to take the situation as an opportunity for a paradigm shift to see how we can live well, and it may be even better, with a lower population density. This is the way for the future on our planet, as we see it.

Just as the age of industrialization has ended for most countries in the world, and we have been following the path leading to knowledge societies for some time now, humanity will also have to regard exponential population growth as a temporary historical development.

To illustrate the demographic development over the past two thousand years, we have included a few graphs in the following chapter of the book. There, we can see that the growth of the world population has increased exponentially in the recent centuries and reached unexpected dimensions.

At the beginning of the Neolithic Age, in 10,000 BC, it was estimated that around two million people lived on earth. This era, initiated by the Neolithic Revolution, is the beginning of sedentary agriculture, the building of organized dwellings, and increasingly larger cities.[402] By 9000 BC, the estimated population had already doubled to around four million people[403]. At the zero point, i.e. beginning of the Common Era, around 188 million people lived on earth.

[402] The classical introduction to this topic is offered in "The Dawn of European Civilization", published in 1925 by V. Gordon Childe.
[403] For a deeper understanding of the drivers of population growth since the Neolithic, we recommend reading: "Guns, Germs and Steel: The Fates of Human Societies, 1997, Jared Diamond. A controversial presentation of the topic can be found in "The Dawn of Everything: a New History of Humanity", 2021, Graeber, David; and Wengrow, David.

Until the end of the European Middle Ages (around 1500 AD), the population grew continuously, and an ever-increasing speed of growth can be registered, which accelerated again from the 19th century onwards due to the onset of industrialization and the introduction of vaccinations and other important measures to improve health, including improved hygiene. In 1900, more than 1.65 billion people already populated our earth. This means that we have had a one thousand-fold increase in the world population since the Neolithic Age. In the course of the 20th century, the population quadrupled to about 6.15 billion. Today, we are easily approaching the 10 billion people mark, i.e. ten thousand times the world population at the Neolithic age.

RISING TO THE CHALLENGE

From our point of view, and in the sense of a desirable paradigm shift, it would therefore make sense if we looked at the so-called "demographic problem" not from one perspective only. We should consider it a useful wake-up call and a challenge, that could even be converted into a blessing. This challenge makes us aware that it is time to take this issue seriously and find a meaningful answer to it. Demographic growth is certainly not a punishment from God. We consider it a call for rising awareness of our responsibility to make good use of our increasing consciousness of the systemic interdependencies of self-regulating processes on earth. The problem lies in our mental "blindness" and in the lack of courage to face reality and to acknowledge things and processes as they are. We have to acknowledge that it is our duty to address what we consider a challenge for us. Looking at things this way, we understand that we do not have a "demographic problem". We are rather in front of a challenge to overcome. First, we have a mental challenge to overcome, and at the second, social and political level, we face a "prosperity challenge", which consists of maintaining the current prosperity for a decreasing population. Considering the rapidly increasing technological potential, we consider it within reach and wishful, to steadily increase prosperity for people, thereby achieving a greater quality of life in Europe and beyond.

With our current politics, however, we are going exactly in the opposite direction, thus obstructing a possible paradigm shift and hindering the unfolding of the growing technical potential in our knowledge societies. All the actions undertaken by our power elites concerning demographic change are leading to a decrease in productivity in our industries. We take in people from other countries and other cultures, with other contexts of experience, who cannot contribute to our prosperity. Through their migration into our countries, they often contribute to a decrease in prosperity in their home countries. This is a well analyzed effect in South-Eastern Europe as well as in many other parts of the world[404]. At the same time, we are increasing social pressure and increasingly destroying our social and natural environment. In addition, most of these people will cause even more costs in the future, when they grow older and will not be able to cover the retirement costs with the capital they have earned. So we are creating increasingly bigger problems for our

[404] We refer here only to one of several possible sources of information: Gunnar Heinsohn, Söhne und Weltmacht, 1. Auflage 2005.

societies. Finally, it is also known that many of these immigrants are missing in their countries of origin. They are missed by their families, and as they are absent, they cannot make substantial contributions to the well-functioning of their own societies.

Remittances sent by migrants are, to a certain extent, contributing to combating poverty in the home countries of the migrants. However, they are a transfer of financial resources that is finally contributing to increasing population growth in the home countries. At the end, remittances are a cure for certain symptoms, such as inequality of income among countries. However, remittances are in no way contributing to improving the situation. They do not lead to the paradigm shift concerning demographic growth that is required at both ends of the capitalist value chain. Thus, remittances are certainly justified socially, but they are playing into the cards of those industries that are looking for quick benefits through cheap labor at the expense of society at large. At the same time, this attitude is sabotaging the growth of productivity and slowing down the ongoing paradigm shift in our societies. Direct investments in the home countries would certainly be the better solution, with lower overall costs for our societies at both ends. This would have to be accompanied by appropriate education and training systems as a direct contribution to the development of the home countries of the migrants. As it stands now, with the current processes promoted by our power elites, the deficient structures of our societies are transferred to the home countries of the migrants, thus consolidating or even increasing the problems created by Western capitalism on a global scale.

For the various reasons mentioned, we strongly advise not to continue as before, in the sense of linear thinking and acting, but to take a new path. This path is already there, we just have to choose it by understanding that we only have a prosperity challenge to overcome. The challenge is simply to maintain our prosperity and, if possible, to increase it, together with improvements in our quality of life. We are capable of covering up this challenge, even though the population is declining. This is absolutely certain. The question remains: Why don't we act?

There is probably not one person in the different countries of Europe, who would seriously doubt that we could not succeed in this transformation of our societies, accompanied by a progressive decline in population. We still have plenty of well-trained engineers. We have a lot of well-educated and intelligent people, who can think, analyze, organize and manage conceptually. We have a lot of well-trained social scientists who can deal competently with social challenges. We have well-trained civil servants, as well as intelligent and well-trained people, who work in the administration, private and public, who can therefore make valuable contributions to organize and manage our societies. We probably don't have to be afraid that tomorrow there will be no more garbage collection, that the letters will not be delivered, that electricity and water will no longer flow, and that tax collection will no longer work. What are we afraid of? Who is telling us that we have to be afraid? It may be that these people are the politicians and other leaders of the power elites, who want us to listen to them and to continue following them. To follow them to where? Down to the abyss?

Despite all the facilities at hand, our societies in Europe as a whole do not have the courage to break away from the usual patterns of thought and behavior, even if it has become obvious that these no longer work. In our societies, people are organized in masses and fear the unknown. All this is corroborated by the increasing authoritarian pressure generated by our power elites, the public media and administrative systems in their hands, such as the legal system, which is increasingly used as an oppressive instrument[405]. People are prevented from facing reality or punished, if they call for action. People are hesitant to break the political bonds and economic clutches to accept or even embrace necessary changes, such as demographic change. Fundamental change, paradigm shift and peaceful transformation in our societies seem to be out of reach.

---

[405] We refer the reader to the increasing number of political decisions in Europe liming free speech or free access to information and media.

People in Europe will have to resist this pressure generated by the power elites and the media. They will have to overcome their deep-rooted fear of the unknown that is preventing them from actively promoting change, initiating the required transformation, and implementing the needed paradigm shift. People will have to end their subjugation to their politicians and the power elites. They will have to become aware that it does not make sense to sit out, manage or administer the problems according to "old" and outdated rules. People will have to become increasingly aware that problems that may grow out of demographic change stem from their fearful way of dealing with them as a society.[406]

We have now presented an important list of challenges that people in Europe are facing. We do not expect people to take on these challenges right away. We also do not have the intention to order or pressure people to accept these challenges. However, we are

[406] The vernacular says: Fear is a poor advisor. As stimulating literature on the topic of fear of change and fear in society in general, we recommend "Fliehen oder Weglaufen" (english: "Flee or Stand") by Horst-Eberhard Richter, 2012.

aware that the pressure for change is coming from the outside, from the external environment. Change and transformation in Europe are going to happen. Our point is, that it would be beneficial, if these changes and transformations were induced deliberately and initiated through consciously taken actions. We have also made it clear, why we do not trust the mindset or good will of our power elites. Their narrow-minded interests are not in line with the interests of the populations and the transformation of societies in Europe.

INITIATING THE PARADIGM SHIFT NOW

As we have been able to show with the examples of paradigm shifts presented here above, paradigm shifts are possible, in Europe as well as in other countries on earth.

Let's now return briefly to the politics under Willy Brandt. Under his government, the concept of "quality of life" was also introduced into politics. This addressed the issue of growth, which is not a value in itself, but only has value and makes sense, if it leads to a better "quality of life" for the population.

Unfortunately, this is no longer mentioned in politics today, or only marginally in order to spread fog, but not to guide political action in reality. Politics in Europe has long since stopped bringing people a better quality of life. Its principal function is limited to crisis management. As we have seen, these crises are not "natural" or necessary. They are self-made, anthropomorphic crises.[407] These crises can also be analyzed scientifically to attain a thorough understanding of their root causes. This is what we have endeavored to do in Part Two of this book.

The paradigm shift in relation to the "demographic problem", the so-called "aging of the population", consists, as a first step, of facing the problem and taking up the challenge. Then, action will have to be taken. Measures taken will have to contribute to general prosperity and well-being. The aim is to consolidate the present achievements and, in the medium to long term, to improve our quality of life even further. Taking up this challenge will require learning from other countries, such as Switzerland, Singapore and

[407] Richard Sakwa also speaks of this in our spirit in the interview recommended for reading, published in GlobalBridge on May 21, 2024.

even emerging China, or from other countries belonging to different cultural areas. The critical step will consist in creating a new perspective and looking at ourselves from a distance, i.e. as if we are watching us through the eyes of another person or nation. This will enable us to completely change our self-awareness and the way we see ourselves, over time. As a consequence, all our attitudes and actions will change and attain a new quality. These are processes well known in psychology, showing that with increasing consciousness, attitudes and actions are also changing[408]. With the thoughtful application of this method, Europe will, in the long run, create a new spiritual center for herself.

This will not require creating a new religion. The religions we are practicing individually are not in the way of such a practice of re-centering the personality of Europe and her people. However, this process of re-centering and re-concentration will bring Europe into a position of self-awareness, making the ongoing paradigm shift and the

[408] John Kabat Zinn has shown the validity of these processes in his book "Coming to Our Senses: Healing Ourselves and the World Through Mindfulness" published in 2005.

transformation in Europe a success. Obviously, this process will take time. But it is necessary, if we wish to escape the downward spiral of our development and the negative impact of our actions, not only internally in Europe, but also globally in the cooperation with other people and nations. We are optimistic and presume, that positive feedback and results will become apparent rapidly, within one generation. It is unfortunate and shameful for institutions, such as the EU, the European Parliament or the Council of Europe, that they neither have the courage, nor dispose of the intellectual standing to provoke such a process of deliberate transformation. For them, it is easier to go to war. What could be more significant for the low moral standards? The most significant and valuable call for the "spiritual renewal"[409] of Europe we know, has been presented by the theologian Joseph Ratzinger, who was later designed Pope Benedict XVI. In a speech given in 2000, concerning the EU Charta of Human Rights[410],

[409] It is significant for the mindset of Europe that its universities and think tanks demand a "renewal of institutions", not a spiritual renewal or a new mindset.
[410] Published by the journal Die Zeit, in December 2000.

he lays out his vision and understanding of Europe and the principal values that he sees at its foundation. Modern Europe did, for Ratzinger, not start with Columbus setting foot in 1492 on the American continent, but with the conquest of Constantinople by the Ottoman Empire of the Turks.

In a paper drafted by Joseph Ratzinger and published in 2005 with the title "The Soul of Europe", he expresses his concern that, notwithstanding the economic success and prosperity in Europe, it is an "inner void" that is at the origin of the deep crisis in Europe. Ratzinger then asks, "Which could be the power that is able to ensure the continuity of Europe's identity through its various historical metamorphoses?". We do not intend to proceed with a review of this speech or the article. Nor do we presume that our readers will share the entire content and all the arguments. Our reference to the reflections of Joseph Ratzinger is, however, a reminder, that Europe is facing serious challenges, while its power elites continue with their linear politics and are busy managing symptoms, thus keeping Europe in a crisis mode.

What we ask for, however, is that people start to ask the right questions seriously. Through debates, followed by deep and thorough reflections, people may progressively abandon the old ways of thinking and acting. We have to understand and accept that Europe is in need of a transformation and urgently requires a mental and spiritual regeneration. Such a process of mental and spiritual renewal will concomitantly lead to actions furthering Europe's transformation and the creation of a new paradigm for Europe.

Obviously, Europe will have to get out of the crisis mode. In our eyes, this will pass through a new definition of the expectations that people have concerning the quality of life. Politics has to be re-centered at the same time. Instead of managing crises, politics will have to support people in their efforts to attain a better quality of life. This new approach to politics in Europe, - we may call it a political paradigm shift -would essentially consist in lowering social costs by increasing trust in people to handle their own affairs. We challenge politics in Europe to offer all people in all countries of our continent free access to quality-conscious health care, access to excellent education and training, not only for elites, but for all people, and access to high-quality housing in an environment that offers people healthy living space in nature for playing, sports and leisure activities. This will certainly not be an easy task for our politicians and power elites. However, that is what we expect them to do for us. And we will dare to hold them accountable. It would certainly be beneficial for Europe to take a look at Singapore, Malaysia and other countries that are making an upward move, without warmongering or stripping other nations and people of their goods and fortunes.

Europe has a lot to learn from others and should not refuse to appreciate rules, which other people and nations they have applied to build successful societies with a higher quality of life than what we have in Europe today. This would represent a political paradigm shift, because for too long politics in Europe has deviated from its primary task. It has forgotten what it is all about and has neglected the welfare of people. It has been a long time since we have noticed politics that would seriously have taken a positive attitude facing the challenges in the most important areas of society. The offers for health care, education and housing are becoming more and more expensive and are at the same time declining in quality.

The current policy approach continues to be based on attempts to extinguish the many fires of crisis, and is generally led by the narrow-minded idea of "limited resources". This way, we are heading nowhere. This is what experience shows us. Politics and the self-proclaimed elites pretend to distribute the "limited resources" fairly. In reality, "distribution" is carried out in an authoritarian manner. People do not have a real choice and are not asked what they really want. Debates with an open outcome do not take place.

It seems, as if Europe and a great part of the Western dominated world is following the example of Germany, a country where the ultimate goal of politics is to guarantee a "subsistence minimum" for all people. This is a goal that is expressed in an intellectually hidden way even in the architecture of the Bauhaus. On the other hand, we would like to attract attention to an attitude, as it has been lived in traditional European societies, such as Wales. The Welsh borne American architect

Frank Lloyd Wright expressed his dismay with the Bauhaus architecture and stated that the aim of his own architecture was to offer people the possibility of pleasure, enjoyment and the comprehensive unfolding of life.[411] This is a significant contrast to the German "subsistence minimum" and represents in our eyes a serious call for a paradigm shift. This is the choice people in Europe should be offered today.

Of course, such a paradigm shift would mean a clear turning away from the current and outdated practice of politics, which obviously sees the *raison d'être*, i.e. the meaning of politics and the state, in generating more and more money and resources for government, in order to have ever greater funds available for ever more "international tasks", including ever more wars such as the one waged in

[411] To introduce this topic and to get to know Frank Lloyd Wright for the first time, we recommend his biography of Robert Carter from 2006. Lewis Mumford has well recognized the danger of this kind of Western civilization and its consequences. For this purpose, we recommend in German "Myth of the Machine. Culture, Technology and Power, from 1986, as well as his early books, such as »The Story of Utopias«, 1922, »Technics and Civilization« 1934, »The Culture of Cities« 1938, »The Condition of Man« 1944.

Ukraine since 2022. This is not the way we consider "just distribution" of resources to be organized.

It is time to fundamentally change this understanding of the *raison d'être* of politics and the state, which was essentially defined mainly by the politics during the era of industrialization in the 18th and 19th centuries, long time after the eras of the Renaissance and Baroque. We see the fundamental *raison d'être* of politics and the state today in securing and, if possible, expanding prosperity and quality of life for the population. This does not include wars of conquest for new habitats or the fight for raw materials. We would like to see the application of scientific and technical knowledge in a contractually agreed-upon international framework. This should enable the free people in Europe to secure their general prosperity in economic and cultural exchange on equal terms with people from other countries and nations. General prosperity and the cultural unfolding of human potential are the aims we have in mind. These are the aims that are setting the benchmarks for new politics. We have to create a social and political environment that constantly improves the quality of life for people to enjoy life in peace in their respective countries.[412]

THE SOLUTION TO THE PROBLEM

According to our understanding of demographic change, which we have briefly outlined here above, a paradigm shift would consist in letting the population develop at their discretion. We agree that most people would be surprised to receive this opportunity and would have to learn to live without

[412] Public Health policy can serve as an example of the failed policies in Europe. There is probably no generation left that has not heard of the so-called "reform of the health system" and has also suffered from it. Services are decreasing in quality, while the costs are constantly increasing. Presumably, this kind of reform will continue to "occupy" future generations.

In the field of environmental policy, we will point out that there is practically no river or stream left in Europe from which fresh water can be drunk all year round without hesitation. Switzerland, Sweden, Finland and Norway may be the examples of the rule. Where the pollution is not caused by industries, it is caused by people, who pollute and overuse waters and seas in ever greater numbers. This is now a worldwide phenomenon. Successful environmental politics and education would lead to different results.

Government and elites telling them what to do and how to behave. In the current situation in Europe, in late 2024, we are living under political processes driven by the international power elites that go straight in the opposite direction. We will briefly illustrate these processes preventing people from exercising their human rights for self-determination with just one recent example. On September 22, 2024, the General Assembly of the UN had to decide on the adoption of a *Global Act for the Future*, including measures of direct interference in people's lives by UN organizations and governments without any democratic legitimization. People are left out in the cold.

In this *Global Act for the Future*, we read under Action 57: "We will strengthen the international response to complex global shocks". A bit further down, we read that to do this, "We request the Secretary-General to: (a) Present for the consideration of Member States protocols for convening and operationalizing emergency platforms based on flexible approaches to respond to a range of different complex global shocks". In the *Policy Brief 2* of March 2023, the UN Secretary-General explained in more detail which emergency rights he would like to have: "I propose that the General Assembly provide the Secretary-General and the United Nations system with permanent authority to automatically convene and deploy an emergency platform in the event of a future complex global shock of sufficient scale, severity and scope. (...) The Secretary-General would decide when to convene an emergency platform in response to a complex global shock". This means that the UN Director-General wants to be equipped with the right to declare a global state of emergency in his or her own absolute discretion and to coordinate the handling of such actual or alleged states of emergency. With the experience gained under the authoritarian management of the so-called Corona pandemic, such suggestions coming from the UN and their member states make the alarm clock ringing.

The open list of "possible complex global emergencies" in the Secretary-General's summary report is not missing out on any issue relevant for freedom and the well-being of people in general. It comprises :

- ➢ Large-scale climate or environmental events that cause significant socio-economic disturbance and/or environmental degradation;
- ➢ Future pandemics with cascading secondary effects;
- ➢ large-scale incidents involving the use of a biological warfare agent (intentionally or unintentionally);
- ➢ events that lead to disruptions in the global flow of goods, people or finances;
- ➢ large-scale destructive and/or disruptive activities in cyberspace or disruptions to global digital connectivity;
- ➢ A major event in space that causes severe disturbances in one or more critical systems on Earth;
- ➢ Unforeseen risks ("black swan").

In the same direction are leading other initiatives, such as the *Council for the Human Future*, which convened in Rome from July 27 to 28, 2024. This *Council for the Human Future* considers the world to be under the constant threat of multiple crises, which will, in their understanding, have to be managed by central institutions or agencies, forming a kind of "world government". Therefore, this Council suggests, in agreement and with the support of various partner organizations, such as the Club of Rome, and based on a paper that has been adopted by the Council to "Give the UN system the competence to enact binding laws to protect our planetary environment".

This is certainly not in our line of thinking and arguing in this book. On the contrary, we suggest that people be directly involved in such decision-making processes. This may slow down such processes and require additional coordination. However, we believe it is worth paying the price. Otherwise, people and humanity at large are paying with their freedom and well-being, which should not be tagged with a price. We therefore ask that public life gradually be organized in a different way, leaving the mass societies behind us and moving towards smaller groups, in which direct participation can be ensured. People will have to be offered access to information that enables them to freely think about controverse subjects and enter into debates about the various rules that might be applied for social and political design. People in Europe have to be brought back to participate, discuss and learn with others globally to see, which rules would be better for Europe in the end. It is therefore important that politicians are progressively hindered from playing their power games and constantly intervene in public and private life. In particular, pressure from economic lobby groups, associations and the power elites will progressively have to be reduced. We are aware that they want to make us believe that the solution to all the vices and problems can only come from them. We do not believe them anymore and bluntly reject their cure of all evils, which consists, in their eyes, in continued population growth.

The financing gap that may open up with a declining population will have to be closed by increasing productivity through investment in science, research and technology. As a consequence, this implies that every active person in the production process will achieve an ever-increasing production surplus. That is the challenge that can be managed and solved technically without major difficulties and will not overwhelm the well-functioning of our societies in any way. Furthermore, this approach is principally valid for all societies globally. As we have learned from Buckminster Fuller, the *universal principles* of the physical functioning of the universe apply everywhere, even in outer space. This is what Kant has been teaching us already in his Critique of Practical Reason.

We know that higher productivity through the use of more intelligent machines and technologies has been the usual path of humanity's scientific and technological development. For several decades, however, productivity growth in Europe has slowed sharply and is constantly declining.[413] This shows that we are moving on the wrong path and in the wrong direction. This means, without any doubt, that we will have to change our previous paradigm, if we wish to preserve prosperity and improve the quality of life.

Currently, we use the profits from productivity growth to cover the ever-increasing costs of immigration, with all the consequential problems of "integration". This functional approach of social engineering for the integration of immigrants leads to ever

[413] Here is just one of many possible sources. The Economic Policy Brief of the VFA – Association of Research-Based Pharmaceutical Companies on June 22, 2023, states: "Productivity: Germany's industry slips into international mediocrity".
https://www.vfa.de/de/wirtschaft-politik/macroscope/

higher social costs, greater expenditure on education, health and infrastructure, and greater pressure on the environment. All these are costs that have no productive outcome for society. They are increasing bureaucracy and the budgets of governments for measures to secure a minimum of social cohesion through technical measures and to maintain a basic level of social peace. It is the usual way of linear politics, treating symptoms and creating consequently new problems downstream.

At the same time, this fervent activism, promoted by huge bureaucracies equipped with immense budgets, makes us blind to the solution that lies openly in front of us. Through a paradigm shift concerning demographic growth, the positive and beneficial effects of a decreasing population, such as decreasing financial costs for our societies and increasing quality of social services, would become reality at short notice. With a decreasing population, fewer hospital beds, fewer daycare places, fewer schools and places at universities are needed. Less investment is also needed in the entire infrastructure system of our modern societies, concerning roads, transport, public utilities and the environmental management.

As we can see, a paradigm shift in Europe in terms of demographic change would definitely lead to a "win-win" situation. Everyone would gain and could draw substantial profit and real benefits of the new policies implemented.

THE KEY TO THE SOLUTION: PRODUCTIVITY[414]

We are all well aware now, that the solution certainly does not lie in further population growth in Europe through ever more immigration. This will only lead to an ever-increasing deterioration of the social situation. This should be obvious by now to any sensible and intelligent reader of the book, as well as to the critical observer of the social, economic and political changes we have experienced over the past decades in Europe.

---

[414] Rene Egli wrote an ingenious book back in 1994, the "Lola Principle", The Perfection of the World", which convincingly shows that paradigm shifts are possible.

We have now understood that the key to solving the challenges posed by natural demographic changes is to count on our own strengths as intelligent and sensitive humans. We have trust in the people in Europe to have the capability to secure and even increase prosperity and quality of life through their own genius. This requires a continuous, intelligently managed, scientifically and technically induced increase in productivity. An intelligent increase in productivity will increase prosperity, as long as the results are fairly shared. Every good entrepreneur knows these links between productivity, income generation and profit. Any educated modern person with common sense can understand this and confirm it.

We do not need to do an inquiry, survey or study to know that our engineers in our companies in Europe, are able to increase productivity in the production and industrial units. VW can confirm this to us, as can Audi, ABB, Alstom, BMW, Bosch, Philips or Siemens. This can be confirmed to us by the entire SME sector and all the successful family businesses in Europe, which have successfully grown their businesses in response to the challenge of increasing productivity for decades. However, all these industries in Europe will not be able to cope with the effects of a contrary policy in the long term.

The current drama is that European industry is being seduced by the wrong policies to prevent productivity growth by integrating immigrants, often low-skilled workers, into work processes. The costs of these policies have to be borne by ever-increasing social budgets. At the same time, these policies ultimately reduce productivity. This leads to fatal consequences in the long term, as the increasing economic crises and growing social problems show.

It is no secret that the social and financial costs of these policies are increasing in all the countries of Europe. Their societies must increasingly devote resources to combating the consequences of the incessantly promoted demographic growth. The industry and the people, who work in the various industries, ultimately have to finance the expensive and very costly population growth caused by immigration. The majority of the population has no benefits of this, neither social not financial.[415] On the contrary, the threat of poverty in old age is a real problem, created by the current wrong path that our politicians are taking. Educational institutions and health care continue to lose quality, and the public infrastructure is deteriorating to a threatening extent.

A successful paradigm shift could have prevented this. This paradigm shift would have consisted of continuously promoting an increase in productivity made possible by the use of ever better technological means and intelligent processes. This increase in productivity would be enhanced by a continuous increase in efficiency of production and management, promoted by the well-trained population in the countries in Europe. This would have led to wonderful results, to a grandiose increase in prosperity and a wonderful quality of life for all, without increasing social problems and without ever more serious environmental pollution.

[415] On this, Christoph Butterwegge published, "The Torn Republic. Economic, Social and Political Inequality in Germany", Beltz Juventa, Weinheim, 2019.

Instead, politics makes us dance around the dead idol of population growth. The problems are growing into dimensions that have become life-threatening to our societies and will soon no longer be controllable.[416]

OUR CALL: TAKE RESPONSIBILITY! ACT NOW!

It will be important and good for all of us to finally act now and initiate the paradigm shift concerning the challenge of demographic change and to take a different, salutary path that will bring us all a better quality of life.

We call for Europe to give the world a positive and constructive example. We have the capacity and should make an effort to show the world in an exemplary way that better modes of life are possible. We should demonstrate to the world that we can live well in our countries, on this earth, even if the population decreases in the future. This would be a positive message coming from Europe to

[416] The globally increasing number of military conflicts and the ever-growing industrial-military complex, fueled by a new arms race, can be seen as warning indications of the increasingly hopeless global situation. Wars are used to cover up the crises. War thus becomes the ultimate crisis.

the other nations, and in particular to the Global South. That would also have been a call for a paradigm shift in the sense of what Singapore has shown: the path from the Third World to the First is possible; for all countries, nations and their people.

In this part of the book, with our essay on the challenge of demographic change, we have placed a lot of emphasis on hints and examples of possible practical solutions. The examples from European and international politics are intended to prove that paradigm shifts are possible and feasible, even under sometimes difficult conditions, and can lead to positive results.

It may be striking that we have given relatively little space to pointing out the negative and obstructive forces. This can be justified by our conviction that paradigm shifts should not be talked into people, nor can they be commanded. A paradigm shift comes about, when appropriate circumstances and the right people come together at the right time, when forces join forces to create something new.[417] We must

[417] In modern physics, a paradigm shift has been carried out in a period that began in the last decades of

learn to understand that these are processes will intervene deeply in the human beings, as well as the functioning of our societies in Europe. Such transformations finally mean profound changes for our nations and cultures.

In the social sphere, the 20th century was the most violent in human history.[418] The 21st century seems to be following this trend. We have analyzed the major symptoms and analyzed the principal causes for the crisis in Europe in the first and second part of our book. We must sadly admit that the retarding and destructive forces have gained the upper hand in our societies in Europe and do not yet want to give way. Norbert Wiener had already in 1950 warned against these negative forces in his socially and politically critical work "The

the 19th century, from Maxwell to Boltzmann and Mach, and which in the 20th century extended through the periods of Einstein, Bohr, Heisenberg to Pauli, and concluded with the formulation of modern quantum theory. This paradigm shift in physics was difficult to achieve and took time until it was finally accepted by all the scientists involved. Tobias Hürter has well traced this process of blurring in his enlightening book "The Age of Blurring (1895-1945)", published 2021.

[418] The War of the World: History's Age of Hatred, from Niall Ferguson, 1st Edition, 2009, Penguin.

Human Use of Human Beings – Cybernetics and Society", in which he insists in the necessity of human control of systems and machines. Norbert Wiener speaks it out clearly and unequivocally: People cannot avoid taking responsibility for their actions and must always take responsibility for their future. It is this approach that we are taking here by appealing to the responsibility of us humans for shaping the context of our own lives and those of our fellow creatures. No excuse, no escape, we are all challenged here.

Even though we know that it is not always easy to initiate and carry out paradigm shifts, we must not back down from our responsibility. Paradigm shifts require a lot of courage and time to implement them, until they are finally accepted by all the people concerned. We must learn to understand that these are social and political processes that intervene deeply in the human being and mean profound changes for our cultures.

In the 21st century, we should summon up the necessary courage a new and not let up in invoking the good forces for a quantum leap out of the crisis in Europe. Through our will and creativity we can open new paths inducing a paradigm shift that can lead to sustainable progress and continuous improvement in the quality of life in our countries and nations.

Part Three

Europe's Way out of the Crisis

Chapter 3

Call for a social and political paradigm shift

Introduction

Currently, the goals and purposes that are driving political development on earth are still mainly driven by the rules and principles enshrined in the Western, i.e. the European and American-driven paradigm. The purpose of our book is to provide a contribution to the efforts to progressively achieve a global paradigm shift in geopolitics. In the chapter on the ongoing paradigm shift towards a new system of global governance, we have shown that this will inevitably lead to change in the way, cooperation among the members of the global community is functioning. Currently, the UN with its agreements and proclamations is coming closest to what we may call a global community. Based on the evidence provided through our analysis in

Parts One and Two, and with a perspective on a peaceful future on our planet, we have to accept that things will have to change. What is even more, we have learned in the chapter on the system of global governance, that things are already changing, unequivocally and irrevocably. The paradigm shift in the area of global governance is ongoing. This shift to a new paradigm will require new rules and principles to be accepted and applied by humanity for the regulation of their societies and nations, geopolitics included. The UN, dominated by the Western powers with their Western mindset, corroborated by Western style international institutions and organizations, does not provide the appropriate environment for the new system of global governance. This need for change of the geopolitical system refers to what the Chinese call the "global community for a common future".[419] The aforementioned document on this subject presented by the Chinese government explicitly states: The zero-sum game is over. This is a clear

---

[419] We would like to remind you of the Chinese government's white paper entitled "A Global Community of Shared Future: China's Proposals and Actions."

statement that we all, in particular Europe and the US, should take into account for future actions.

In Parts One and Two of our book, we have proceeded with an evidence-based analysis of the current situation. Progressively, we have built up the foundation for evidence-based suggestions for change and transformation that make sense. On the basis of this solid foundation, we have become confident enough to ask ourselves what it takes to move forward on the path of successfully meeting the complex challenges of a transformation of our societies. The historical reconstruction of the specific mindset in Europe has led us to gain insight into the main factors that are driving Europe's actions. We have shown that the specific desire for progress and unlimited material growth through the application of scientific knowledge and technology are at the root of Europe's mental constitution.

The analytical parts in our book also provided evidence, that Europe has come to a point, where it has to act now. In modern science, such as cybernetics and life-sciences, such as biology and chemistry, these points, where the pressure on the system requires change, are called *bifurcation points*. The system at a "bifurcation point", if it has the will to survive, has to adjust through modifications in the dynamics, as well as the direction of self-regulating processes. Consequently, Europe will have to learn from modern science how to better manage her societies, as well as its actions in geopolitics, to induce a future upward spiral of continuous improvement of the quality of life for its people. This might become Europe's contribution to a peaceful and prosperous life on spaceship Earth.

We presume that not only Europe, but humanity in its entirety, has entered into an era of change and has reached a *tipping point*, i.e. a *bifurcation point*, in its evolution. Such *bifurcation points* are temporal moments or spaces in time, in which processes are pressing to develop further. The processes may move in different directions, depending on the action and interference of the active catalytic forces. It is therefore important not to let this moment pass by, thus missing the opportunity. Europe, together with the other members of humanity, has the possibility of influencing these ongoing global social and political processes through a joint act of willpower as the principal catalytic force. It is human action promoted by human willpower that is able to move the ongoing transformation of our societies in Europe and beyond in certain, desired directions. Through willpower Europe has the potential to orientate processes of the self-regulating system of humanity evolving on earth.

Europe has the capacity to avoid a situation, where she will flip by sheer chance from one paradigm to another. Europe, in a synergetic move with humanity, will consciously have to take responsibility for this shift to a new paradigm. This is the capacity offered to human beings by the gift of freedom inherent in the human constitution.

WAYS OUT OF THE DILEMMA

So where should we start to get out of this seemingly untamable and generalized "growth trap"? What can we in Europe do practically? What should be the first step to take?

Objectively speaking, population growth certainly has the greatest potential and the greatest leverage to start lifting Europe out of its crisis. Reversing the unlimited population growth is the first and most effective step. It will create the highest impact and have the most rapid social and political effects. Over time, it may even enable the recovery of threatened resources and bring "healing" to damaged social structures. Thus, a new approach to the demographic challenge will certainly be a first and effective step out of the crisis in Europe.

If we have followed the argumentation in this book with attention, we should have become sensitive to our suggestion and will appreciate that this first step will explicitly focus on human action in society. We are not promoting a functional or technocratic approach. Our intention is to indicate to Europe, as an integral part of humanity, a way back to taking her fate in her own hands. This process of rising consciousness and becoming aware of its fate will lead Europe to the urgent integration of the various social, economic and political structures into a new system following new rules. The outcome of these processes is critical for the increasingly harmonic functioning of the living environment in Europe. These processes of integration within Europe will eventually also lead to synergies within humanity as a self-regulating system. Currently, the opposite happens. The actions coming from Europe and the US have effects that are a cause for global suffering, illness and destruction.

Following this path of integration, Europe must not be driven anymore by the limited scope of the present forces, such as the exclusive drive for power and money. We have made it clear by now that we are not prone to improving the quality of life through the sole application of technological means. Evolution is expected to continue under increasing responsibility and with the conscious, catalytic impulses of human intellect and mind. We have an optimistic view of the human being and the potential of humanity. We trust humans to be capable and willing to find constructive and sustainable solutions to the challenges they are facing. We do not trust the politicians, self-proclaimed global leaders and power elites and will not follow them anymore.

Implementation of this first step concerning demographic change, to induce a paradigm shift in Europe, will almost immediately change the situation. This first step consists essentially of a process of communication and joint decision-making. This process will contribute to trust-building and an increasing sense of coherence among people. These are well-known effects of group-building processes. This is very different and contrary to the manipulation and control of the masses that is currently the rule in our societies in Europe. These processes will show people that they can take and subsequently implement decisions without being manipulated by their politicians, self-proclaimed leaders and power elites. This will create trust within people and their groups to rely on their own forces and capabilities. People will feel the impact of such a decision directly as a result of human action based on their own experience.

Concerning demographic change, decisions taken by people, that are leading to a paradigm shift, will almost immediately produce direct impacts. Within one generation already, it will become obvious that fewer people need less energy, will need and consume fewer resources to shape their living environment, will produce less waste and wastewater, and will take up less space for habitation. We may call these results "self-evident". The generalized and indiscriminate growth we are used to, which covers all areas of life, will decline immediately.

This first step taken, it will show that people are capable of finding adequate solutions to their problems. People will learn to trust in their own capacities. Through this kind of action, people will understand that solutions to problems can be found in joint and peaceful efforts within social groups and accepted political settings. No threats, violent actions or wars are required. This kind of human action will change the social and political attitudes in Europe at short notice, with sensitive effects that will reinforce mutual trust and understanding. This is the kind of European integration that will lead to improving the quality of life in the long term.

The readers, who have followed us so far, may well understand that we are suggesting here principles of human action, that are not promoted by our power elites. On the contrary, these power elites are afraid of people taking action on their own and without their control. Unfortunately, we are increasingly living in a situation of repression of free speech and free human action in

Europe. The power elites try to turn the freedom bell back.

Therefore, the action taken will have to overcome political forces of resistance in Europe that are still furthered through the ever-present public, as well as the mainstream media. Human social and political action that is undertaken with the interest of promoting a peaceful transformation of our societies will have to recur to methods of social action, as they have been applied by Mahatma Gandhi with his *Satyagraha* methods and by Martin Luther King Jr. with his *Montgomery bus-boycott* mass protest movement. In both cases, conscious, courageous and charismatic humans have taken responsible action with considerable results. In the present situation of repression, only through this kind of human action by civil society can sensitive changes be induced, which will lead to a new paradigm in Europe and for humanity. The new paradigm will not be generated in parliaments or other presumably representative institutions managed under the surveillance of our power elites.

We are aware that there are numerous groups and movements that have developed various methods of peaceful protest and are operating platforms for mediation in conflicts and promoting dialogues for peaceful development. In Germany, we know of the Berghof Foundation with her vision of "*A world changing for the better through constructive conflict transformation.* In the US, there are also various active groups, such as Popular Resistance, that have acquired broad experience in organizing campaigns and participate globally in coalitions on a broad range of issues. Africa, Latin America and Asia are vibrant with grassroots associations and civil society movements that are working to temper the negative impact of global politics managed by our current power elites. These civic organizations are the promoting forces and privileged partners for initiating a paradigm shift in Europe leading to a better future and sustainable improvements in the quality of life. They are usually focusing on concrete results for their constituent members and communities, and are creating an impact on the quality of life within their social groups.

It should have become obvious by now, that we are calling for a new civil movement taking actions of civil engagement that may even comprise civil disobedience, if and when required. We do this, because we consider this the most effective means to start inducing and strengthening our quest for a paradigm shift. It is not the only means, but certainly one of the most effective.

On our way to utopia, we will meet many obstacles and many people, who will tell us that what we intend to do and what we are looking for is nonsense and not realistic. We are clear about the point that we do not follow the way of Aldous Huxley and of Thomas Moore, who told us that utopia can only be realized on an island. We live on this earth only, and we have only this earth to live on. There is no alternative to this. Hence, there is no alternative to our quest for a paradigm shift on the way to utopia.

Let's take a brief look at reality - at our reality of the past few years. What would have happened, if people had applied the methods of Gandhi's *Satyagraha* and of Martin Luther King's Jr. *Montgomery bus-boycott* mass protest movement? For example during the so-called Corona pandemic. People could have refused to wear these ridicule, denigrating and completely useless masks; they could have refused any kind of additional vaccination; they could have enjoyed life without traveling. No government could have done anything against their populations. These would have been acts of passive civil resistance. In cases, where it is a matter of life and death, i.e. the question of war and peace, would it make sense, if people refused to pay taxes, or refused to go to work until critical steps to peaceful action were enabled and taken? The most important measure people can take right now is to stop watching TV and use public media. These are the prime tools for manipulating the masses. People have to learn to get information by doing their own searches on the internet and by talking to their neighbors and peers in their relevant social groups. These should become our primary information sources.

We are aware that everybody will tell us that this is not realistic. We do not believe this and will not listen to this objection anymore. We are aware that we have been manipulated and lied to for much too long. What we experience on a daily basis is that wars are possible, they are "realistic" all over the globe every day at a large scale, bearing huge costs in human lives and for the environment. This is realistic and realized by humanity, in our name. In December 2014, a number of important public figures in Germany published a call for a change in the policies against Russia: "War again in Europe? – Not in our Name". If this call had been listened to, hundreds of thousands of human lives in Europe would have been saved, millions of people would not have become refugees, and the endless suffering of innocent people would have been avoided. Obviously, our power elites had other interests and more important things in mind. Is it not only our right, but also our duty as citizens and human beings, to take action under such circumstances? Do we not have the right to take action against the wars promoted by our political leaders and power elites? These are questions we should raise again and again, without fear.

The ceaseless and uncontrolled enrichment of a very limited number of people and financial cartels is happening on an incredibly large scale every day. We know that during all the crises of the past decades, the rich and affluent have become richer and more affluent every day. This is realistic and realized, with most citizens in Europe and beyond remaining tacit. These citizens are living under constraints in their mass societies. They are put daily under social and economic pressure by society and are forced to accept public actions of repression and war as "natural". Over the past decades, under US hegemony and Europe's proclaimed "superiority", the pressure in all areas of life on the billions of ordinary people has increased globally every day. This is confirmed by our experience every day and wherever we live.

We humans can think, and we are what we are thinking. Obviously, we have to change what we are told to think and to believe by our self-declared leaders and power elites. We have to understand that everything is unrealistic, until it happens and is realized. This is called the principle of manifestation[420] or incarnation, i.e. bringing things to life and making things real. We agree with Buckminster Fuller that there is a *Critical Path*

[420] David Spangler has written in his book "The Laws of Manifestation", 1978, an informative introduction to this subject.

to take. That's how the first human being reached the moon and returned to earth. It is the path of the ten thousand steps, of which each step is critical. However, we believe that this is the only way to achieve our goal of inducing a new paradigm in Europe and to the benefit of humanity. Let's join Nelson Mandela on his "Long Walk to Freedom"[421].

On the basis of these considerations, we call for a move towards the realization of our convincing suggestion made in this book. Europe is called to start her way towards a paradigm shift and transformation of her societies with a first step in the area of demographic change. Would it not make sense for civil society in Europe to open a debate on demographic trends and the potential to change them, and start living with self-regulating demographic trends in the future? The solutions coming from civil society might look different from the measures that are currently suggested by our self-proclaimed leaders and power elites, to be driven through by governments and parliamentarians. To do this, we, as civil society, will have to take action. Only human

[421] This is the title of the biography of Nelson Mandela, published in 1994, which we highly recommend.

action can provide the basis for the unfolding and renewed flourishing of human potential. Science and technology will assist us in our endeavors to produce energy for heating and light, when we sit in meetings, do our jobs in our factories or businesses, or are dwelling in our homes. However, science and technology will not bring a solution to the challenges humanity is facing. Such methods, as they have been applied by civil society movements under Gandhi, Martin Luther King Jr., and Nelson Mandela, will lead to social and political conditions enabling us to establish new rules that align the design and functioning of our societies with the goal of a better quality of life. The utopia of an ever-optimizing quality of life will offer the appropriate perspective for our actions.

Our politicians and leaders, as well as people from all kinds of industries, will do what they can to hinder the realization of this utopia. They will continuously try to persuade us that more growth in all areas, especially the growth of the economy, is crucial for better well-being. They will say that this growth can only be achieved through higher population growth. Is that really right? Is this causal relation correct? Or do these people follow their egoistic, short-sighted, and short-term interests to attain their short-term egoistic advantages from unlimited and one-sided growth? We will not accept any more being persuaded by these people and groups, whose interest is single-minded economic growth to increase the income of the financial cartels. They will continue to tell us that growth has to be based on the ever-increasing consumption of energy and natural resources, and can supposedly only be generated by ever greater masses of people.

We will refuse to be the masses they intend to manipulate every day through their media for the realization of their short-sighted interests. We will let them know that we are well aware that their approach to growth through weaponry and expansive wars has negative consequences for Europe, for humanity and for our earth. We know that these domineering and hegemonic politics promoted by Europe and the US create exponentially ever greater negative social impact and long-term environmental damage. We will tell them that we refuse to follow them down their out-worn path.

Would it not be possible to make prosperity, quality of life and well-being possible for the people of Europe, even with a declining population? This is certainly possible. However, it is not part of the options of the power elites. According to what criteria would a free human being, which we all want to become, evaluate prosperity, quality of life and well-being? We presume that it will even be possible to increase prosperity, quality of life and well-being for all people on this earth, without giving in to the pressure for ever greater material and economic growth and for ever larger populations. Wouldn't this also correspond to an irreversible change from the industrial age to the age of the knowledge society?[422]

The critical key to success is, that we in Europe take responsibility for steering the processes of progress and growth according to rules that bring us closer to the goal of an ever higher quality of life, even with a decreasing population. The means to this end lie in increasing productivity, which is a

[422] An introduction to the topic of the knowledge society with detailed references to the literature can be found at:
https://de.wikipedia.org/wiki/Wissensgesellschaft

natural outflow of the human mind and a direct result of scientific and technological progress.

This has become a truism and shows us that we are on the brink of a new humanity. In fact, the paradigm shift has already been induced by the catalytic forces of willpower at work. The paradigm shift is already ongoing, without the consent of the Western power elites. The dreams of the Renaissance are going to be accomplished. This means that it is possible to achieve more and better products by increasing productivity and improving production processes, while at the same time decreasing the use and consumption of resources. It should be clear to everyone that the increasing robotization of production and the use of "artificial intelligence" (AI) mean that there are no foreseeable limits to the growth of productivity. Has this not been the aim we have always been looking for since the Renaissance?

Let us engage in this new experiment of humanity, and we will soon realize that we can live better with a smaller population, attaining a higher quality of life and greater well-being.[423] This result should not even surprise us, it makes sense immediately. This is common sense! It is certainly worthwhile to try this experience now. This is not the great re-set promoted by the WEF. We refuse to embark on their functional and technological approach that is dictated by the egoistic strive for power and money of the domineering power elites. We encourage people to take human action. This is the only way out of the crisis mode. Let's ask people from other cultural areas what they think of this idea. That will certainly further us more, than always coming up with our "Western" solutions promoted globally by the power elites, who are pretending to know what is best for everyone.

The material wealth within the framework of this new path will be drawn from the potentially infinite growth of scientific and technical capacities, and can at wish be continuously furthered by means provided by

[423] Hans-Peter Duerr has repeatedly drawn attention to this fact in his lectures and books. For this purpose, we recommend reading his book "The Myth of the Civilization Process", 2005.
http://www.denkwerkzukunft.de/index.php/stiftung/index/Duerr.

them.[424] A mentally and psychologically maturing humanity will reach, at a certain point in time, a situation of saturation concerning their wish for material growth. There exists a natural saturation point for mentally healthy and consciously living people. There is no natural need for overweight in an affluent society. Hence, we will certainly succeed in attaining a higher quality of life and more well-being with a decreasing population. The funds generated by industries can be distributed to fewer people and the available prosperity for the people will continuously increase. This will also mean that the Malthusian fear of a limitation or an end of available resources will decrease to finally cease completely. External, materially oriented growth will lose importance in order to give people more space.

---

[424] A term that is usually used for this refers to productivity growth, as a central concept of growth theory. Productivity growth means a positive change in the output of production in relation to the factors of production used for it, such as labor, capital, and environmental resources, over a certain period of time. To put it simply, one could say: "doing more with less"; i.e. achieving more by using fewer resources.

This will provide the opportunity for people to develop a living environment that suits them for further personal pleasure, as well as their mental health and spiritual growth. Indiscriminate, exponential economic and material growth will not remain the measure of all things anymore. Rather, the focus will be placed on social and cultural development. The focus of people will shift towards their responsibility and the well-being of humanity. The conscious willpower leading to self-determination will be at the origin of the processes setting new rules for Europe and her role in international solidarity and cooperation. The new era will see human beings attaining a new level of personal integration and mental maturity.

Wouldn't this also be a model that could make sense for other societies, not just for Europe? For China, India, Bangladesh, or Brazil and Malaysia, as well as for many countries in Africa, most of which are suffering from the exponential growth of their populations, which is accompanied by an unprecedented destruction of the natural environment and degradation of the living environment. The export of this new European model might be an opportunity for the formation of new international partnerships. The EU should cease to promote her limited vision in line with the narrow-minded example of its own development model, which has lost its credibility. This has become even more evident since the authoritarian rule of our power elites during the so-called Corona pandemic. This has definitely become obvious since the new open war and the subsequent shift to a war economy in Europe.

The model of Europe is exhausted and has emptied itself. At the global level, it is void of all moral credibility. The warmongering EU of 2024 will have to stop her outdated policies. The EU must contain and eventually stop the promotion of international politics that are hiding behind the Western domineering value-system and the pretended promotion of good governance. It is a well-known fact in the education of children and youth that the most important factor relies on the adults setting a good example. The EU is no longer setting a good example for the world. Europe and the EU in their crisis mode have become, with the expired historical evolutionary process since the Renaissance, a warning to the global community. The hopes, that were linked to the creation of the EU and to the historical and political processes of European integration, have been disappointing, proven to be vain, and may finally counter the freedom of people. Following the initial decades full of hope and even euphoric aspirations, Europe has been set back by the US and NATO to become a pawn in the strategy for global hegemony. After 9/11 of 2001, the hopes proved to be in vain. The detrimental outcome of the historical process of the European integration is a warning. It shows what happens, when one gives up sovereignty and abandons its moral obligation of responsibility for the well-being of societies and nations at the expense of the purely egoistic, self-centered interests of power elites. At the end, the really substantial result that came out of the initial fifty years following European integration and the creation of the EU has been an increasing level of material and economic prosperity. Socially and politically, Europe shows increasing symptoms of decay, decadence and even isolation. As it has become apparent now, even the economic results have been only temporary in nature. Since the war against Russia, the EU and her member states have entered into a war economy. Hence, even material prosperity is sacrificed on the altar of transatlantic solidarity and the promotion of wars through NATO. The benefits are reaped by the Anglo-American financial cartels and the owners and shareholders of the military-industrial complex. Europe and its people are left out in the cold.

In their own interest, Europe and the EU will have to cease the promotion of their limited vision that is globally perceived detrimental and only in line with the narrow-minded, egoistic interests of a limited group of people. Europe and the EU will have to shift their politics and cease to encourage the emergence of societies that no longer know how to feed people, that can hardly offer them clean water, where people in the cities can no longer breathe clean air and cannot hide from the omnipresent noise. The EU has been a worthwhile attempt to promote the principles of free association and international partnership. These are rules and principles indicating into a direction for a paradigm shift that could lead Europe to a future with new hope for a better quality of life and new partnerships.

The New Paradigm: New Ways of Life

The outdated paradigm of unlimited material growth, the "scientific-technological age" into which we started to grow since the Renaissance and which we have been practicing with ever-increasing fervor over the past 100 years now, is coming to a natural end. Many of us do not want to see it yet. Many are still blinded by the forces that make them believe in the illusion of happiness through infinite material growth and progress driven by science and technology.

A successful paradigm shift will consist in a progressive and conclusive move away from weaponry towards livingry. This will comprise the intelligent use of the scientific-technical capabilities combined with the hitherto still hidden potential for infinite regeneration of energy and resources. Management and production processes will have to be realigned with the needs inherent to human action. Redundant work and relevant jobs will have to be cancelled. Bureaucracy will have to be reduced. This is not only desirable, but feasible. A good example is provided by the initiative taken by Professor Paul Kirchhof in Germany, to simplify the extremely complex, cumbersome, time-consuming and cost-intensive taxing system in Germany. Professor Paul Kirchhof, a renowned specialist in the field of tax management, presented in 2011 a convincing concept for its simplification to the public. This laudable initiative has been blocked for narrow-minded political reasons. Society as a whole is paying a high price for such political nonsense that is in the interest of politicians, parties and the power elites to hide their deficient, but very costly bureaucracy and self-centered utilization of the taxes perceived. The governments and state budgets are constantly increasing without any change for a higher quality of life in sight. The ever-increasing tax income of the nations in Europe is utilized by the governments and the political parties to increase the social budgets in the hope of expanding their political power. That's the rule of the game. The greatest part of the potential made available by the increasing scientific-technical capacities is wasted by government, bureaucracy and related agencies and institutions.

The Mises Institute in the USA has put on the agenda of its most important actions, the takedown of America's central bank, the Federal Reserve Bank (FED). The Mises Institute criticizes strongly that "almost everything we hear about the Federal Reserve comes from those who think the Fed is essential to the prosperity and stability of the American economy. This isn't true, of course. In fact, the opposite is true. The Fed has been the source of booms, busts, and the ongoing impoverishment of Americans since its founding". The critical look of the Mises Institute at the Federal Reserve has been summarized in the documentary *Playing with Fire*, which shows how the Fed uses its power to damage the economy, increase inequality, and impoverish ordinary Americans. The film also looks at how the Fed has expanded its power since the financial crisis of 2008. *Playing with Fire* reveals what the Fed is, how it was born, and why it is so dangerous. Perhaps most important of all, *Playing with Fire* explains why Americans need to end the Fed. The American Mises Institute is consistently putting on the table for discussion the topic of *The FED and War Finance*. In 2006, an audio was produced to draw attention to the fact that "in the debate on American foreign and economic policy, the topic of financing is hardly ever raised. If tax increases are politically impossible, but the government still wants empire, the printing is there to assist". We suggest closely watching the role of the European Central Bank (ECB) in the funding of the EU. Where does the money come from for the euphemistically called "European Peace Facility" that has been created to fund the European and NATO-driven war in Ukraine against Russia? Whoever has the courage to face reality and the truth will understand that the FED and the ECB are cut from the same cloth. They have been created for the same purpose and goals. These are issues to be tackled by civil society in Europe, once it has heard the wake-up call and is ready for future action.

At present, the breathing space that could be made available to people to unfold their social creativity, or for socially relevant actions, such as debates serving to establish new rules for shaping a humane economy and society, is deliberately constrained by the power elites. People, who are left without surveillance through the media, might start to think and act in their own interests. This is what the power elites fear most, because it would run counter to their narrow-minded and egoistic interests.

This book cannot provide an operating manual with precise instructions concerning a paradigm shift leading Europe on its way out of its crisis mode. However, we thought it was not fair to say nothing about actions that might be taken and social and political methods that might be applied by people, who are eager to advance Europe on the path of her liberation. Liberation from their own, self-made traps and mental "prisons", as well as liberation from the political and economic clutches of the big brother on the other side of the Atlantic Ocean.

We also did not pretend to write a book on the mental or psychological cures Europe and her people might take to become more conscious. However, we agree with C. G. Jung that the paradigm shift for Europe will comprise a process of increasing consciousness and healing. This implies three essential elements to retain. First, we will have to accept that this process of increasing consciousness and healing will not happen with one single stroke. It will take time.

Second, from the perspective of the required transformation, Europe cannot remain stuck at the level of the symptoms of its crisis. Effective and sustainable solutions cannot happen at the level of symptoms. Healing of symptoms means not healing, but rather shifting sources of illness from one symptom to another. This would mean, at best, to gain time during the ongoing illness, i.e. the crisis mode. Third, the process of increasing consciousness and healing we are suggesting implies the application of a holistic approach, where the physical goes together with the mental or spiritual.

By the way, this is a strong reason that corroborates our choice for demographic change in our societies in Europe to become the first step towards a paradigm shift in politics. The new approach to demographic change will have a holistic impact, because it concerns economic, as well as social and political aspects of change and the healing of our societies. Demographic change is not a one-dimensional issue. Working on demographic change cannot be limited to functional measures. It will require a profound change in the mindset of the humans involved. This is a critical element for the long-term success of the process that should not be underestimated. The current perception of demographic growth is part of the phylogenetic heritage of our species. It has been ingrained in the human mind since the dawn of existence and its evolution on earth.

This means that such a change can only be induced through the use and application of the human mind and mindful willpower. Consciousness and the deliberate utilization of willpower are relatively recent outcomes in the evolutionary process of humanity.[425] This shows again that humanity and evolution are currently approaching a *bifurcation point* that will turn into the path of the *anthropocene*. In the future, humanity will progressively become the master of its own fate. Seen in this way, the paradigm shift is a process of maturation for humanity and the human mind. It is a process that cannot be fully understood by intellect. It has to be grasped intuitively during its ongoing realization, as it

[425] We recall here our previous references to Erich Neumann's "The Origins and History of Consciousness", as well as to the publications by Konrad Lorenz on the same subject, but looking at it from the angle of comparative behavioral research.

is becoming part of the human experience. This means that the coming epoch, in Europe as well as on a global level, will comprise and lead to an increasing consciousness and higher spiritual knowledge[426]. Such an evolution towards increasing consciousness and higher spiritual knowledge will progressively lead to synergies and harmony. The wishes and desires of people will lead to increasing synergetic energies in the mechanisms and structures that organize social and political systems. We suggest not using the term "democracy" for the outcome and the new system. This is a Eurocentric term. Its use would hinder the required opening of the processes towards the paradigm shift in Europe, which will at the end become global.

These processes, combined and implemented globally, will lead humanity to organize life in our societies with increasing consciousness. This will lead to progressively improving the mechanisms and structures for their functioning, moving them ever closer to the

[426] We refer here once again to R. Buckminster Fuller, who is not suspected of being esoteric. "Brain is different from mind" he let us know in his "Critical Path".

requirements of humanity as a self-regulating system on earth. This evolutionary process cannot be managed by a technological switchboard. Human action will be at the core. This reconciliation between technology and human demands and actions will lead progressively to an improving balance in social and political life. The outcome will consist of positive results, i.e., a sustainable increase in prosperity and quality of life for all, without increasing social problems and without ever more serious burdens on the environment.

In conclusion, we call for an end to politics that continue to let us dance around the dead idol of unlimited growth of the world's population, as well as the economy and material wealth. Humanity has reached a *bifurcation point* in its evolution and will have to consciously change its path towards the *anthropocene*.

THE CRITICAL QUESTION: HOW DO WE WANT TO LIVE IN EUROPE?

It will be important and good to act now. It will be beneficial for all of us, if we in Europe were to show in an exemplary way that alternative paths of development and human evolution exist and can be chosen. Europe will do good at providing humanity with an example of a society composed of peacefully cooperating countries to further their mutual benefits. Europe should show that an improving quality of life can be achieved on this earth, even if the population is declining and without the ever-growing need for continued material growth at a high rate. This would be an important European contribution to a paradigm shift. Europe will have to demonstrate that it is ready, in all sincerity, to join in with other nations and people to create conditions for a better future on this planet. We presume that such a contribution from Europe for a paradigm shift, in the sense of a credible and viable path of development for all nations and their people, would be welcome globally. This would open up, at the same time, the potential for new partnerships.

The new paradigm of our epoch and of future social transformations must be based on ever-increasing knowledge and rising awareness.[427] This will, over time, put an end to the unlimited growth of societies, based on unlimited demographic growth and uncontrolled exploitation of natural resources. We all know that, even if many still don't want to admit it.

The path humanity has followed so far has been guided by the question: how can we continue to grow? Economic growth was set as the benchmark and seen directly in connection with population growth. A positive correlation has erroneously been set between demographics and productivity.

We have shown here above that Bentham's principle of "the greatest happiness principle" might have been valid until the assembly lines

[427] Lewis Mumford emphasizes this point in a particularly emphatic way in the concluding chapters of his book "Hope or Barbarism," where he considers the "new man" to be the prerequisite for the "new world culture." He would probably have agreed with us if we assumed that this "new world" would be realized more and more as a result of a cybernetic process of feedback and self-optimization.

of Ford's car production.[428] At the latest with the assembly line production and the accompanying rapid technical progress of the means of production, this principle has proven to be wrong. Since then, at the beginning of the 19th century, Bentham's principle has turned into an inverse trend, producing increasingly negative effects. The industrializing, modern states in Europe and the US have slept through this point in time. They have overlooked this *tipping point*. They didn't see the need for a *bifurcation*, a move in a different direction. The principal interest of the financial and other power elites was focusing on getting many consumers for the products of their industrial mass production. Government was eager to get more money into their coffers to spend it on "welfare" programs, making people believe in their benevolent power.

[428] S. h. Buckminster Fuller, also in his references to the application of the calculations of Malthus (1766-1834), an economist, statistician and official of the British colonial administration. He draws the lesson from statistical calculations that it is a "fateful necessity" that humanity blindly obey the law of unlimited reproduction.
https://de.wikipedia.org/wiki/Thomas_Robert_Malthus.

Experience has shown that our power elites do not wish to loosen their grip on people. As long as it serves their short-sighted interests, they will be ready to chain people in useless economic, bureaucratic and administrative processes, or try to convince the masses through their media of the need for producing ever more useless products that are littering the world and our oceans.

At the latest after the First World War and the mass killings of people, humanity should have turned to a new paradigm. With the rapid increase in productivity through the use of ever more efficient machines and production techniques, industrial and agrarian production could have been decoupled from the need for an increasing population. The technocratic answers, which always tell us that the earth can "support" 15, 20, or more billions of people, fall short here. It's not about what we can do, but what we want to do and achieve as humanity.

So the real question that we should ask ourselves in Europe, but also as humanity, is: How do we want to live?

Europe certainly disposes of the scientific and intellectual resources to progressively move forward on the path towards a new paradigm. Europe will have to uncover her dormant mental capacities, of which it has made decreasing use since the Renaissance and the Baroque era. In this way, Europe could again become a role model for other societies, this time on a positive footing of partnership and sustainability.

Through a paradigm shift concerning demographic development, the pressure on nature and the aggression among people and nations would naturally decrease. Peace and an enhanced quality of life are always possible. Europe must become willing to face, consciously and with courage, the complex challenges ahead.

The biggest obstacle lies within ourselves. It is the fear of breaking new ground. Let us overcome this fear and this narrow, materialistic vision of our human world. So, let's end the present misconception in Europe through a first pragmatic step building on a new mindset. Experience will convincingly show that material growth does not require unlimited population growth. Let's switch to a new paradigm of infinite regenerative growth and an ever-improving quality of life. Let us trust that we, as increasingly conscious and free people in Europe, can take responsibility for this new path of development. This will also become Europe's contribution to humanity on her way to a more rational course, building her future on the ever-extending use of knowledge and her mental forces. We all in Europe and beyond have our responsibility here.[429]

EUROPE'S LACK OF COURAGE FOR UTOPIA

Many people are still convinced that this process of material growth, a development driven by science, technology and industry, will never come to an end. Furthermore, most

---

[429] It is worth mentioning sources from China showing that we can always count on China for a peaceful and constructive transformation of our societies. In a "White paper", i.e., a public discussion paper, the Chinese government refers to the results of its "green development" policies and its proposals on improving governance in the field of global ecological development. A report on this was published in Global Times China on January 19, 2023, by Li Xuanmin and Fan Anqi; (https://www.globaltimes.cn//author/Reporter-Li-Xuanmin.html).

people do not see a reason, why this material growth should come to an end.

This attitude of people is relatively easy to explain. In the first place, it has to do with the innate strive for ever more possessions. People do not see why they should not aim for more material wealth. The psychoanalyst Erich Fromm has shown, in his 1976 book "To Have or to Be?", how an innate unconscious drive is used by society to promote the quest for ever more possessions and for ever more material growth. He also explains in some detail the psychological consequences that this quest for "Having" ever more, is creating in the human being. At a secondary level, this striving for ever more material growth can be explained by people's leaning toward comfort. People wish to lead a life following the *principle of least effort*. People expect, without much reasoning, that more possessions are a precondition for leading a good and easy life. People tend to take, what they consider the easiest way, to achieve goals. They try, according to their understanding, to avoid constraints and problems as much as possible. This behavior is neatly mirrored by the behavior of entrepreneurs in the capitalist economy, who fundamentally and primarily strive for the realization of quick profits.

We would all agree, that our deep-rooted pursuit of happiness and a simple life also includes material prosperity and the wish to lead a life in material abundance. At the moment, when technology is capable of fulfilling all material wishes without much constraint, this wish for ever-increasing possessions will have the opposite effect. It is well known that material possessions in abundance tend to become a burden. They require ever more attention and maintenance, and they create ever more fear of loss.

In addition, being the owner of material possessions leads to envy of the neighbor, who may even have more than oneself. Obviously this innate drive for material possessions cannot be changed easily. It is part of human's natural behavior. A more rational attitude and increasing consciousness of one's own behavior will change this attitude progressively. We agree that the current short-sighted behavior can only be changed, if people become aware of their attitude, and if they begin deliberately setting their wishes and priorities differently. Such behavioral changes require a change of mindset and will follow rising consciousness and awareness of the consequences of one's own actions. Education can play an important role in inducing and furthering these processes of change.[430] As we know, the current paradigm in our societies has been underpinned by an educational system that reproduces "one-dimensional" humans that are trained to focus their efforts in life primarily on the gain of power and money. It is not without reason that government, as the principal tool of the power elites, has a quasi-monopoly on education. This is the most effective instrument to educate people to become "good citizens" as well as "good consumers", i.e., to obey government and submit to the interests of the power elites. This creates increasing uniformity of content and conformity of procedures in education. Higher education in Europe, as we know, is increasingly dependent on private funding. In the US, this has been the habitual functioning

---

[430] The psychologists Margot and Willy Wahl have created an inspiring website, because they are convinced that education is key to the transformation of our societies: https://seniora.org/home/ .

of universities and higher education institutions since the foundation of the American nation. This has opened the door for the financial and power elites to streamline education and training according to their interests. Economically and politically, this has been a very successful approach. It has created a power elite with a narrow and almost exclusive focus on the gain of ever more money and power. Europe is following the same trend with some delay. The Bologna Process, which has been promoted in Europe since 1999, goes in the same direction. General and humanistic education are increasingly limited, while functional education and training are strongly promoted.[431]

In the interest of a social and political paradigm shift in Europe, people will have to become aware of the triggers that are pushing their desires and priorities. Increasing awareness will progressively lead to a behavioral change in favor of more independence of external influence. People

[431] Bernd Schoepe, member of the Union for Education (GEW) in Germany, has published over the past decade a series of critical articles illustrating the effects of the Bologna Process. More references can be found there.

will be less likely to fall victim to the attempts of the power elites to create artificial needs[432] that are far from essential or critical for their well-being. Increasing awareness will lead to reducing greed and other destructive attitudes in our societies.

In line with our argumentation, instead of short-term profit for individuals, the long-term and continuous increase in prosperity and quality of life in Europe will move progressively into the focus of people. While this may seem to be partially in contradiction to Adam Smith's views, expressed in his famous work of 1776 on the "Wealth of Nations", in which he declares the individual drive for property and prosperity to be the driving forces for capitalist action. We do not reject the essence of this explanation of a liberal economy through the individual drive of personal satisfaction. However, we suppose that human evolution has brought us to a *bifurcation point*, where humanity is challenged to deliberately change a

[432] One of the best-known and most-analyzed examples is provided by Coca-Cola. It's not about matching desires, but about creating them. You can learn this in every good marketing course of a business school.

phylogenetically developed attitude. The human mind has to demonstrate its capacity to go beyond the characteristics it has acquired over the course of developmental history, i.e. natural evolution. This is a principle that comes concomitantly with the new era of the *anthropocene*. Humanity cannot pretend to have become master of her destiny without taking responsibility for her actions. Such a change in attitude makes sense today, given the current situation, in which humanity as a globalized society finds itself at a threshold and *bifurcation point*. We should not regard everything that is in the book of Adam Smith, or that has been interpreted into it, as universal principles. As we explained earlier, there are no universal principles for human cultures. Such a thing as human rights exists only in theory. Human rights are not morally good. They only consist of words and do not have an intrinsic value. They are just a declaration, and they attain their value only through the reality of actions being guided by them. We all know that human rights are much too often disregarded and interpreted in line with specific and often egoistic interests. We understand the psychological roots of their disregard, but we refuse to call this attitude morally justifiable or good. We are not willing to consider violence, criminal acts and war as normal. And we are not willing to justify them. What we call human rights must be determined and approved by the majority of people, and then enacted by them. Without self-regulation through the catalyst force of willpower, brought to a bearing by the majority of people, human rights or human dignity cannot be determined and cannot be realized in practice. Sole reference to the willpower, that may be motivated by the ego-centric interests of the power elites, will not be accepted anymore.

We understand that a child, who has to grow up in the slums of one of the world's big cities can be happy, if he or she finds enough food during the day or has enough water to wash herself a little. Such a child can no longer imagine how nice it can be to play with friends on the beach, take a bath in a clean river of a forest, play on a meadow, or ride a nice bike on a forest path and go to a clean school with her friends, where she is meeting friendly teachers. These things are no longer part of the child's experience, and hence this child can no longer have the desire for them.

This simple example shows, how people are getting used to circumstances characterized by a lack of, or a poor quality of life. This is what happens currently to all of us in Europe, while the media and the power elites tell us that this is "the normal way of life". This principle, of removing experience from perception, functions in all of us, as long as we do not become aware of it. People are used to managing their lives to find moments of happiness and love, even under adverse circumstances. However, this does not mean that we should accept these deficient or bad conditions for children that have to grow up in slums, or for most humans that have to cope with the often adverse circumstances of their professional and public lives. We, who know better, should do everything in our power to ensure that people can once again develop a desire for healthy living conditions, in which they can lead their lives increasingly in freedom of choice for a better quality of life. This idea of a "better life" naturally affects all important areas of life, such as education, health and housing, in which even in the rich countries more and more cutbacks and restrictions are being recorded. Don't forget, we are living in a crisis mode in Europe, with war among our countries and a war economy being put into action. Don't be blinded by the color pictures on TV, showing our "sovereign" power elites in action, and the often psychotic movie stars on the way to heaven.

In order to move away from the old paradigm of mutual exploitation through European-style politics striving for dominance of individuals over other individuals and of groups over other groups, we must recognize and admit that the current path of unlimited material growth cannot lead to general welfare and happiness in the long term. If the present situation with its crisis mode is considered the normal way our societies are normally functioning, then we will have to change what is considered "normal". Is it normal, or even "natural", that individuals strive for individual gains at the expense of others? Will actions that are guided by such principles lead to general happiness and a better quality of life for all? We don't believe in this kind of natural laws or universal principles. These laws and principles have been established by our power elites and continue to be promoted in their own interests. That is what we understand. This implies that we are all challenged to bring up the courage to find ways to create a new paradigm for well-being and a constantly improving quality of life for all of us.

We are aware that we are talking about a utopia here. But we think that's appropriate and right. We refer here to the behavior of the scientist in the technical field, who is looking for something new, something that has not existed before. We must turn to this search for new and better ways of life again and again in the social and political spheres. Yes, we acknowledge that striving for the utopia of a better life is the goal. Even if we know that we will never quite reach this goal, we should strive for it here on earth, here and now, not in the distant heavens. We believe that it is part of human nature to always strive for a good quality of life and for happiness.

In this sense, we would have liked to live in Europe with the European Union coordinating her member states to follow the example of Singapore, or other exemplary countries. This would have meant that the EU would have been striving to provide all people with free access to the best education system, the best health system, the best housing situation, and to offer the best quality of life to all citizens in Europe. We would have liked to hear these aspirations openly spoken out as objectives for the development of the EU. Such a Europe would have followed the visionary spirit inspired by the Renaissance of Leonardo da Vinci. We would have liked to see an EU that does not get involved in wars, does not finance wars, and does not increasingly produce and export weapons for war. We would have liked to live in an EU that does not want to punish other countries with sanctions, that does not want to impose her "values", her hierarchical governance systems, and her destructive and parasitic way of life on other countries. Following our analysis, we still maintain that this is a desirable utopia for Europe. Therefore, we ask for an EU that measures her performance by the quality of life it enables people to enjoy, not by successes on the battlefield.

Unfortunately, Europe and the EU have not chosen this path to optimizing the quality of life for their citizens. Although, the experiences that have been made in the course of this process of social and economic development over the past six centuries have obviously not always been positive for humanity and its living environment.

Therefore, there still remains in Europe enough room for the development of good ideas and the implementation of good actions.

For now, the negative effects and disastrous impact of European and US-driven global developments have become increasingly apparent. This has become all the more true, the further this development of uninhibited growth has spread globally and intensified. To this day, many economists have the one-sided idea that this development has created wealth that was previously considered impossible. This may be true, as long as we talk about wealth in terms of monetary income and property of a limited number of individuals. However, the created wealth is not shared and is not equally accessible. Furthermore, its creation is attained only through a high price to be paid by humanity and her living environment. We should also not fail to observe the fact that this wealth is by and large limited to things we can buy with money. This approach does overlook the fact that before the total economization of the world's societies, many things and services were free.[433] This scientific and industry-driven growth, induced and stimulated by Europe, has now spread to the entire globe. The total and comprehensive economization of human living conditions is finally the ultimate goal - the utopia of this capitalism driven by Europe and the USA. In this sense, and according to the ideas of the economists and politicians educated under this system, humanity seems to be on the right track. A healthy community life is not part of this picture of the complete economization of human life. The picture shows us the lives of the masses. In this sense, the ultimate goal of the capitalist movement induced and dominated by Europe and the US has been reached. With our analytical approach, we have been able to show that this detrimental path is coming to its natural end. The paradigm shift for the social and political transformation of our societies is already under way and taking pace. We have to do our

[433] Jörg Guido Hülsmann has just published a book analyzing the interdependence between "Abundance, Generosity, and the State: An Inquiry into Economic Principles", 2024. There we can learn how the state has become the enemy of good neighborhood, of generous friendship and cheerful parenting.

best to make this transformation as peaceful and smooth as possible.

ACTIONS TO BE TAKEN

It cannot be denied any more that we will have to change perspective. We must not try to solve our global problems exclusively with the same means, by which they were created. That can't go well. Einstein already knew this when he said that a problem cannot be solved by the same thinking that created it. Understanding Einstein requires a different mindset than understanding Newton.

We will not only have to come up with the right questions. We will have to change our minds in a way to create new answers to existing challenges. Here below, we are formulating a few questions that may lead in the right direction.

What steps do we need to take if we want to say goodbye to the current paradigm of this kind of uncontrolled and unlimited material growth? Which are the steps to take to start our journey to new pastures and new ventures? How can we arrive at a paradigm of "infinite regeneration" and the use of cosmic, and thus also earthly, energies and forces? How must the interaction of people and their nations be shaped in order to achieve a united effort to realize the utopia of an "ideal society", i.e., a movement towards constant improvement in the quality of life for all people?

Sure, we are a modern global society today that has been promoted and formed essentially through scientific and technological development. Nobody will deny that. So it will make no sense to throw away or abandon all this knowledge and the inherent capacities that science and technology offer us. Rather, we are certainly well advised to take advantage of the opportunities and possibilities they offer us. However, it will be critical to first find a commonly validated orientation for the way out of our current model of progress and inhibited growth. To do this, we must find together defining rules that help us to decide in open discourse on the purpose of our joint way into a shared future. We will have to question the potential and desired benefits we hope to obtain through the use of science and technology. To do this, we should not abstain of utopian and visionary thinking. We understand well that the so-called "realistic" and linear thinking of our power elites and leaders will not further us on our newly defined way to progress. The upward spiral has been realized over the past centuries almost exclusively at the technological level. Seen from a global perspective, humanity is increasingly destroying her natural, as well as the social and political basis for a sustainable living environment and peace among people and nations. Freedom is increasingly constrained by the justification that people are not capable of taking responsibility. The arguments are that the world today has become too complex and difficult to understand for ordinary people. Therefore, our noble elites and leaders must take over. That is the WEF policy, inherent to its road map for *the Great Reset*. We do not believe in the value and righteousness of this policy. First, because we are not convinced that these so-called global leaders and elites know better or are smarter than other people. And furthermore, we are not convinced of their moral highness and good intentions, which are supposedly guiding their intentions and actions. Obvious experience teaches us that much of what we are told cannot be true and is not right. People are increasingly becoming aware of a *tipping point* in human evolution, where direction may have to be changed radically, induced at the roots of the crisis. It has become clear by now that the world will, in this sense, once again have to be turned upside-down. People and individual nations must once again determine their own destiny. The dictates of the old power elites do not promise good results for the future.

We need to develop social and political units that have the capacity to integrate people in processes to deliberately overcome fear and manage their lives in a fruitful way to live in peace. We will also need to create social and political platforms to figure out the rules, by which decisions should be made to determine the newly defined "progress of mankind." This may probably lead to a decrease of unilateral power and a reduction of the concentration of financial resources in the hands of a privileged few. And finally, we must always ask each other, how it will be possible for us to reach consensus on the most important questions. Only consensual answers to existing questions and challenges will help us to move towards a better and more peaceful coexistence on this planet and to shape our societies for a shared future. The dominance of unilateral approaches based on power and financial resources must not be accepted anymore. Freedom will have to be redefined in a steady debate in face of the existing challenges. Yes, we understand that the elites of the present dominant system need arms and wars to maintain their position and increase their power. Do ordinary people need war technology and wars to improve their quality of life? These are questions to be raised in public debates. They cannot be answered by guided interviews, where the answers are known at the outset. The answers provided in the public debates organized by civil society will have to be taken into account. Progressively, the tide will have to turn.

The paradigm shift must therefore certainly consist in not continuing to use this scientific and technological development unhindered for further unchecked and indiscriminate growth with the exploitation and use of natural resources without well-considered control. Buckminster Fuller explains convincingly in his *Critical Path* how humanity is depleting non-regenerative natural resources, that have taken millions of years to build up, in just a few years. This kind of irrational growth serves the principal purpose of increasing power and financial resources in the hands of the global leaders and power elites sitting in the WEF meetings. This paradigm of growth has to be discontinued.

The exploitation and use of natural resources must no longer be driven forward without well-considered, jointly responsible management. The earth's natural resources are there for everyone. They are made available to us by others who hold them in trust for humanity. These natural resources will have to be made available to all people according to real needs and on the basis of transparent decisions following commonly agreed rules. Any priority attributed to individuals and their businesses will have to be validated publicly. Natural resources and their use must not be in the hands of large corporations and cartels that are responsible only for their owners.

Humanity will find her way out of the dilemma, once the current system, dominated by the use of force, by the concentration of financial resources, and by the hegemonic use of military power, is progressively be brought to its end.

As we said earlier in this chapter, scientific and technical progress, i.e. the increase in technically applicable knowledge, will continue to provide humanity with important tools and instruments for future development. In our emerging "world society", however, these scientific and technical forces must always operate under the control of the people and nations concerned. Humanity as a whole must face up to this task at each level of our societies. There cannot be an *outer world* or an *inner world* anymore. Responsibility is local, regional, national and global. Responsibility cannot be taken by others for others. Freedom is a function of responsibility and requires human beings to take charge of their lives in their respective societies. Europe or the US will not bring the solution to others, they can offer help and assistance and bring their non-coercive, and non-violent contributions. Finding a common path to the new paradigm will require a step-by-step approach, because we are deeply plunged into crisis mode. We will have to tread this new path peacefully and with courage. This will require talking to each other and building ever-new trust among people and nations. The wars and conflicts that are inflicted globally do not point in the right direction. Mutual trust and confidence will be the foundations on which human actions will be relaunched within Europe. This will bring Europe back into a position, where it may make a useful contribution to a peaceful and prosperous living environment, in which humanity will successfully cope with the great challenges of our era.

**Guai - The Breakthrough
the Determination**

*The best way to fight evil is to make vigorous
progress toward good.*

I Ching, The Book of Changes, translation and
edition by Richard Wilhelm

Epilogue – Final Considerations

We do certainly not pretend to present ourselves in this book as the great specialists of the EU integration process, the policy of NATO enlargement, or even of American foreign policy. For all these fields and areas, there are specialists, who are far superior to us in knowledge and insight.

However, we are convinced that it is our strength to see, understand and also present things, procedures and processes in a broader context, taking a wider view of the complex interdependency of issues and events. In addition, one of our advantages is that we are not dependent on any institution, we are not paid by anyone for our work. In this sense, we owe nothing to anyone, only to our own conscience.

For a critical view of the integration process of the EU, we recommend the work "The Origins and Development of European Integration: A Reader and Commentary", published by M. R. Stirk David Weigall in 1999. In this book, plenty of additional sources for further reading and deepening the insight into this subject are provided. Here above, we have already referred to the work of Eckart Conze and others, who have worked and written on the process of European integration in various aspects. On American foreign policy, we have repeatedly sought advice from Henry Kissinger, as an elder statesman and knowledgeable insider.[434] Kissinger has been at the core of American foreign politics for the greatest part of his long life. We know well that Kissinger is a highly controversial figure. But the point is here: American Foreign Policy is highly controversial, and for many good reasons, as we have shown in our book. However, while Kissinger was one of the persons, who actively shaped American foreign policy after the Second World War, he was not an imperialist, but did his best to promote a balanced and pragmatic American approach to geopolitics. The best source on American foreign policy are certainly the publications of the Council on Foreign Relations (CFR), where one can find all the information required to understand the development of US foreign policy positions over the past century, albeit from a sole American perspective. For a critical observer of current developments in US foreign policy, excellent analyses can be found daily on Global Times China and are sufficient for a first insight. On the issue of NATO enlargement and extension towards

---

[434] Refer to *Kissinger: A Biography*, published in 1992 by Walter Isaacson. This is not an "authorized biography" and ends with the year 1969.

the Russian border, many discussion papers and studies with different points of view have and are being published; we do not want to highlight one individual source here.

It is time that we make a few personal statements to reply to questions that may arise concerning my qualifications to write this book. As an attentive observer of current political and social processes, and as a trained economist, political scientist and social anthropologist, I personally have all the prerequisites and analytical skills to arrive at a good understanding of international relations. In addition, I have worked a lot for the EU over several decades, but also for other international organizations such as the World Bank, the UNDP *(United Nations Development Program)*, and the African and Asian Development Banks. So, I also know these institutions from the inside, I know to some extent how they are organized and according to which rules they function. The German and Swiss governments were also among my customers. In my forty-year professional career, I have provided consulting and advisory services in more than fifty countries on four continents, mostly for governments and their institutions, but also for private companies and banks. I know much of what is talked about in the present book from my own experience. I have always learned a lot in my work as an advisor, talking and listening to many people in a great variety of countries, who look at Europe from the outside, or who have looked at Europe from the outside, such as Poland, the Czech Republic or Hungary, when they were not yet members of NATO, i.e. before 1999, and when they were not yet members of the EU, in the years after 1990 to 2003.

So, I take the right to make clear statements, because I assume that I have a sufficiently good understanding of the history, background and interdependencies, about which I have written in this book. I have the academic training that qualifies me for this work. In addition, I have sought out many written sources and carefully analyzed them. In my professional career, from 1982 to 2022, I have gained intensive practical experience in coping with a large number of diverse tasks in the context of reform processes in many, often very diverse countries. The reader will appreciate that I make these personal statements here with the purpose of providing some authority on the analysis presented in this book and on the argumentation and narrative developed.

We have made it clear by now that with this book, we are primarily pursuing the goal of providing information to the European public, opening their eyes about their own situation, as well as for their responsibility. We do not know who will read the book, how it will be understood and received, and what impact it will achieve. But we know that it will not only be read in Europe. Earlier publications of related subjects and of similar argumentation have in any case met great interest abroad, especially in China, Russia and India, but also on the African continent.

Our goal was to present a book that is easy to read and whose argumentation is clear and concise, even if the content and subject matters are often quite complex. The most important message is that Europe has gotten into an existential crisis through its own fault and its own making. We consider the crisis in Europe to be part of its historical destiny. We believe therefore that Europe must pull herself by her own forces out of the entanglements, into which it has ever deeper fallen over a period of more than a century, as a result of its own actions, failures and deficiencies.

We also wish to indicate that in such a difficult situation, it is important and can be decisive for Europe to understand, who its friends and who its foes are. Support for one's own efforts should not be rejected, if it helps to find one's way out of the existing difficulties. Due to the internal discord that was common in Europe for a long time, it has been easy for other, ambitious nations, such as the USA, to interfere in the internal shaping of Europe. For centuries, the large countries and states in Europe have repeatedly quarreled through wars and have thus allowed themselves to be brought into ever new and ever greater dependencies. Until today, Europe has not been united. The process of European integration is historically seen as still young. There still persists a lack of a healthy self-image of Europe as a common cultural space with shared political interests. The egoism of the nation-states is still prevalent and more important than the formulation of common goals and intentions. In fact, until today, Europe has not been able to draft its own geopolitical and economic strategy that would have been commensurate with its existing potential. The EU is constantly drafting and publishing many concept papers. As long as unity and a sense of a common purpose are lacking in Europe, there cannot be any valid common strategy. The only strategy that exists has been dictated by the US right after 2001, and is closely linked to NATO. This is a highly significant fact for the persisting political weakness in Europe.

A brief overview of various EU agendas that have been declared but have never been seriously addressed or implemented would serve as a striking illustration of this fact of a missing integration in Europe.[435] As a consequence, the entire regulatory framework for politics and economics within the EU and other international organizations will eventually have to be redesigned according to new rules in the interest of self-identification. Europe will have to create a

[435] The ambition of the 'Lisbon Agenda' or 'Lisbon strategy' of 2000, has been for the European Union (EU) 'to become the most competitive and dynamic knowledge-based economy in the world, capable of sustainable economic growth with more and better jobs and greater social cohesion'. Nobody in the EU has ever taken this agenda seriously. Other, and "more important" individual agendas of the different EU member states have taken the fore.

self-image that will be shared by its people and nations. Posting the EU flag all over the continent will not be enough. Identity is created through shared experience. The member states of the EU share the experience of the past century and its devastating wars. Europe will share the experience of the war against Russia. Will this be a good foundation for a shared future in Europe? We seriously doubt this vague hope that some may have.

Seen from a global perspective, it is in no way enough for the UN Security Council to be equipped with new members. It is obvious that the UN Security Council with its over-representation of the former European powers is still reflecting the situation after the Second World War and is corroborating the dominant hegemonic position of the US. New platforms with new rules for decision-making must be created. The old hierarchies and mechanisms of control of power and money, according to which the important geopolitical decision-making processes have been managed so far, have long since ceased to be appropriate and are outdated. We would add to this that, in our understanding, the nation-states will also not be able to provide the required framework for politics that will reach into the future. We have all been witnesses to the processes of eroding democracy in the nation-states of Europe. They are, in fact, missing an anchor point in Europe. The nation-states are the backbone, but European unity will be required. The example of the EU shows, however, that a magic formula for unions of nation-states does not exist. Integration of nations and states will be the way to go in the future. However, this requires a political and mental maturity that does not yet exist. This is, at least, what we can say about Europe. We make this statement without reservation.

Geopolitics are in a transformation, as we have shown in the chapter on the New System of Global Governance here above. The EU and Europe are part of this process of transformation and the ongoing paradigm shift in geopolitics. However, the EU and Europe are in their current condition no sovereign actors within this ongoing process.

Europe's aim must be to once again regain a position to have a formative influence on geopolitics. This impact on geopolitics cannot be created through a hegemonic alliance with the US and NATO for dominance or through weapons. A sustainable and respected geopolitical impact has to be built on trust. It has to be created intelligently and with a fresh spirit and courage. Europe will have, once again to determine, who her friends are and how to deal with them. Europe must gain a new self-image, not in the face, or in confrontation with a provoked enemy, as the war initiated against Russia in Ukraine shows. We should not forget that a good part of Europe's present collective memory is built on wars. Europe will have to acknowledge this fact. However, the future will have to be sought through a deep transformation and a paradigm shift that concerns the identity of modern Europe created since the Renaissance.

Partnership would, in our eyes, provide an excellent principle to be taken as a starting point for the formation of a new self-image for Europe and the EU. We have strong affirmation for the partnership principle in many countries during the time of our international advisory and consulting services for the EU. When partnership among friends was still in the foreground of EU cooperation, we were met with respect, esteem and goodwill from all sides. Now that the EU's foreign policy has been aligned with NATO and the USA, the quality of encounters and meetings with people has completely changed. General mistrust, suspicion and often even cynicism are increasingly dominating relationships. Of course, EU leaders have done their best during this period to recruit new officers selected to promote their NATO and US-driven policies. The partners have, however, understood that EU policies are no longer primarily a matter of shaping a common future, but that the EU's selfish economic and political interests have moved to the foreground. The EU's partners also understand well, who are the partners in the background, who influence Europe in determining her interests. Europe is no longer considered a sovereign, but rather a dependent geopolitical player of the USA.

Europe must find its way back to a new, sovereign self-image, both for herself and in the eyes of her partners. Europe's new self-image must be based on the self-confidence, that it will be possible to shape the living environment on its small continent, which is merely an appendix on the Eurasian continent. The future living environment in

Europe will have to be built the way people want it to be and according to rules that are not prescribed by others. We have to look for friends, who support us in our efforts to shape life in Europe creatively, who do not want to dominate us, or who want to dictate us and subdue us to foreign interests. This is not an easy task, and it will certainly be difficult, looking at the economic dependencies, to which we are currently exposed in Europe. The pressure is already enormous, although Europe has always been told that it can rely on the support of its friends in any situation. If we consider the price Europe is currently paying for its "friendship" with the US and NATO, then this claim must be questioned, or even better, directly doubted, and finally rejected as false. Why? Because the price of this friendship has been enmity toward former friends, partners and even geographic neighbors. The US and NATO have forced Europe into a block that prohibits it from choosing its partners and friends freely and according to its very own interests. In Europe, people have increasingly become aware that their fate is externally determined. Europe has long since ceased to be able to decide in sovereignty over its own fate.

We assume that people in Europe can find out very well in open discourses what they estimate as important and precious to them, and what is in their interest. For this they do not need foreign masters or self-proclaimed leaders of the power elites. However, for Europe to take its chance and come back to a mode, where it will take its own sovereign decisions again, it will have to say goodbye to the crisis mode in order to escape the massive pressure created by an uncontrolled fear of change and self-transformation. The EU may be considered a symbol for Europe's integration. Considered mentally, however, Europe has not yet reached a level of maturity, is not integrated and not conscious of her situation of almost complete economic and political dependency. Europe is very much afraid of looking into her own eyes and facing her situation. It is obviously suffering from a distorted self-image. Europe is increasingly integrated economically, driven by the process of incorporation into the US economy. However, Europe is not yet an integrated unity, neither socially, politically, nor mentally. Hence, its actions and effectiveness remain at the bureaucratic and technocratic levels. They are characterized by

Europe's the fear of taking responsibility and being in charge of its own existence and destiny.

In the future, Europe will have to refuse action, which leads further into ever more difficult entanglements. Past experience has shown that it is detrimental to Europe's future to assume responsibilities that are not its own and implement tasks that do not serve its long-term interests. The cultural variety in the countries of Europe, which still exists and which people in Europe still have the pleasure to enjoy, is under the pressure of uniformity. Europe, with its cultural diversity and the different European models of life, is culturally threatened by ever-new coercion and by ever-stronger influence towards a cultural uniformity and Americanization. The obstruction and suppression of cultural and intellectual diversity are taking on ever greater dimensions of threat. EU regulations, often under pressure from the US, are increasingly squeezing the precious cultural diversity in Europe. These regulations tend to lock individual and creative European communication patterns into narrow-minded and one-dimensional borders. This has already become evident, in particular at the time of the Corona policy, when people were forced to follow rules that they did not know, where they came from, or who had set them up[436]. An epidemic, a so-called pandemic, was conjured up, of which there were no symptoms, except for the fear that has been planted in the citizens of Europe by so-called global power elites[437].

These processes of public manipulation have taken on ever increasingly threatening forms, since the European public has been forced to demonize Russia and turn culturally against China[438]. These are extremist attitudes and authoritarian political processes that cannot be accepted in any way in open and free societies. They all represent attitudes and rules of action that cannot find any

[436] Refer to Rand Paul's "Deception: The Great Covid Cover-Up", published on October 10, 2023.
[437] It is official now that Anthony Fauci, in charge of Corona policies under President Trump, has been lying not only about the origin of the Coronavirus, but has also suggested protective measures that have been an outgrow of his private, single-minded intentions. Refer to: InfoSperber, 23.02.2024; refer to:
https://www.infosperber.ch/gesundheit/anthony-fauci-hat-ueber-das-corona-virus-gelogen/
[438] Think of the suppression of Confucian institutes and other cultural initiatives in Germany and Europe.

justification in reality, but are imposed on the people in Europe by power elites, who think they do not have to justify themselves. During the so-called Corona pandemic, the international community was given rules of action by individual "Western" nations and "Western"-dominated institutions, such as WHO, that could no longer be questioned. Even China and India were following the advice and obeying WHO "prescriptions" by foot. These events have been striking symptoms of the current global crisis, driven by Western forces. They are examples that show, how the future system of global governance must not be regulated, if it is to enable an improved quality of life for all and the development of more freedom. Such Western driven politics will definitely not lead to an increasingly peaceful and prosperous coexistence of all nations and peoples on this planet.

This book therefore wants to raise awareness, which is the most important prerequisite on the path to creating a new European self-confident self-image. In the Analytical Psychology of C.G. Jung, this is called "the individuation process", i.e. knowing progressively and with increasing self-trust, who you are. Such a self-consciousness of Europe and her people is the critical prerequisite for self-confident actions to be taken in the future. The conclusive purpose of this individuation process will be to create self-conscious integration in Europe. This will be a new form of European integration that will not be limited to material progress and economic growth. The essence will lie at the mental level. This confirms the argumentation developed in this book, based on our historical reconstruction of processes that have shaped the prevalent mindset in Europe. The principal root causes of the crisis in Europe have been brought to light. This prepares the ground for sustainable solutions.

EUROPE'S WAY OUT OF THE CRISIS

We see Europe in an extremely difficult situation today. It will be very challenging for Europe to find its way out of these difficulties on its own. In freeing itself from this "political and economic trap", into which Europe has fallen, it will be very helpful to find the support of friends and partners. Europe will have to look for new friends, or revive proven partnerships. In order to form new partnerships, Europe will have to develop her own strategy and set her own goals, because friends and partners will want to know where the journey together is going to be headed.

The paradigm shift that Europe will have to undergo will require Europe to seize any opportunity to reposition herself geopolitically. To do this, Europe must progressively develop its own sovereign profile. Europe must redefine her role in the emerging multipolar world. This also means that Europe should not integrate herself into new alliances for the time being. Joining other alliances presupposes a healthy and confident self-image, which must first be developed again in Europe.

After the collapse of the Soviet Union and German reunification, the window for such a new role for Europe was open for a short time. However, it seems that Europe and the EU have not been ready at that time. The EU has been occupied by other important processes and has not yet consolidated its internal structures[439]. After the attack on the

[439] Remember that these have been the internal processes leading to the Maastricht Treaty under EU

World Trade Center in 2001, the US intensified its foreign policy with the aim of achieving and consolidating its hegemonic dominance[440]. The United States was the only superpower to emerge from the Cold War. The time had come to consolidate this hegemonic position. Europe and the EU have, in the eyes of the US, been considered the principal pillars to definitely take over the Eurasian continent. Europe has globally been considered the privileged partner in the implementation of the American strategy of geopolitical hegemony. Europe went with the USA to Iraq and Afghanistan, and EU Member States also took over the task of bombing Libya on behalf of the USA. The reception of Syrian refugees in Germany and the deal with Turkey to manage the flow of refugees are also part of this period. Europe had fallen straight into the American fairway, without the possibility of determining its own fate. Of course, this has also affected relations with

President Delors, and the subsequent introduction of the Euro currency.
[440] A very informative source of information is Gore Vidal, with several fascinating and elucidating books. One striking example is offered in Gore Vidal's "Perpetual War for Perpetual Peace: How We Got to Be So Hated. American Imperialism, Book 1", 2002.

Europe's existing partners. Europe's international relations have been massively damaged over the past decades, especially by the increasingly aggressive sanctions policy driven by the US. Europe's economies have suffered and been increasingly de-industrialized, while the US' nationalist economic policy has invested heavily in its re-industrialization at home. The economic warfare of US-driven policies in the energy sector in Europe, in particular since the war in Ukraine, has delivered a final blow to the economy in Europe. Russia has, intentionally and with strong support from managed Western and European media, mutated into an enemy, with whom Europe entered into an open war. China has been declared a major adversary, because it does not want to subordinate itself to American interests. Europe has been forced to join American political positions unconditionally. As a result, the geopolitical image of Europe has suffered great damage. This also applies to individual countries in Europe, in particular France, which is increasingly pushed out of Africa. The diplomatic damage to Europe through the alignment with American politics and the expansive NATO strategy is huge. Europe has lost its face and most of its international reputation and credibility. As an international policy advisor, I personally can confirm this statement from my own professional experience in the international political arena, without reservation.

In such a situation, as we briefly outline it here, the well-known saying fits very well: "If you have such friends, you don't have to worry about enemies". This is especially true for NATO. If Europe wants to play its own, independent and sovereign role as a global partner in the future, then it must detach itself from NATO and gradually withdraw.[441] This also means that previous friendships no longer have to remain valid unconditionally

---

[441] It is astonishing to see how the small and not very rich country of Hungary, as a member of the EU and NATO, does not want to subordinate itself to the constraints of these institutions without resistance. In a news item in the Hungarian online magazine *Hungary Today* on May 24, 2024, we read that Hungary refuses to participate directly in the war against Russia. Hungary puts forward a very intelligent argument, insisting that NATO stands for itself as a "defensive alliance". Therefore, members cannot be forced into wars of aggression. This shows that alternatives to unconditional submission to the dictates of the USA and NATO are possible.

and in their existing form. It also means that previous enmities can be ended. New relationships will have to be established to replace old ones in a steady process. Europe does not need this NATO for its prosperous and peaceful development. Europe is not threatened, neither by Russia nor by China, and not yet by the USA. NATO has mutated into an instrument that primarily does not serve Europe's security, but is subordinate to the geopolitical interests of the USA and its hegemonic aspirations. The decoupling of Europe from NATO will therefore be the first pragmatic and decisive step toward a paradigm shift in Europe. This is the prerequisite for Europe to play a new, sovereign geopolitical role in the future. If Europe leaves NATO, or if at least its major European nations, such as France, Germany, Italy, the Netherlands and Spain, will take this decision, then the paradigm shift will immediately have been set into motion. Therefore, this is the first and decisive step to breaking free from the clutches of the USA. Thereafter, the priorities in economic cooperation will also have to be redefined. Due to the intense economic integration between the US and Europe, this will take time. However, the dominance and almost exclusive economic fixation on the USA will have to be gradually scaled back, to the advantage of intensifying economic relations with other countries, above all with China, India and Russia. Europe must create a new balance between the old and large partner, the USA, and the new partners from Asia, Eurasia, Latin America and Africa.

The crisis for Europe is undeniably here. It can no longer be denied. Two possibilities are open, two paths, of which only the second will be a successful way out of the crisis. Either Europe can continue as it currently does, and submit to the hegemonic striving of the USA driven by NATO, i.e. ultimately operate without direct sovereignty, neither of the EU nor of the member states. Europe will then become part of a new world order, but remain a fully incorporated part of a Western, US-dominated bloc, without the possibility of playing an independent and sovereign role. This way, Europe will always remain a junior partner of the United States, to whose bloc it will belong.

In an alternative scenario, Europe can work her way out of the crisis on its own, remembering her own interests, setting her own sovereign goals again, and developing her own strategy and road map into a future shared with new partners.

EUROPE'S NEW SELF-IMAGE, GROWN OUT OF HER HISTORY AND CULTURE

Once again, we will briefly recall the purpose of this book and explain our principal motivation for writing it. The primary interest does not consist of pointing out the problems. Rather, we intend to show ways that can lead to feasible solutions for the identified problems and existing challenges. The working of the intellect requires, however, that the point of departure be clarified. Hence, we started with an analysis of the situational context and its historical background. We started the book with reference to the Treaty of Versailles and its consequences for Europe under US hegemonic leadership. At this very moment in history, the seeds have been planted, and the major problems, characteristic of the crisis in Europe, have grown out. In the next step, we provided details on the processes related to the creation of the EU and her administrative and political structures, showing closely the influence the US has taken on these processes and how this informed the specific organizational structure of the EU. In the following step of our analytical approach, we identified the principal root causes of the current problems and challenges that Europe and the world are facing. Only through the knowledge of the root causes and their impact can appropriate measures be identified that will lead to sustainable solutions for existing problems. One important reason, why we recall the process we followed with our analytical description is the following: We want to spell out that this book has been drafted in a creative process, without fixed ideas at the beginning. When we drafted this book, we entered into a process, in which the outcome has not been known at the outset. We are glad that we can say now that, through an intellectual and analytical process, a deep understanding of the current crisis in Europe has been created. We are convinced that only on the basis of such an honestly led scientific and intellectual endeavor can thorough understanding be achieved and meaningful orientation for future action be provided. Our endeavor has focused on the crisis in Europe, and we have set our sights on two major areas in which a paradigm shift is imminent. One area is concerning the transformation of Europe and its societies towards a steady improvement of the quality of life. The other area is concerning the upcoming new system of global governance. In both areas, pragmatic solutions for a paradigm shift and the successful transformation of Europe and its future role have been presented.

It is our sincere wish that the societies in Europe will, in the future, steadily improve the quality of life for their people. This refers to the inner aspect of the transformation of Europe. Concerning Europe and her role as an actor in the international arena, we wish for Europe to become a creative and respected partner in the future system of global governance.

We see ourselves now, reaching the end of our intellectual and analytical process, in a confident position to make well pondered and convincing suggestions for measures to be taken by Europe to find her way out of the crisis. From hindsight, we perceive that through the creative intellectual and analytical process, we have gone through a fruitful personal process of learning that made us gain new insights and find a new understanding of reality. This outcome of our endeavor confirms our personal attitude and conviction that intellectual honesty is an indispensable ingredient in research. We feel reassured now, that only an evidence-based scientific method and a transparent analytical process, combined with intellectual courage and personal honesty, can lead to results that may convince other people of their value as an orientation for future action.

We have shown how Europe got into this crisis, and we feel now entitled to point to concrete measures for Europe to find her way out of the crisis. On the basis of our honest and transparent analysis, we are confident that we can provide qualified orientation for action to be taken. Our political leaders and the self-declared figures of our present power elites have, locked into their narrow and egoistic mindsets, not been able to come up with such qualified advice. If you refuse to see things as they are, how can you talk about improving a difficult situation? The hypocritical and dishonest power elites are not the advisors Europe needs in today's crisis. They are leading Europe ever deeper into the crisis and are always in search of inflating their personal egos, presenting themselves as the indispensable angel-like saviors.

The Critical Step out of the Crisis in Europe

Europe will have to dig up its unique genius, bring it to light, and unfold it. Europe then has to grow a healthy, self-confident willpower, if it wishes to come back into a position to take its fate into its own hands. This is the moment we have had to wait for more than a century now. Until the First World War, only individual states and monarchic empires had taken responsibility for themselves and for the pursuit of their specific interests. Europe was divided, and the nations repeatedly fought each other in fierce wars. The 'Hundred Years War' between England and France and the Thirty Years War, still from pre-modern times, then the Napoleonic Wars, are striking examples of the war-torn history of Europe. The Habsburg Empire owed its expansion and dimension either to wars of aggression in Italy, in Central

Europe, on the Balkans, or defensive wars against the Turks. In the 20th century, these wars reached their inglorious climax with the two Europe-driven world wars. Europe emerged weakened in 1919, and even more so in 1945, while the USA was able to present itself as the new global empire that emerged to become the new globally dominant power. It is therefore an important part of the truth to say that the European powers have gotten into their current crisis through their own failure, which has come to a head in our time.

These considerations require us to express explicitly that we are fundamentally in favor of European integration and will continue promoting its successful realization. However, Europe must urgently free itself from the clutches of NATO. Europe will have to establish its own defense organization that will coordinate with NATO. However, the new European Defense Alliance will exclusively operate under European leadership and command. This first step will require of Europe to overcome US resistance through an energetic act of political will. It may well appear that such an energetic undertaking will have to wait for a new generation of political leaders to enter the stage in Europe.

The present generation of political leaders is submissive to the trans-Atlantic partnership that is exclusively operating under US command and leadership. This scenario will have to come to an end. This political act of Europe will be critical and, in consequence, open the way for negotiations leading to a new, sustainable and effective European security architecture.

This is the first, but critical, step for Europe to eventually find and redefine her own way. Only thereafter will Europe be in a position to lead her own process, creating a climate of peaceful coexistence in Europe shaped according to rules set by Europe as a sovereign political power. This new situation will, at the same time, open the way to new partnerships. Europe will progressively regain credibility as an honest broker in the international political arena.

If we want to reach a deep understanding of the situation in Europe, we must recall the results of our previous analysis and also ask ourselves, why this crisis is currently coming to a head and what the concrete reasons for the culmination of the situation are. Again, the answer is not difficult to find, if we are courageous and dare to be honest. Europe's crisis is coming to a head, because the United States has increasingly fallen into its own self-made crisis. The US crisis arises, on the one hand, from internal contradictions that increasingly call into question the financial viability of its own hegemonic and military ambitions. In fact, the FED, the so-called American Reserve Bank, finds it increasingly difficult to fund and refinance the immense American debt load.[442] We will illustrate the situation with a brief reference to the Mises Institute of the USA. Let us quote one of its economists and specialists on the subject. "An Unprecedented Monetary Destruction Is Coming", writes Daniel Lacalle on September 18, 2024, on Mises Wire. He recalls that, according to Bloomberg News agency, "Global money supply has soared by $20.6 trillion since 2019. Additionally, global debt surged by over $15 trillion in 2023, reaching a new record high of $313 trillion". We don't have the time to go deeper into the details of this very timely article. Nevertheless, we draw attention to the fact that the level of debt, which is intrinsically linked to the money supply by the central banks, has increased over the past decades even more in Europe among the EU member states, most notably France, Italy, Spain and Germany. We remind you of these facts just to emphasize once again the outcome of our analysis, which brought to light the dimensions of the present crisis in Europe.

In addition, the crisis of American hegemony also has to do with the growing countervailing forces of other nations and alliances. The US is not ready or willing to accept a retreat from its hegemonic position. It does not modify or adapt its present line and strategy. The US is prepared to use any means in this crisis to avoid losing its dominance. It is taking up any challenge, presuming that it will be able to even emerge stronger from this global crisis. The mechanisms deployed by the US in pursuit of maintaining and even extending its hegemonic power have been examined and explained in detail in our book "War and Business", published in 2024. It shows that proxy wars are increasingly favored by the US, because it alone cannot sustain all the confrontations and wars it manages on a global scale. In addition, the US resorts increasingly to instruments and "financial weapons" offered by the Bretton Woods System established in 1944, one year ahead of the End of World War II. One of the means the US is deploying with ever more fervor are economic sanctions, in combination with, what Jeffry Sachs and others call the "Weaponization of the Dollar"[443].

Due to the almost absolute subordination of Europe, within the framework of NATO, to the strategic aspirations of the USA, the complex and globally virulent crisis of the USA has today become the crisis of Europe. This US-driven global crisis is marked by its intensity, its severeness and, in the long term, by its extremely destructive course. Europe is in the center of this US-driven crisis. It is, so to speak, in "the eye of the hurricane" that has been building up with increasing intensity since 2001.

If we look at the situation this way, then it also becomes clear what must urgently be done to find a way out of the crisis. Europe does not have to decouple herself from the USA. This will not be possible and is

[443] Refer to Saleha Mohsin, Economist at the London School of Economics (LSE) "How the Weaponization of the Dollar changed the World Order", 2024.

ultimately not even desirable. The United States will always remain a privileged partner of Europe within its network of international relations. However, the US cannot maintain the role of the dominant or single most important partner of Europe. Obviously, Europe must resist the hegemonic ambitions of the USA. Europe must not allow herself to be made a henchman for the wars of the USA, which are now being waged worldwide via NATO's military platform and continue to be propagated and prepared. The functioning of NATO has taught the US to build similar structures globally to dispose of a perfect war machine for limitless warfare.[444] NATO is the key element of the Business Model for the American hegemonic aspirations.[445]

As we have explained in Part One of our book, we have identified war as the critical and ultimate symptom of the crisis in Europe. The current war, led by NATO with direct

---

[444] In line with our argumentation, Sevim Dağdelen, Member of the Bundestag and specialist for the Middle East, has recently published a comprehensive book "NATO: A Reckoning with the Alliance of Values", 2024.
[445] Refer to "War & Business. The American Success Story of the past century", 2024, Georg von Goldbach.

engagement by European nations against Russia, is the culmination of a historical process driven by the US after the Treaty of Versailles, signed in 1919.

THE ROLE OF MODERN SCIENCE

We now have to come back briefly to our descriptive analysis concerning the root causes, which we have conducted in Part Two of this book. In line with our argumentation, we have painted a complex and colorful picture with several key elements and interdependent forces. We have shown that the drive for progress and the belief in unlimited material growth, driven by science and technology, in combination with the drive for global geographic expansion, have grown out to become a complex of destructive forces. This general growth pattern covering everything at all levels and pushing at ever new limits has its historical roots in Europe. It has been in Europe, where modern sciences originated, and where colonialism, as an intrinsic part of capitalism, has taken its origin. This is where the narrow-minded approach to science has found its way with its exclusive focus on "objectivity" preached in the 17th and 18th centuries. This process has led to fantastic results in science and technological development.

The intensifying application of scientific research in production technology in the 19th and 20th centuries has been the driving force behind industrialization in Europe and the Western hemisphere. For several centuries, Europe and the US considered themselves and were seen by other peoples and nations as the "masters of the world". Until the 1920s, practically all Nobel Prize winners in the natural sciences were educated in Europe and exerted their impact on the technological and economic development in Europe and the countries in the Western hemisphere[446]. All the knowledge needed for the initial formation of modern sciences comes from Europe. Oppenheimer, who led the team to

[446] We are aware that Japan started its industrialization in the second half of the 19th century. This makes that Japan is since then considered "Western", at least what concerns industry and the economy.

Modris Eksteins also points out the link between science and cultural development in his historic novel, "Rites of Spring: The Great War and the Birth of the Modern Age", published in 2000.

build the first atomic bomb for the US military, was trained by Max Planck in Göttingen and Niels Bohr in Copenhagen. This European origin and the development of the foundations of modern science up to the Second World War apply to practically everything from mathematics to chemistry, physics and astrophysics.

In the period after the Second World War, i.e. after 1945, the USA perfected European science and, in particular, continued the technological application of the results of the sciences intensively and pragmatically[447]. Not only did all the knowledge required to build the atomic bomb come from Europe to the USA, but also the knowledge in other cutting-edge sciences. A striking example is provided by the work of Norbert Wiener[448] and John von Neumann, both former members of the

[447] Sigmund Freud made an interesting observation about the American pragmatism in his lectures on psychoanalysis given in the USA in 1909. He explained that he did not dare talk about dreams and dream analysis in these lectures, because this must remain incomprehensible for such a "pragmatic people" as the Americans. Everyone knows that dream analysis is at the heart of Freud's psychoanalysis.

[448] Norbert Wiener, "Cybernetics or Control and Communication in the Animal and the Machine", 1948.

Vienna Circle, who jointly created the science of cybernetics in the US. As an impact of the Second World War and the forced emigration of a great part of the European scientific community, most Nobel Prize winners in the natural and economic sciences have since 1945 come from the USA. Not only the sciences have been perfected in the USA, but also the belief in progress without end and in all areas has been raised to new heights in the USA.

As a result, sciences and research have ever more grown into one-sidedness, in which priority is given to the development of technology as a means for dominance over and the exploitation of nature with the interest of making quick economic profits. In the social sciences, behaviorism is a striking example of the focus on functionality and tangible results. Behaviorism, as the American version of psychology, has led to "social engineering", a social science created with the aim of increasing the power of humans over humans themselves. This is often referred to as the trend for "auto-domestication" of humanity. Obviously, this process is closely linked to what we call today the *anthropocene*, i.e. humans ruling over nature and humans creating their own living environment. Behaviorism[449] considers "auto-domestication" as an ultimate goal, eventually making humans perfectly obedient citizens, who are always willing to sacrifice the expression of their free will to the ordered functioning of society that is in line with the interests of the ruling power elites.

It seems, that the old saying, that "War is the Father of all Things", still bears a lot of truth in it and can still be applied to certain aspects of our time. It is well known that the most important technological innovations of the past century have either been developed directly out of the needs of warfare, or have been able to prove their "value" and importance in related processes. Just think of the aircraft industry, of electronic communication tools, or of today's drones for military use. It is part of the American doctrine and at the center of their character

---

[449] An excellent analysis of Behaviorism has been provided by Noam Chomsky in his book published under the title "The Essential Chomsky". In this book, Chomsky presents his detailed and thorough analysis and review of the seminal book "Verbal Behavior", published in 1957 by B. F. Skinner. This book of Skinner stands at the origin of Behaviorism.

as a nation to always strive for more power and greater wealth[450]. For this purpose, every means is justified, even if it requires the US to wage wars in every corner of the globe. Greater prosperity for all is more of a by-product of these global political and economic operations. A good example of this approach to empire-building is offered by John D. Rockefeller, who was considered a deeply religious Christian. He missed out on no opportunity, using all the means at his disposal, to ruthlessly eliminate his competitors, who stood in his way of building up his own business as an Empire. The aggressiveness that characterized him, together with his irrepressible drive for business success, was the key to his wealth and power.[451] Most Americans and Europeans still consider Rockefeller a great person and role model for the American spirit.

[450] Gore Vidal has published a whole series of books illustrating the American character. Several other sources have been quoted in our book.
[451] This contradictory personality is very convincingly shown in Robert Greene's book "The Laws of Human Nature", of 2019, in the chapter on "aggressiveness". The English original is "The Laws of Human Nature, 2018.

We are aware that scientific research and its overwhelming technological effects have resulted in an infinite amount of good and useful results for humanity. We can say without hesitation that it was in Europe, over the past six centuries, that the modern, individualistic scientist has been formed. This applies in the same way to the individualistic capitalist entrepreneur. All this represents, indisputably, a great step in the development of humanity. The dilemma that Europe has found itself in at the same time, however, has its origin in the fact that Europe has not yet found a balance. In using an image, we might say that Europe has euphorically been carried away by the illusive promise to leave the shackles of a life depending on nature. The dream of an eternal life, which some people are still dreaming of, comes to mind.

The narrow focus on the one-sided scientific and technological development, combined with the capitalist fervor for ever-increasing and quick profits, prevented Europe from developing a well-balanced character. This has led European and American people in general to come out of balance. The focus is on pleasure provided by material wealth and physical enjoyment, which in our day also includes media entertainment. The character of modern man in Europe is missing the integration of a counterweight that can only come from a reliable spiritual foundation.[452] The purpose of life will find its affirmation only through this side of human life. Material progress, as important and useful as it may have proven, cannot answer the question, "What is life?"[453] We will provide more insight into these processes in the concluding chapter of our book. The one-sided character of Europe has led to a situation, where social and political developments in Europe and the US have not kept pace with science- and technology-driven progress.

European integration is certainly an important step in the right direction to free Europe from the old constraints and contradictions on her way to finding new rules for her development. This important step indicates, at the same time, very clearly

[452] The attentive reader will not overlook that, with our indication of the lack of balance, we are hinting here in a rather subtle way at the need for the spiritual balancing powers between East and West.
[453] We refer here to the book "What is Life,", published in 1944 by Ernst Schrödinger, who was a member of the eminent circle of scientists laying the foundation of modern physics in the early 20th century.

what the challenge is for Europe in our time to actually break free of the old framework. This challenge is concerning the sovereign restructuring and shaping of European societies. This process must be carried out, building on new rules that will lead to a balance of energies in a progressively self-regulated system of freely uniting European nations and peoples. The use of force, aggressive behavior and striving for dominance or mutual exploitation must progressively diminish. The persistence of these negative forces and energies shows us that a common positive and constructive purpose does not yet exist in Europe. In 2024, when we draft these lines, the fight against Russia and China has been declared the common purpose of Europe and the West. It is all too obvious that this is profound and hypocritical nonsense. In psychology, such a fictitious declaration of an enemy, is called transference and externalization of an internally existing problem. How stupid Europe is! And this in the 21st century, after so many destructive wars waged in Europe. Such an attitude is certainly not a sign of historical and political maturity.

Proceeding piecemeal and cluttering are not the methods to apply in such integrating systemic processes. The time has ripened now to take all the courage required to face this challenge of establishing new rules in going through systematically and rationally processes of open communication. Europe has to seize the emerging opportunity to overcome its current crisis. Please remember our words: *every crisis offers a chance for new happiness*.

We consider this the appropriate moment, where we find it important to recall the special responsibilities Europe has to bear as a result of its history. For the formation of a new self-image of Europe, it is essential to understand the great loss Europe has suffered as a result of the National Socialist ideology and the racism promoted by European fascism. As a result of this National Socialist and Fascist ideology, including its pronounced anti-Semitism, Europe has suffered a great loss. The majority of Jewish scientists left Europe behind. A minor part remained in Great Britain or emigrated directly to Palestine. The majority of the Jewish-European educated middle class, together with a great number of cultural bearers, emigrated or were fleeing to the USA. Europe has profoundly been impoverished, scientifically and in particular culturally, due to anti-Semitism[454]. Today, we can only understand this retrospectively, with the help of works such as the autobiography "The World of Yesterday", published by Stefan Zweig in exile. He lost his civil existence twice. First, with the collapse of the Habsburg monarchy through the First World War, and then through persecution by the National Socialist regime in Europe, from which he, like thousands of other Jews, could only escape by emigration and flight. Emigration has brought a large part of the wealth of European science to the USA, while another, perhaps even larger, part has been silenced in the extermination camps. These events are deeply engraved in the collective and historical memory of Europe. They are not only the cause of great shame, but they have also caused enormous damage to Europe, its science, economy and culture.

[454] We recall here the fact that anti-Semitism had become part of the fascist European movement. However, anti-Semitism has been part of the Christian driven ideology of most of European peoples and countries.

They have changed the face of Europe and life on the European continent forever.

We should not conceal these historical and cultural roots of today's crisis. It is important for our self-image that we understand the origins of the present European crisis in their complexity. This will prevent us from looking for simple-minded, linear solutions, or creating fictitious enemies with the aim of avoiding facing our real problems.

Europe will have to build its future on the experience of its past that is engraved in its collective historical memory. In this way, we will consciously create rational conditions for taking on due responsibility. The responsibility, we mean, is not limited to a moralizing retrospective dimension, but comprises responsibility for creating a better future for all people on our planet. Hence, we call for Europe to take responsibility for its past in order to create a new self-image that is built on growing self-knowledge and consciousness. This will enable Europe to find the courage and confidence to make a valuable contribution for a better future on our continent and on the planet.

EUROPE IN SEARCH OF HER SOUL

Following his cathartic process of personal integration, which had come in motion in C. G. Jung in an intensive form in the years from 1914 onwards, he increasingly began to focus his scientific interest on the question of the human soul. This was already clear in his Red Book, which he had drafted from 1914 to 1928, and left after his death to his family, who only had it published in 2009. In 1934, Jung published a book entitled "The Reality of the Soul" in the Psychological Treatises, Volume IV. Jung himself wrote the introductory essay to this anthology. There, he wrote in the last paragraph: "Psychological research has not succeeded in revealing the often veiled image of the soul, because it is unapproachable and obscure, like all deep secrets of life".

We have heard this warning and are happy to heed it. This means that we did not want to attempt to portray the soul of Europe in our book. That would be presumptuous and absurd.

During the work on our book, however, it became clear to us that much of what Jung talks about and deals with in his books and treatises also has significance for Europe and can contribute to a deeper understanding of the causes of its current crisis.

In the following short essay, we will look at the insights gained in our book and read them through the lens of Jung's Analytical Psychology. In order to avoid the temptation of getting involved in a lengthy treatise, we will limit ourselves to following the essential points and line of argumentation of our analytical presentation in this book. Ultimately, the critical factor will be, whether we have actually succeeded in promoting a better understanding of the crisis in Europe and in clarifying its major root causes. This has been our claim since the beginning of the book.

In the sense of Analytical Psychology, and basically like any analytical science, we started at the level of symptoms. In a kind of historical reconstruction, we traced the emergence of the symptoms of the crisis. This corresponds, if you will, to a phenomenology of the present situation in Europe[455]. Of

---

[455] We have earlier mentioned Modris Eksteins book "Rites of Spring: The Great War and the Birth of the Modern Age", 1989, where he applies a similar

course, we have concentrated on a few, very central points and events here.

In a second step, we went in search of the root causes of the crisis in Europe. In the process, without much ado, and as a result of the analysis of the symptoms, we came across a few critical phenomena. We do not hesitate here, after careful consideration, to refer to these root causes as archetypes of Europe's collective memory, using the terminology of Analytical Psychology. In this way, we follow with our analysis and research directly the work of Jung and his school.

According to our understanding, and we have of course cross-checked our assumptions through various lines of argumentation and sources, there exist three primary archetypes that form the mental framework and are characteristic of Europe's self-understanding. The first archetype consists of individuality, characterized by Ego consciousness, as opposed to the unconscious or pre-conscious. We have frequently referred to the unconscious in our book as the "collective

approach to the time between 1912 and 1945. We have to draw the attention to the fact that Eksteins remains, in our view, largely at the symptomatic level.

historical memory" of Europe, or its "collective unconscious". The specific form of the collective historical memory is unconsciously driving Europe's social life and political actions. Joseph Campbell, an early scholar of Jung, shows in several of his books under various ankles and aspects that the unique form of Western individuality has a peculiar primordial root[456]. Western individuality grows out of the old Persian, Mesopotamian and Egyptian cultures, religions and mythologies and takes a clearly distinctive form, from what he calls the "Eastern" form of individuality. On his side, Sigmund Freud drafted, just a few months before his death in 1939, four complementary writings, which he published as his last book under the title "The Man Moses and the Monotheist Religion". In the summary of this book, Freud explains that the majority of people, at least those who have grown up in the Judeo-Christian tradition, are driven by an inborn need for a strong and authoritarian father figure. In the Analytical Psychology of Jung, a close colleague of Freud until 1913, this father figure is recognized as the Ego that

[456] The reader may refer to chapter 1 in the book the "Myths of Light", 2003, Joseph Campbell.

has grown out through a process of differentiation out of the primordial psychological unconscious. In his book "Aion", on which Jung worked for several decades to finally publish it in 1951, he presents the various forms the symbol of individuality takes in the Judeo-Christian tradition. The transformation of the symbols refers to the transformation of the collective unconscious in Europe during the Christian era. Jung shows in his thorough analysis that this transformation of the symbols consists of a process of growing consciousness in the individual. This transformative process eventually leads to a critical and psychologically effective differentiation between Ego and the unconscious. The seeds for the birth of the psychology and specific character of modern man have thus been sown. The "death of God" proclaimed by Nietzsche in the outgoing 19th century has taken its origin in this conjunction of the psychological differentiation that took a decisive step during the Renaissance. The era of the Middle Ages has finally been overcome. In conjunction with the translation of the books of Aristotle at the onset of the

Renaissance, the conditions for the birth of modern man were created in Europe.

In the following eras of the Baroque and the Enlightenment, initiated in Europe through the French Revolution, the way for the creation of the "rational", modern man of science has been opened in Europe, characterized by the belief that scientifically everything can be known and technically everything is feasible. It is this complex psychological transformation that is at the origin of Europe and modern man. This new form of human individuality is considered specific to Europe. The personality of the "rational man" is not only characteristic of modern science, but is at the root of Western-style capitalism as well.

In second place, we have identified the archetype of "progress". This is an archetype that, in our understanding, derives its power equally from the unconscious, collective memory of Europe. Strictly speaking, the critical factor that is effective in "progress", lies probably in its inherent drive for constant change and improvement of circumstances. With reference to Oswald Spengler, we would call this the "Faustian character" and its inherent forces. These forces work in modern man unconsciously. It is these forces that always drive the European people to new and higher performance in order to move forward despite any resistance. The figure of Faust, in the second part of the tragedy, stands exemplary for this untamable spirit with its irrepressible urge for conquest of land and victory over enemies.[457]

The third archetype that we have uncovered, while working on our book, is the pursuit of growth - of infinite and limitless growth, always and forever, concerning all aspects of life. Strictly speaking, in psychological terms, this archetype is considered an expression and symptom of the fear of death. Seen through the lenses of modern Psychology, unlimited growth is the psychological means by which European man hopes to escape death.

With the recognition of these three archetypes at the root of the "soul of Europe", we have certainly not fully grasped the character of modern man, nor drawn a comprehensive picture of Europe. However,

---

[457] We refer the reader once again to "The Decline of the West", published by Oswald Spengler in 1918.

we believe that, focusing our analytical description on the impact of these three archetypes, has proven useful in providing enlightening insights. We have been able to provide evidence for the effectivity of the essential driving forces that grow out of these fundamental archetypes. The complex interdependency of these forces was also brought to light in the characteristic way they have shaped the specific mindset of Europe. We could show that these forces are underlying Europe's self-image and are effective at the core of its attitudes and actions.

As a reminder, we see the United States as a European offshoot and an actor that expresses the archetypes of Europe in an extreme manner. Europe and the USA are cut from the same cloth. Nobody should overlook this fact.

We have to point out here that we have not investigated the question of where these archetypes come from and how they came into being. These are questions of religion, ontology or metaphysics that are not in the scope of our book. According to Jung, these questions do not make much sense, because they refer to "the deeper secrets of life". We also do not know whether and how these archetypes may be at work in other cultures. However, we assume that the identified archetypes have found their special expression in Europe and have unfolded only here their very specific impact.

So, what does it mean, when we say that Europe is in search of her soul? Our intention has primarily been to show, how these unconscious driving forces bear fruit and lead to specific outcomes in certain areas of private and public life. We have identified the issues of global governance, together with economic action and social development, as important areas, where these archetypes and their forces show their effectiveness. In Global Governance, the impact is visible in the confrontation with potential partners in the geopolitical arena, which is increasingly leading to Europe being involved in wars. In economic action and social development, the impact is tangible in its destructive consequences for the natural and human environment. The persisting high level of consumption of raw materials and non-regenerative resources in Europe is considered a symptom of the first order.

With our evidence-based analytical description, we intended to provide indications as to what the effects are that arise from these driving forces. We have included these indications to show how Europe could deal with these driving forces, that have grown out of the underlying archetypes, to avoid negative impacts in the future. We have frequently been talking about the need for a paradigm shift and transformation of the mindset that is characteristic of Europe. We consider this the most imminent challenge now, which is in front of Europe. As we have said, this paradigm shift and transformation should be induced and put into action with consciousness and awareness of the root causes of the crisis in Europe. This will be of help in finding a way out of the crisis. This will also provide direction for the relevant actions leading to a better quality of life in our societies, an increase in social cohesion, and an improving quality of partnership with our peer nations on this planet.

We are aware of the complexity of all these facts and psychological references and have to remain honest. So, we agree that our title of the book, pretending that Europe is in search of its soul, can be seen as an insinuation. First, we cannot even affirm with clarity who Europe is, with its more than 30 nations and more than 500 million people. We can also not know what Europe is going to do in the future. Has Europe understood its crisis? Is Europe ready to recognize that it is living through a deep crisis? If so, does it want to escape this crisis? Or is Europe "tired" and caught up in a process of self-dissolution and self-destruction? Ultimately, we cannot give conclusive answers to all these critical questions.

Notwithstanding, we assume that it is a natural instinct that Europe and its peoples and nations want to preserve themselves and secure their existence. So we assume that Europe will look for a way out of the current crisis. So much for our first premise.

Based on this premise, it was our intention in the book to show ways that at least hints at what Europe could do to find a way out of the crisis.

In line with the approach we took in our book, we assume that, looking for a sustainable way out of the crisis, it makes no sense for Europe to start working on the symptoms. This is what is characteristic of the "linear" action of politics, and cannot lead to sustainable solutions. We therefore believe that Europe must begin at the root causes for a successful process of resolving its crisis in the long term. This is our claim for sustainable solutions to the various crises. In our understanding, Europe needs to become increasingly aware of and understand the root causes of its own behavior and actions. An essential prerequisite for a transformation in Europe is therefore an increasing consciousness of the existence of the root causes and the forces that emanate from the underlying archetypes.

Europe must become increasingly aware of the forces that unconsciously are at work in it. The archetypes are emanating effects that find their specific expression in Europe's attitude and the consequent social and political actions. Just as, in the understanding of Analytical Psychology, where a healthy maturing individual progresses on his process of integration and increasing awareness, so too must Europe gain new consciousness and self-awareness. Through this process of self-understanding, increasing self-confidence will come to the fore. This will liberate forces that can creatively be deployed on finding a way out of the crisis leading Europe to a new way of life and the creation of a living environment offering a higher quality of life.

According to these assumptions, Europe must gain a new self-image through increasing awareness of its motives and the forces that determine its behavior and drive its actions. This then also means redefining one's relationship with potential partners in geopolitics. Once Europe becomes aware of the forces of these archetypes, it will increasingly be able to control her thinking as well as her actions to redefine its destiny[458]. The clearest possible self-awareness of Europe, concerning its own situation and of the working of the unconscious forces out of these archetypes, is the prerequisite for a successful transformation and for a sustainable way out of the crisis.

With our book, we wish to further this increasing consciousness and self-awareness of Europe.

---

[458] A useful reading to this issue is the book of Joachim Bauer, "Selbststeuerung: Die Wiederentdeckung des Freien Willens, 2015. (our translation: "Self-Control: The Rediscovery of the Free Will").

So we call out to Europe: Know yourself!

If Europe follows this advice for increasing self-awareness, that is carved over the entry to the Apollo temple of Delphi, then she will be able to reshape her destiny.

On the basis of our insights, we would like to give Europe additional advice: Trust in your genius, be courageous and confident, and build your actions on mutual trust and partnership!

In our book, we have provided concrete information for pragmatic steps to take, that will promote Europe on this path of liberation.

Bibliography

Abelshauser, Werner; Wunder gibt es immer wieder: Mythos Wirtschaftswunder, in: Aus Politik und Zeitgeschichte, 68 (2018) 27, S. 4-10.

Amodei, Dario; Machines of Loving Grace: How AI Could Transform the World for the Better, October 2024.

Ansprenger, Franz; Auflösung der Kolonialreiche, 1989.

Armstrong, Karen; The Great Transformation: The Axial Age, 2005. Deutsch: Achsenzeit der grossen Zivilisationen, 2006.

Attali, Jacques; Biographie: C'était François Mitterand, Paris, 2007.

Bateson, Gregory; Geist und Natur. Eine notwendige Einheit, 1987.

Bateson, Gregory; in Ökologie des Geistes, Teil VI, Krisen in der Ökologie des Geistes, von Versailles zur Kybernetik, Vorlesung von 1966.

Bateson, Gregory; Ökologie des Geistes, 1985; English edition: Steps to an Ecology of Mind, Collected Essays, 1972.

Bauer, Joachim; Selbststeuerung: Die Wiederentdeckung des Freien Willens, 2015. (our translation: "Self-Control: The rediscovery of the Free Will").

Bell, Daniel A, Amitav Acharya, Rajeev Bhargava, Yan Xuetong (eds.); Bridging two Worlds, Comparing Classical Political Thought and Statecraft in India and China, 2003. University of California Press, series: Great Transformations.

Benjamin, Craig G.; Foundations of Eastern Civilization,

Berger, Jens; Wer schützt die Welt vor den Finanzkonzernen?, Frankfurt, 2020.

Bernstein, Richard J.; Beyond objectivism and relativism: Science, Hermeneutics, and Praxis, University of Pennsylvania Press 1983.

Bittner, Wolfgang; Die Eroberung Europas durch die USA, 2015.

Blankart, Charles B.; Föderalismus in Deutschland und in Europa, 2007, erschienen in der Reihe „Neue Studien zur Politischen Ökonomie", Nomos Verlag.

Blankart, Charles B.; Öffentliche Finanzen in der Demokratie: Eine Einführung in die Finanzwissenschaft, Gebundene Ausgabe, 2017.

Bloch, Marc; Die Feudalgesellschaft, Neuausgabe 2019, Französisches Original von 1939.

Bono, Edward de; Lateral Thinking: a Textbook of Creativity, 1970.

Bono, Edward de; Laterales Denken : Ein Kursbuch zur Erschliessung ihrer Kreativitätsreserven, 1971.

Bördlein, Christoph; Einführung in die Verhaltensanalyse (English Edition: Introduction to Behavioral Analysis), 2015.

Born, Max; Der Mensch und das Atom, in:
Ausblick auf die Zukunft, 1968.

Bozo, Frederic; Deux stratégies pour l'Europe,
Paris, 1996.

Bracher, Andreas; Europa im amerikanischen
Weltsystem, Bruchstücke zu einer
ungeschriebenen Geschichte des 20.
Jahrhunderts, 2001.

Bracher, Andreas; Völkische
Selbstbestimmung und Dreigliederung, in der
Zeitschrift Perseus, der Europäer, Jg. 6 Nr. 8,
Juni 2002.

Brandt, Willy; Frieden sichern und Mauern
überwinden – Ost- und Deutschlandpolitik
1955–1989. https://www.willy-brandt-
biografie.de/politik/ost-und-
deutschlandpolitik/

Braudel, Fernand; Die lange Dauer. in:
Schriften zur Geschichte, Bd. 1: Gesellschaft
und Zeitstrukturen. 1992, S. 49–87. Ganz
wichtig in unserem Zusammenhang ist „Die
Geschichte der Zivilisation vom 15 bis zum 18
Jahrhundert, 1982.

Fernand Braudel, "Civilization and Capitalism", 1967.

Braudel, Fernand; Histoire et Sciences sociales : La longue durée, in : Annales, Année 1958, pp. 725-753.

Braudel, Fernand; L'Identité de la France, auf Deutsch herausgegeben als «Frankreich, Band 1: Raum und Geschichte / Band 2: Die Menschen und die Dinge / Band 3: die Dinge und die Menschen, 2009.

Braudel, Fernand; La dynamique du capitalisme. Paris, 1985. Deutsch als: Die Dynamik des Kapitalismus, 1991.

Braun, Eduard; Pseudoliberale Staatsinterventionen und die Neoklassik . Gedanken zum Homo Oeconomicus und zum wahren Wert der Dinge, Mises Institute, Mises Wire, 11. April 2022.

Bricker, Darrell and Ibbitson, John; Empty Planet: The Shock of Global Population Decline, 2019

Briggs, John und Peat, F. David; Die Entdeckung des Chaos, 1997; das Original ist 1989 unter dem Titel „Turbulent Mirror" in New York veröffentlicht worden.

Brzezinski, Zbigniew, The Grand Chessboard: American Primacy and its Geostrategic Imperatives, 1997.

Brzezinski, Zbigniew; Die einzige Weltmacht: Amerikas Strategie der Vorherrschaft, 1999.

Burkhard, Jakob; Kultur der Renaissance in Italien, Erstveröffentlichung 1860.

Butterwegge, Christoph; Die zerrissene Republik. Wirtschaftliche, soziale und politische Ungleichheit in Deutschland, 2019.

Campbell, Joseph; Thou art That. Transforming Religious Metaphor. The spiritual meaning of Biblical Stories, Miracles and Parables, 2002.

Campbell, Joseph; Understanding and Interpretation of Mythology. The Website of the Joseph Campbell Foundation: https://www.jcf.org/.

Campbell, Joseph; Myths of Light, 2003,
Joseph Campbell.

Fritjof; Tao der Physik, 1977.

Carstens, Peter; Deutsch-Französisches
Projekt: Ein Kampfflugzeug für 100 Milliarden
Euro, in der FAZ vom 21.01.2020.

Carter, Robert; Frank Lloyd Wright, A
Biography, 2006.

Chomsky, Noam; The essential Chomsky,
1959.

Chomsky, Noam; Sprache und Geist, 1970.
Darin der Anhang aus *New Left Review*
(Nummer 57, September/Oktober 1969).

Chomsky, Noam; Rules and Representations.
Behavioral and Brain Sciences, 1980. .
Deutsch: Regeln und Repräsentationen, 1980

Chomsky, Noam; Gespräch mit C. J.
Polychroniou zum Thema „Warum China,
nicht Russland die US-dominierte

Weltordnung bedroht", auf Deutsch am 09.07.2022 in Telepolis; Original in Trouthout.

Chomsky, Noam; in Asia-Pacific-Forum vom 31.12.2012, Revenge Of History: Chomsky on Japan, China, The United States, And The Threat of Conflict in Asia".

Clark, Christopher; Die Schlafwandler: Wie Europa in den Ersten Weltkrieg zog, 2013.

Clark, Christopher; Von Zeit und Macht, 2918.

Club of Rome, Grenzen des Wachstums, 1962.

Conze, Eckart; Hegemonie durch Integration: Die amerikanische Europapolitik und ihre Herausforderung durch de Gaulle, in: Institut für Zeitgeschichte, Vierteljahreshefte für Zeitgeschichte, Jahrgang 43 (1995), Heft 2.

Couvée, Leonard; Verslumung als Folge von Metropolisierung, 2016.

Covey, Stephen R.; Die 7 Wege zur Effektivität, Original von 1990, deutsch 1996.

Dagdelen, Sevim; Die NATO: Eine Abrechnung mit dem Wertebündnis, 2024.

Dangeleit, Elke; Deutschland finanziert Erdogans Umsiedelungspolitik in Nord- und Ostsyrien, Online Magazin Telepolis, vom 24. Januar 2020.

Davis, Irvine Mike; Planet der Slums, Department of History an der University of California, 2005; Planet der Slums ist 2019 auf Deutsch erschienen.

Denson, John V.; "A Century of War" wurde 1997 als Vortrag zum fünfzehnjährigen Jubiläum des Ludwig von Mises Institute gehalten und Mises.org veröffentlicht.

Desjardins, T. ; François Mitterand: un socialiste gaullien, Paris, 1978.

Deutsch, David; The Beginning of Infinity, 2012. Is bringing some light to the discussion about "progress"

Diamond, Jared; Guns, Germs and Steel. The Fates of Human Societies, 1998.

Doering-Manteuffel, Anselm; Amerikanisierung und Westernisierung, Version: 2.0, in: Docupedia-Zeitgeschichte, 19.08.2019.

Dresdener gesammelte Kommentare zur Sicherheitspolitik – dgksp-diskussionspapiere – vom 14. April 2021.

Duerr, Hans-Peter; Der Mythos vom Zivilisationsprozeß, 2005.

Egli, Rene; Das Lola Prinzip, Die Vollkommenheit der Welt, 1994.

Ehrlich, Paul R.; The Population Bomb, New York: Ballantine Books 1968; dt. Übers.: Die Bevölkerungsbombe, 1971.

Eksteins, Modris; Rites of Spring: The Great War and the Birth of the Modern Age, 1989.

Evans, Richard; The Pursuit of Power, Europe 1815-1914, 2016.

Ferguson, Niall; Colossus: The Rise and Fall of the American Empire, 2004.

Ferguson, Niall; Eine Nation ist kein Individuum, und ein Individuum ist keine Nation, am 31.12.2021 in der NZZ.

Ferguson, Niall; Empire: How Britain Made the Modern World, 2003.

Ferguson, Niall; The Ascent of Money: A Financial History of the World, 2008.

Ferguson, Niall; The Cash Nexus. Money and Power in the Modern World, 1700–2000, 2001.

Ferguson, Niall; The War of the World: History's Age of Hatred, 1st Edition, 2009.

Ferguson, Niall; Civilization. The West and the Rest, 2012.

Fix, Andrew C.; The Renaissance, the Reformation and the Rise of Nations", Audible Audiobook series: „The Great Courses" produced by „The Teaching Company", 2005.

Focus Magazin Nr. 8, 2009; "Alles schon gelaufen?", Wem gehört Deutschland?

Foreign Affairs, Volume 103 Number 3, No Substitute for Victory, 2024. https://www.foreignaffairs.com/united-states/no-substitute-victory-pottinger-gallagher

Fortes, Meyer; The Political Systems of the Tallensi of the Northern Territories of the Gold Coast, in African Political Systems, M. Fortes and E.E. Evans-Pritchard (eds.), First Edition 1940.

Frankopan, Peter; The Silk Roads, The New History of the World, 2015.

Freud, Sigmund; Vorlesungen zur Einführung in die Psychoanalyse, 1917.

Friedrich, Marc und Weik, Matthias ; Komplette, legale Enteignung per Gesetz, 2019.

Fröhlich, Stefan; Die transatlantischen Beziehungen, Deutschland, 2017.

Fuller, R. Buckminster; Critical Path, 1981;

Fuller, R. Buckminster; Ideas and Integrities, 1963.

Fuller, R. Buckminster; Nine Chains to the Moon", 1938.

Fuller, R. Buckminster; Operating Manual for Spaceship Erath, 1969; deutsche Ausgabe: Bedienungsanleitung für das Raumschiff Erde und andere Schriften", 2011.

Gluckman, Max; The Limits of Naivety in Social Anthropology", 2017.

Goethe, J. W.; Faust, Tragödie Erster und Zweiter Teil, 1986.

Goldbach, Georg von; Europe lost her Sovereignty. History-Background-Perspectives, 2024.

Goldbach, Georg von; War & Business : The American Success Story of the past Century. Background – Script – Empires, 2024.

Goldbach, Georg von; The New System of Global Governance: The ongoing Paradigm Shift, 2024.

Goldbach, Georg von; Europe on the Way to Her Apocalypse. History-Background-Perspectives, 2024.

Goldbach, Georg von; Europa auf dem Weg in die Apokalypse. Geschichte-Hintergründe-Perspektiven. (German Edition), 2024.

Granet, Marcel; Die chinesische Zivilisation. Band 2: Das chinesische Denken. Inhalt, Form, Charakter, Ersterscheinung deutsch 1985. Original: „La pensée chinoise", Paris 1938.

Greene, Robert; Die Gesetze der menschlichen Natur, 2019; das englische Original „The Laws of Human Nature, 2018.

Greene, Robert; Gesetze der Macht. engl. The Laws of Power, 1998.

Grenoble University, Ecole de Management (GEM) de Grenoble, Energie for Society, Université de Grenoble, Politiques énergétiques : comment éviter une dystopie européenne?, 2024.

Griffin, George Edward; The Creature from Jekyll Island, 1994.

Grün, Arno; Dem Leben entfremdet, 2019.

Grün, Arno; The Insanity of Normality. Toward Understanding Human Destructiveness, 1987.

Grün, Arno; The Betrayal of the Self: The Fear of Autonomy in Men and Women, 2007.

Guelzo, Allen C., et al.; The History of the United States, 2003, 2nd Edition, 2013.

Guilford, J. P.; The Structure of Intellect, in Psychological Bulletin, Volume 53 N° 4, July 1956.

Habermas, Jürgen; Theorie des kommunikativen Handelns, 1981.

Hahn, Robert; Herrschaft von Lissabon bis Wladiwostok", 06.07.2022.

Halbwachs, Maurice; Les cadres sociaux de la mémoire, 1925.

Hall, Stuart; The West and the Rest:
Discourse and Power, 1992.

Hayek Friedrich A. v.; Weltwirtschaftliches
Archiv, 36. Bd., 1932.

Hayes, Sam W. and Morris, Christopher
(eds.): Manifest Destiny and Empire:
American Antebellum Expansionism, 1997.
Heer, Burkhard; Umwelt, Bevölkerungsdruck
und Wirtschaftswachstum in
Entwicklungsländern, 2013.

Hegel G.W.F.; Tagebuch der Reise in die
Berner Oberalpen, 1796. In: K. Rosenkranz,
G.W.F. Hegels Leben [1844]. Darmstadt 1969:
470–89.

Heinsohn, Gunnar; Söhne und Weltmacht, 1.
Auflage 2005.

Heisterkamp, Jens (Hg.); Die
Jahrhundertillusion. Wilsons
Selbstbestimmungsrecht der Völker,
Sammelband, 2002.

Hellmann, Gunther; Zwischen Gestaltungsmacht und Hegemoniefalle: Zur neuesten Debatte über eine neue deutsche Außenpolitik, in der Reihe „Aus Politik und Zeitgeschichte, 11.07.2016.

Heylighen, Francis; , Accelerating Evolution, 2007, in Modelski, Tessaleno and Thompson, William (eds.), "Globalization as an Evolutionary Process: Modeling Global Change", Rethinking Globalizations, London 2007.

Hobsbawm, Eric; Zeitalter der Extreme, Weltgeschichte des 20. Jahrhunderts, 1995.

Horkheimer, Max und Adorno, Theodor W.; Dialektik der Aufklärung, 1944.

Horsman, Reginald; Race and Manifest Destiny: The Origins of American Racial Anglo-Saxonism, 1981.

Hülsmann, Jörg Guido; Abundance, Generosity, and the State: an Inquiry into Economic Principles, 2024.

Hummel, Diana; Der Bevölkerungsdiskurs: Demographisches Wissen und politische Macht, 2000.

Hungary Today, Online Magazin vom 24. Mai 2024.

Hürter, Thomas; Das Zeitalter der Unschärfe, 2021.

Jordan, Pascual; Wie sieht die Welt von morgen aus?, 1958.

Jung, C. G.; Biographie: Erinnerungen, Träume, Gedanken, 1962.

Jung, C. G.; Modern Men in Search of a Soul", auf Deutsch „Der moderne Mensch auf der Suche nach einer Seele", von 1933.

Jung, Carl Gustaf; "Civilization in Transition", 1946, BBC broadcast.

Jung, Carl Gustaf; The Structure of the Unconscious, 1916.

Keynes, John Maynard; Krieg und Frieden: Die wirtschaftlichen Folgen des Vertrags von Versailles, 1920.

Koestler, Arthur and Smythies, J. R. (eds); Revolutionizing the Sciences of Man, 1968.

Koestler, Arthur; Jenseits von Atomismus und Holismus – Der Begriff des Holons, in, "Das Neue Menschenbild – Die Revolutionierung der Wissenschaften vom Menschen", 1970, Hrsg. Arthur Koestler und J. R. Smythies.

Kohlenberg, Kerstin und Schieritz, Mark; am 23. Oktober 2014, in DIE ZEIT Nr. 44/2014, Die Superwaffe des Mr. Glaser, Sanktionen gegen Russland und den Iran: Wie amerikanische Finanzbeamte zu Wirtschaftskriegern werden.

Kolk, Bessel van der; The Body Keeps the Score: Brain, Mind, and Body in the Healing of Trauma, 2014.

Konersmann, Ralf (Hrsg.); Kulturkritik: Reflexionen in der veränderten Welt, Reclam 2001.

Konicz, Tomasz; Türkei: Merkels zivilisatorischer Tabubruch, Online Magazin Telepolis, vom 25. Januar 2020.

Koselleck, Reinhard; Vergangene Zukunft. Zur Semantik geschichtlicher Zeiten, 1989.

Kreitner, R. & Kinicki, A; Organizational Behavior, 2004, New York: McGraw-Hill.

Krohne, Heinz W.; Psychologie der Angst, 2010.

Kuhn, Thomas S.; The Structure of Scientific Revolutions, 1962.

Lacalle, Daniel; „An Unprecedented Monetary Destruction Is Coming", published on September 18, 2024, on Mises Wire.

Lau, Jörg; "Regelbasierte Weltordnung. In 80 Phrasen um die Welt", 01. Juli 2020.

Lee, Kuam Yew; From Third World to First, 2016.

Lévi-Strauss, Claude; Das wilde Denken, 1976.

Li Xuanmin and Fan Anqi; Government of China „White paper", in Global Times China, 19. Januar 2023, https://www.globaltimes.cn//author/Reporter -Li-Xuanmin.html.

Lieven, Dominic (ed.); The Cambridge History of Russia, 2005.

Lohmann, Sascha; in SWP-Aktuell 2019/A 31, Mai 2019, Extraterritoriale US-Sanktionen.

Lorenz, Konrad und Wuketits, Franz (Hg.): Die Evolution des Denkens. Zwölf Beiträge, 1983.

Lorenz, Konrad; Das sogenannte Böse: Zur Naturgeschichte der Aggression, 1963.

Lovelock, James; Gaia. A New Look at Life on Earth, 1972.

Lukács, Georg; Die Zerstörung der Vernunft, 1955.

Mackinder, Halford; Artikel „The Geographical Pivot of History, 1904.

Mahlmann, Matthias; Philosophische Grundlehren, 7. Auflage, 2022. https://www.rwi.uzh.ch/elt-lst-mahlmann/rechtstheorie/kant/de/html/unit_u2.html.

Mandela, Nelson; The Long Walt to Freedom, 1994.

Marschall, Tim; The Future of Geography, 2023.

Mausfeld, Rainer; Warum schweigen die Lämmer?, 2018.

Mauss, Marcel; Manuel d'Ethnographie, 1926.

Mayer, Thomas; Die Ordnung der Freiheit und ihre Feinde: Vom Aufstand der Verlassenen gegen die Herrschaft der Eliten, 2018.

Meadows, H. Donella; Thinking in Systems, 2008.

Mereschkowski, Dmitri; Leonardo da Vinci, 1951.

Merk, Frederick; Manifest Destiny and Mission in American History: A Reinterpretation, 1963.

Mises, Ludwig von; Human Action: A Treatise on Economics, 1949.

Mises, Ludwig von; Theorie des Geldes und der Umlaufmittel, 1912.

Mises, Ludwig von; Vom Wert der besseren Ideen, Vorlesungen, 1958.

Mittasch, Alwin; Von der Chemie zur Philosophie, 1948.

Mohr, Daniel; „Viele amerikanische Investoren, Der Dax ist fest in ausländischer Hand", FAZ vom 26.01.2017.

Mohsin, Saleha; How the Weaponization of the Dollar changed the World Order, 2024.

Morland, Paul; The Power of Demography to Understand Our World, 2019.

Mumford, Lewis; The Original American edition: The Transformation of Man, 1956.

Mumford, Lewis; Mythos der Maschine. Kultur, Technik und Macht, 1986.

Mumford, Lewis; Technics and Civilization, 1934.

Mumford, Lewis; The Condition of Man, 1944.

Mumford, Lewis; The Culture of Cities, 1938.

Mumford, Lewis; The Story of Utopias, 1922.

Needham, Joseph; Moulds of Understanding, 1976.

Needham, Joseph; Needham Research Institute, Science and Civilisation in China, since 1954.

Needham, Joseph; Wissenschaftlicher Universalismus, 1979, das Kapitel „Der Zeitbegriff im Orient", s. 176-250.

Neubauer, Heinz; Grundlagen der Systemtheorie, 1989.

Nietzsche, Friedrich; Genealogie der Moral, 1887.

Ortega y Gasset, José; "La Rebelíon de la Masas", published in 1929. English in 1930 as "The Revolt of the Masses".

Pany, Thomas; Syrien-Krise und EU: Katastrophale Armut und Auswanderung als letzter Ausweg, 22. February, 2024.

Perry, Markus; Understanding Organizational Culture: A Systems Theory Perspective, 2023.

Pfluger, Walter; Ronga – Ein Beispiel politischer Komplementarität, 1987.

Popper, Karl; The Open Society and its Enemies, 1945. Deutsche Ausgabe in 2 Bänden, „Die offene Gesellschaft und ihre Feinde", 1957 und 1958.

Prigogine, Ilya; Order through Fluctuation. Self-Organization and Social System, 1976.

Ratzinger, Joseph; "The Soul of Europe", a speech given in Munich, Bavaria, in december

2000, published in 2005, in Die Zeit, German weekly magazine.

Reid, Anna; Borderland, A Journey Through the History of the Ukraine, 2015.

Reinhard, Wolfgang; Die Unterwerfung der Welt: Globalgeschichte der europäischen Expansion 1414 – 2015, 2017.

Richard, Wilhelm; Weisheit des Ostens, von 1951.

Riemann, Fritz; Basic Forms of Fear. A depth psychological study, 1975.

Richter, Horst-Eberhard; Flüchten oder Standhalten, 2012.

Richter, Horst-Eberhard; Moral in Zeiten der Krise, Originalausgabe 2010.

Riegel, Tobias; Syrien – Die unendliche (Lügen-)Geschichte", 20. Februar 2020.

Riemann, Fritz; Grundformen der Angst. Eine tiefenpsychologische Studie. 10. überarbeitete und erweiterte Auflage, 1975.

Riesman, David; "The Lonely Crowd", published in 1950.

Risk Management Network, Neue Ära der Großmachtkonflikte – Erosionsprozesse der geopolitischen Welt, am 7. Oktober 2019. https://www.risknet.de/themen/risknews/ero sionsprozesse-der-geopolitischen-welt/.

Rübel, Gerhard; Grundlagen der monetären Aussenwirtschaft, 2009.

Rügemer, Werner; Die Kapitalisten des 21. Jahrhunderts. Allgemeinverständliche Notizen zum Aufstieg der neuen Finanzakteure, 2018.

Rügemer, Werner; The Capitalist of the 21st Century, 2019.

Rügemer, Werner; USA im Niedergang? – Aber in der EU so mächtig wie noch nie, Artikel im Online Magazin „Nachdenkseiten" vom 23. April 2019.

Sachs, Jeffry; Agenda der US-Aussenpolitik",
am 20. Dezember 2023, auf dem Online
Magazin Telepolis:
https://www.telepolis.de/features/Kriegsdeba
kel-und-viel-Geld-Die-geheime-Agenda-
hinter-der-gescheiterten-US-Aussenpolitik-
9584068.html?seite=all.

Sachs, Jeffry;
https://www.jeffsachs.org/newspaper-
articles/

Sakwa, Richard; Frontline Ukraine: Crisis in
the Borderlands, 2022.

Sakwa, Richard; The Lost Peace: How the
West Failed to prevent a Second Cold War,
2023.

Sakwa, Richard; Wir sind an der Beerdigung
der alten Schule der Diplomatie, Interview
vom 21. Mai 2024 in GlobalBridge.

Schmalz, Stefan und Ebenau, Mathias; Auf
dem Sprung – Brasilien, Indien und China,
2011.

Schmalz, Stefan; Chinas neue Rolle im globalen Kapitalismus. in: Prokla 40 (4):483-503, 2015.

Schöllgen, Gregor; Das Zeitalter des Imperialismus (in Oldenbourg, Grundriss der Geschichte, Band 15), 2000.

Schuldt, Christian; Zeitalter der Krisen, Bundesverband „Energie, Wasser, Leben", 2021.

Sieren, Frank und Vossenkuhl, Josef, et al; "Zukunft? China! Wie die neue Supermacht unser Leben, unsere Politik, unsere Wirtschaft verändert", 2020.

Sieren, Frank; Shenzhen – Zukunft Made in China: Zwischen Kreativität und Kontrolle, 2021.

Sigrist, Christian; Regulierte Anarchie, 1967.

Sinn, Hans-Werner; Der Mythos vom Marshall-Plan, 03.02.2023.
https://www.hanswernersinn.de/de/marshallplan-brackmann-hb-03022023

Sinn, Hans-Werner;
https://www.hanswernersinn.de/de.

SIPRI – Stockholm International Peace
Research Institute. SIPRI:
https://www.sipri.org/databases/armstransfers.

Skinner, B. F.; Verbal Behavior, 1957.

Smith, Adam; Der Wohlstand der Nationen,
Erstveröffentlichung 1776.

Spangler, David; The Flame of Incarnation,
First edition, 2009.

Spengler, Oswald; Der Untergang des
Abendlandes, erster Band 1918, zweiter Band
1922.
Spethmann, Dieter; Deutschland verschenkt
seinen Wohlstand, am 19.01.2011 in der FAZ.

Spykman, Nicholas J.; Geography and
Foreign Policy", published in The American
Political Science Review, Vol. XXXII, Nos. 1
and 2, February and April 1938.

Steinbuch, Karl; Falsch programmiert – Über das Versagen unserer Gesellschaft in der Gegenwart und vor der Zukunft, 1968.

Steiner, Rudolf; Band GA 335 der Gesamtausgabe.

Steiner, Rudolf; Gesamtausgabe Band GA 185, Vorträge von 1918.

Stephanson, Anders; Manifest Destiny: American Expansionism and the Empire of Right, 1995.

Straubhaar, Thomas; Der Untergang ist abgesagt: Wider die Mythen des Demographischen Wandels, 2016.

Streeck, Wolfgang; "Gekaufte Zeit: die vertagte Krise des demokratischen Kapitalismus", 2013.

Thomas, Anthony; Rhodes: the Race for Africa, 1997.

Tiger, Lionel und Fox, Robin; The Imperial Animal, 1976.

Todd, Emmanuel; La Défaite de l'Occident, von 2024.

Todd, Emmanuel; Weltmacht USA: ein Nachruf, 2003.

Tofler, Alvin ; Revolutionary Wealth, 2006.

Toynbee, Arnold J.; "Things Not Foreseen at Paris; The Future in Retrospect", Essay drafted in 1934.

Verovšek, P.J.; "Collective memory, politics, and the influence of the past: the politics of memory as a research paradigm", published in: Taylor & Francis; "Politics, Groups and Identities, 2016, 4 (3). pp. 529-543.

Vidal, Gore; Perpetual War for Perpetual Peace: How we got to be so hated. American Imperialism, Book 1", 2002.

Wallerstein, Immanuel; Aufstieg und zukünftiger Niedergang des kapitalistischen Weltsystems. Zur Grundlegung vergleichender Analyse. In: Senghaas, Dieter (Hrsg.): Kapitalistische Weltökonomie.

Kontroversen über ihren Ursprung und ihre Entwicklungsdynamik, 1979 und 1982.

Wallerstein, Immanuel; The Capitalist World-Economy, 1979.

Wang, Mingming; Between Nations and the World: Marcel Mauss's Conceptualization of Civilization and Envisioning of Human Science", in 2018, Chinese Journal of Sociology, 38(4): 1-53.

Wang, Mingyuan; Why Have Repeated Efforts to Revitalize the Northeast Failed? – Rethinking the Twentieth Anniversary of the Strategy of Revitalizing the Old Industrial base.
https://www.readingthechinadream.com/wang-mingyuan-on-chinas-northeast.html.

Wang, Qi; On the cultural constitution of collective memory", 2008.

Warburg, Paul M.; The Federal Reserve System: its origin and growth; reflections and recollections; 2 volumes, New York 1930.

Weidenhausen, Gerd; Buchbesprechung, in Die Drei, Nr. 5.: Wolfgang Bittner, Die Eroberung Europas durch die USA, 2015.

Wendt, Reinhard; Vom Kolonialismus zur Globalisierung: Europa und die Welt seit 1500, 2016.

Wiener, Norbert; The Human Use of Human Beings – Cybernetics and Society, 1950.

Wilhelm, Richard; Die Seele Chinas, 1925.

Wilhelm, Richard; The Soul of China", 1928.

Wilhelm, Richard; Chinesische Wirtschaftspsychologie, Leipzig 1930.

Wilhelm, Richard; Wisdom of the East, 1951.

Willke, Hellmut; Global Governance, 2006.

Willke, Helmut; Atopia, 2001.

Wuketits, F. M.; Review: Herausforderungen durch die moderne Biologie, in Philosophische Rundschau, Vol. 30, N°. 1/2 (1983), pp. 1-23.

Wulf, Andrea; Alexander von Humboldt und die Erfindung der Natur, deutsch 2016.

Wüthrich, Werner; Europäische Integration, in dem Schweizer Magazin «Zeit-Fragen» von 2011 bis 2012.

Zeit-Fragen, Nr. 38, 2010: Studie zur „Geschichte der EU – Teil 1.

Zhao, Tingyang; Alles unter einem Himmel - Vergangenheit und Zukunft der Weltordnung, 2019.

ZHAO, Tingyang; All under Heaven: The Tianxia System for a Possible World Order, 2016.

Zinn, John Kabat; Coming to Our Senses: Healing Ourselves and the World Through Mindfulness, 2005.

Zürcher Kantonalbank, CBO, Census, OMB. https://www.zkb.ch/de/blog/anlegen/us-staatsverschuldung-rekordkurs.html.

Zürn, Michael; A Theory of Global Governance: Authority, Legitimacy and Contestation, 2018.